CANADA
TOMORROW'S GIANT

BRUCE HUTCHISON

With a New Introduction by **VAUGHN PALMER**

Maps by **RAFAEL PALACIOS**

OXFORD
UNIVERSITY PRESS

OXFORD
UNIVERSITY PRESS

Oxford University Press is a department of the University of Oxford.
It furthers the University's objective of excellence in research, scholarship,
and education by publishing worldwide. Oxford is a registered trade mark of
Oxford University Press in the UK and in certain other countries.

Published in Canada by
Oxford University Press
8 Sampson Mews, Suite 204,
Don Mills, Ontario M3C 0H5 Canada

www.oupcanada.com

Library and Archives Canada Cataloguing in Publication
Hutchison, Bruce, 1901–1992
Canada : tomorrow's giant / Bruce Hutchison ; with
an introduction by Vaughn Palmer.

(The Wynford Project)
Includes index.
Originally published: 1957.
ISBN 978-0-19-900261-0

1. Canada—Description and travel. 2. Hutchison,
Bruce, 1901–1992—Travel—Canada. I. Title.
II. Series: Wynford Project

FC75.H88 2012   917.04'633   C2012-902404-X

Cover: Charles Fraser Comfort, *Edmonton, Skyline of the North*, 1951. McCord
Museum, Montreal, M2000.83.56.

Printed and bound in the United States of America

1 2 3 4 — 15 14 13 12

Introduction to the Wynford Edition

Vaughn Palmer

The headline in *Maclean's* magazine in late 1955 said it all. "Bruce Hutchison rediscovers the Unknown Country," it declared, invoking the name of the bestselling book that made Hutchison's reputation and defined the country for a generation.

Now Hutchison had gone on the road again, him driving and dictating, wife Dorothy alongside taking notes whenever a usable notion struck him. Their spring journey spanned three months and roamed over ten provinces, including new arrival Newfoundland, which had joined Confederation since the tour fourteen years previously that gave rise to the *Unknown Country*.

Perhaps it was not an "ideal way" to compile the material for a book, Hutchison reflected in his memoirs. He confessed to feeling "less satisfied" with a work completed in competition with the deadline pressures of his other jobs: editor, columnist, and award-winning editorial writer at the *Victoria Times* and freelance magazine writer — one of the country's most prolific — never mind the relentless demands of the fabled garden and woodpile.

But if the perfectionist Hutchison could always see a way to improve his writing, the results "satisfied the publishers." *Maclean's*, which had the inspiration of sending him to revisit the country in the first place, commissioned a fifteen-part series, starting in late 1955 and continuing through to the next summer. The next year, a tightened, rewritten version was published as the book you are holding in your hand. Longman's, Green and Co. shipped out advance copies with the gift of a seedling Douglas fir, bright and "shiny as a jewel," a point the reviewer would ultimately get by reading to the last sentence of the book.

Canada: Tomorrow's Giant produced another bestseller for Hutchison, and in 1958 the Governor General's Award for Creative Non-fiction, his third. For this was not simply a travelogue; it was a prose portrait of the country by one of its foremost stylists. Hutchison later characterized it as an old man's book: "As they grow older all men find successive layers of reticence and caution encrusted on them like the annual rings of tree growth, protective covering for the ego." The intervening years had tamed the *Unknown Country's* "youthful hyperbole," substituting what a friend jokingly called "lowperbole."

But for all his mock-fretting about showing his age, the fifty-four-year-old writer was merely halfway through his reporting career during the spring 1955 trip. His career began in 1918 with the coverage of a YMCA swim meet and continued until he published his last column, an analysis of Bill Clinton's campaign for the US presidency, the month before his death in 1992.

Tomorrow's Giant is the more mature, but also the more realistic, portrait of the country, then in the midst of the postwar decade, transformed from the one Hutchison toured in haste in 1941—an emerging modern nation. Alberta is still ranching country and farmland, with the "invisible cauldron of oil and gas beneath it." Quebec, unrecognizable in his painfully dated account of the Gaspé, shows traces, here and there, of the Quiet Revolution to come: "The stark smokestacks, the towns clustered around these grimy altars of commerce, the logs in booms or mountainous pyramids, the paper streaming off the rollers, the people no longer following the plow but punching the time clock, all inform the traveler of Quebec's new age." British Columbia, in its own solitude, is isolated by geography as much as a contrary outlook. Returning to their home province via Prince George, the Hutchisons found the lone route to the west coast cut by a spring flood, forcing them to undertake a 3,200-kilometre detour, back through Alberta then southward to the US before reaching Vancouver via Seattle.

Along with the portrait of the emerging giant invoked in the title, there are the prose poems (as they were dubbed at the time) interspersed between the main chapters, paeans to the simple and sometimes amusing verities of maple syrup, the Canadian Shield, the big trees.

Hutchison did much of his book writing on his great Canadian getaway in the seclusion of his own lakeside "camp": "The shack is usually made of cardboard, fastened to a rock, by a few rusty nails, built like an incompetent swallow's nest or a gopher's hole, and supported by some obscure principle unknown to science."

But here and there, one meets the Canadians themselves. The Hutchisons made an extensive detour to meet one particular couple, doctors Julius and Hanna Kratz, refugees from Nazi Germany who were ministering to the health cares of a mostly Aboriginal population in Fort Vermilion, Alberta. The writer extracts a single, vivid detail from their stirring story: "Dr. Julius recalled with a wistful smile that, on reaching Canada, he had been asked to write down on an official immigration form how long he and his wife intended to remain. He had seized a pen and joyfully scrawled one word—'Forever.'"

"We would not forget them," reflected Bruce as he and Dot headed back out on the road. Nor, reading their story as recounted by Hutchison, will you.

Publisher's Note

Canada: Tomorrow's Giant was first published in 1957. This facsimile edition faithfully reproduces the original text of the first edition. In the six decades since, society's attitudes toward Canada's First Nations peoples and indeed the very terms used to denote those societies have changed greatly. So have historical views of first contact between Europeans and the First Nations, relations between French and English Canada, as well as social attitudes in general toward gender and ethnicity. *Canada: Tomorrow's Giant* is, like any creative work, an artifact of its time, and it is only fair to say that the twenty-first century reader may stumble across the occasional expression no longer in common use.

FOR DOROTHY, faithful companion on a long journey through Canada and life

THE WHOLESOME SEA IS AT HER GATES,
HER GATES BOTH EAST AND WEST

Lines graven above the doorway of the
Canadian Parliament in Ottawa

FOREWORD

*F*ifteen years ago I wrote a book about Canada and called it The
Unknown Country. Today that country is still largely unknown to
its natives and almost totally unknown to the world in which it is
destined to be a leading power not long hence. Or if known at all
abroad, it is known for all the unimportant reasons. The important
ones—much more difficult to come by and, indeed, stubbornly con-
cealed from foreigners—were my primary concern in writing the
present book.

But if Canada, so simple and obvious on the surface, is complicated, contradictory, and deceptive below the surface, it is not the
country I found on my first inspection. Fifteen years have altered
it outwardly in many places beyond recognition and inwardly everywhere.

Perhaps in this brief period no other nation has altered so much
as Canada. It might be truer to say that Canada became a nation in
mind, as it was long a nation by constitution, only yesterday or the
day before, its inhabitants a distinct and distinguishable race.

The intention of this book, and the long travels preceding it, was
to rediscover Canada, if I could, not as an expert but as an ordinary
traveler. Those who want a technical description of Canada can
find it in a bulky literature growing by the hour. They will not find
it here.

Nor will they find all of Canada here. The land is too big for one
book or a thousand books. My modest purpose will be served if the
reader cares to join me in a casual, disordered tour across the nation
and some of its wilderness—not by the main highways but mostly
on the side roads—and thus encounters, among their own surroundings, a curious and little-understood people with a surprising past
and a future rather important to mankind.

If the reader learns something of these sixteen millions who have mastered half a continent against almost impossible odds, and if he is encouraged to look further into the subject for himself, the writer will be content.

In my various journeys I was assisted by countless Canadians whose names, unlike their hospitality, are forgotten. I am indebted to the officers of the excellent Travel Bureau in Ottawa; to leaders and officials of the provincial governments; to the able editors of Maclean's magazine, who have generously allowed me to use material gathered, in the first place, for them; to Jean Ellis, without whose skilled help in preparing the manuscript and apprehending at least its worst flaws the job would have been impossible; above all, to my wife, without whose company, support, and humor on the rough stretches I could not have attempted or survived my explorations.

B. H.

Victoria, B.C.
June 1957

CONTENTS

Contents

CANADA
TOMORROW'S GIANT

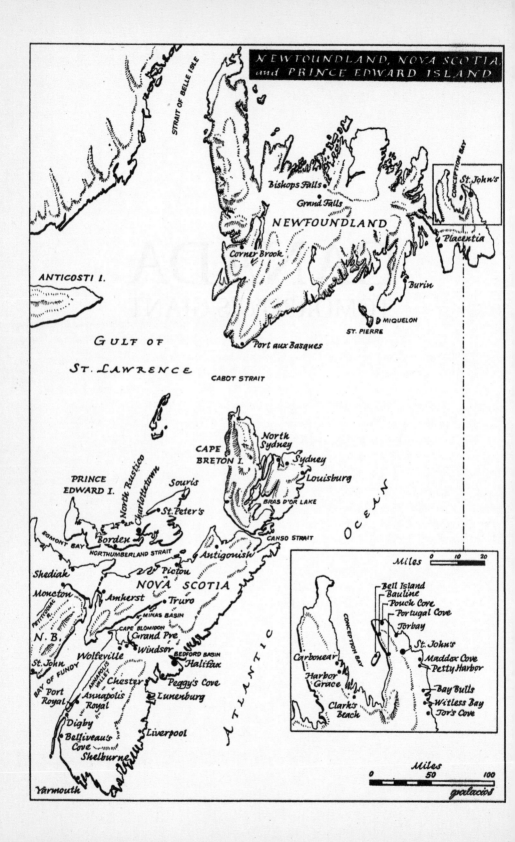

CANADIANS

*N*o one has yet defined the Canadian in words. What of it? He defines himself in action. Primarily he is a man of action rather than speech because he has to be. The Canadian cannot articulate; he acts—seldom with any considered principle or logic, almost always by instinct and pragmatic test. He is doubtless the most pragmatic of human creatures, the least given to theory, and he is skeptical of nearly everything, especially himself. More than most men, he is the amalgam of repeated trial and error, the result of more experience, disappointment, and hard-won games than any foreigner suspects.

Some three centuries of toil, adventure, war, blunder, narrow escape, experiment, and the slow mastery of a land designed for different owners have produced at last a Canadian character perhaps too young and certainly too reticent for definition.

If definition could be made and articulated now, it must soon become obsolete. The nature of the Canadian, though it contains some hard, unalterable ingredients, is still in the flux and accretion of youth. Nevertheless, it is growing fast, hardening and taking a definite shape quite distinct from the nature of other peoples, even the American neighbors next door.

Something strange, nameless, and profound moves in Canada today. It cannot be seen or labeled, but it can be heard and felt—a kind of whisper from far away, a rustle as of wind in prairie poplars, a distant river's voice, or the shuffle of footsteps in a midnight street. It is less a sound than a sense of motion.

Something moves as it has never moved before in this land, moves dumbly in the deepest runnels of a collective mind, yet by sure direction toward a known goal. Sometimes by thought, more often by intuition, the Canadian people make the final discovery. They are discovering themselves.

That passion of discovery which once sent birchbark canoes down unmapped waters, pushed railways across the Rockies, and dragged men to the frozen sea turns inward to explore a darker terrain. The nation labors in the travail of self-discovery and, by this labor, proves that it is in truth a nation, the home of a people.

The land, beyond men's narrow flares of light, is as it always was and will be to the end. A traveler sees the same eastern river that the Frenchmen saw, the cold, metallic lakes, the rounded glacial stone and little trees of the Shield, the big prairie sky, the mountains, the western jungle, and all that harsh splendor, mystery, and loneliness long known to his fathers. Only the inhabited fractions of the land are changing, a small part of the whole. But all the people are changing; or, unchanged, are finding themselves.

They build cities and spread concrete where grass grew yesterday. They drop new towns upon the tundra from airplanes, cut the Arctic horizon with smokestacks, bore through buried forests for oil, and turn the currents of the continent from their ageless courses. Yet all this hungry pursuit and apparent success could mean little until the Canadian found himself.

The sovereign question of Canadian life has always been whether anything lay here to be found, any separate and valid quality of our own, any indigenous substance to justify a nation.

That question has been answered in our time. It has been answered not by the nation's leaders and policies, but by the little, unknown people, of whom the great names, the great towns, the day's news, and all the known things are merely the shadow and reverberation.

The little people perceive for themselves a decisive event in the nation's history, unnoticed when it came to pass, undated, and still only half understood. In these last twenty years at most, probably in ten, they crossed the grand portage and watershed of their long march when no man saw the crossing. They crossed it blindly in the darkness; they left no stone or stake to make their crossing and saw it behind them by a backward glance.

Until then the foreigner might predict and the Canadian admit to himself that a nation, or the semblance of nation strung in shreds and clusters along four thousand miles of emptiness, could not permanently resist the magnetism of its mighty neighbor. Even today, in the full tide of material progress, the Canadian still asks himself whether his work is ultimately doomed by the neighbor's friendly economic penetration.

This doubt is as old as Canada, but can no longer be considered in its old context. For if American penetration is increasing, the permanent stuff of life, and the means of preserving it, have been found in Canada.

Where found? In the politics of Ottawa? In sudden prosperity, opulent living standards, and the resounding clamor of the boom? Not there. No great thing was ever found there.

Look for the answer in the eyes and minds of the nameless Canadians. Listen to their casual talk, their shy hints, their secret hopes. Ask some fisherman in his boat, a farmer in his field, a logger in the woods, a factory worker in the city bus what he is thinking about Canada and you will get the same reply in different words, accents, and languages.

The Canadian whose father accepted Canada as a spiritual dependency of some external power is thinking of it now solely as a nation in its own right. Though the nation is diverse, confused, self-centered, a little dizzy and smug from success at the moment, it is essentially whole. It has become cognate and organic. The Canadian knows, better than his father knew, that he belongs to it and no other.

Historians tell us that a purely negative and centrifugal movement, a traumatic recoil from the American Revolution, began the Canadian experiment. A sterile force somehow fertilized the cold northern ovum. Maybe so. Today, however, a positive centripetal force is at work. No one will doubt it after he sees Canada, at first hand, from coast to coast.

What is this force? As usual, the Canadian cannot define it or his place in it. He can say only that he is everywhere building something of his own, no better than other men's work, possibly not as good, but still his own. He follows a homemade dream. He has followed it long enough now, against more obstacles than any stranger can guess, to be nothing but a Canadian. That definition serves him well enough.

——————◆——————

CHAPTER ONE

The Misty Island

THE TWINE loft was propped on lurching stilts beside a frozen sea. Its stove distilled the odors of cod, tar, paint, salt, and sweat, the native reek of Newfoundland, long impregnated in the shed and its owners. This tiny refuge of warmth and habitation contained six men, a ton of coiled fishnet, and the latest chapter in a North American story four and a half centuries old; also, if one could read it, the intimation of a new America, a shift in the whole balance of its affairs, the rapid emergence of a new power athwart the United States, and the appearance of a new American race, called Canadians.

The men in the twine loft of Bauline, like most North Americans, were ignorant of such things. Canada remained a mystery to them, as to all its peoples—a nation outwardly so simple, inwardly so complex, diverse, and unfathomable. The eyes and minds of these men were turned away from the continental mainland, and they felt themselves to be no part of the new race. (Besides, they had troubles of their own. With patient desperation they watched the icefloe, of a full mile's width, that ground the whole eastern shore of Newfoundland, beached every boat, chocked every cove, and left the fish hordes uncaught in the second week of May.)

The youngest fisherman, his cheeks pink from the salty wind and not yet graven, like the other faces, by time and weather, was mending a net. A wooden needle danced in his fingers like a living creature, and he hummed a merry tune.

A man of gigantic girth and face roughly carved out of roast beef, the veteran net-maker of Bauline, lolled on a stool and observed the apprentice with silent condescension. His working days were over, but in his prime he could weave a complete cod trap in only six months.

Beside him sat the replica of a Chinese idol, carved in dark teak, who peered out of rheumy eyes and chewed tobacco with toothless gums. Slowly and painfully he brought himself at last to the point of utterance.

"Why, 'tis easy now," he said in that odd accent derived from Devon, Ireland, and the talk of foreign sailormen. " 'Tis easy indeed fer fishin' when they've de engines and all. We used to row at de oars, five men, you see, to de boat."

He held up his hands to show me how they had been twisted by the oar handles in fixed, circular grip like talons.

"De young," he added, glancing at the apprentice, "don't know nawthin' about work in Newf'nland." (He pronounced the name in a slur, like all Newfoundlanders, the emphasis heavily on the last syllable.) "Why, nawthin' a-tall. Dat's de trut' of it and no mistake."

The retired net-maker permitted himself a grunt of approval. The others laughed, as Newfoundlanders are always laughing at some private joke of their own. But the captain of the crew, a towering man of square, crimson features, allowed that the work was hard enough, even with engines in the boats.

"Me fadder," he said, a glint of bitterness in his beach-pebble eyes, "worked all of his life and not a penny to show fer it. And his fadder before him. And his fadder, too. 'Tis always dat way wid fish."

He spoke of fish as if the word itself explained the history of his folk. So it does. The cod swarm brought men here in the beginning and still holds them on this barren island shore against climate, poverty, and the magnet of the continent.

Why, I asked, did he and his fellows stay here when they could get good jobs on the mainland? The question seemed to take him by surprise, almost as an affront, and he gave me a suspicious look. These men were Canadians by recent constitutional contract, though not otherwise, but no one, I dare say, had ever asked them about Canada before.

"Sir," the captain said after reflection, "I'll tell you wot it is—we lives a good life and 'tis de only work we knows. A good life indeed when a man's his own boss and nobody to tell him come or go, and de fish ready to de trap and de price fair."

His voice took on the tone of a craftsman's pride: "Dawn to dark we pulls de traps and a woman workin' on de stages, makin' fish, fer every man afloat. Man and woman, we've bin happy here a long, long toime."

I glanced through the door at the place where men and women of this breed have been happy for a long, long time. The flat-topped houses of Bauline had been fastened like the nest of some monstrous sea bird to the base of a naked cliff. No discernible street, only a rough track, wriggled between the houses, and nothing moved on the cramped sea-shelf but a few sheep and two lean cows. The little church and, beside it, the newly painted school told their story of these people's struggle for religion and learning. A shaft of cut stone held the names of twenty-five men from the fifty-two families of Bauline who had died in two world wars for Newfoundland and the British Empire—not for Canada. Beyond this scant acre of man's possession stretched six thousand miles of coast-line, the solid ice, the solitary island, and the misty sea.

No such scene or people could be found anywhere else in Canada.

Roses were blooming that day on the Pacific shore. The coast jungle was noisy with the click of ax and the mutter of chain saws. Fruit blossom foamed down the interior valleys. Snow dripped from the lips of the Rockies, and the swollen western rivers writhed in sudden freshet.

Plows sliced the black prairie earth, wheat sprouted, cattle nibbled the new bunch grass, oil flowed from the breast of the central plains, miners' drills punctured the northern tundra, last year's crop moved in endless procession of freight trains to the Lakehead, and ships with bellies full of grain wallowed toward the St. Lawrence.

Along the great river and northward, among the rocks, lakes, and little trees of the Shield, the cities, towns, and camps of central Canada felt the reviving touch of spring, heard the steady beat of an industrial revolution, began another year of ravenous growth.

Down in the Maritimes the maples opened their scarlet buds, fishermen tended their lobster pots, the fleets of the North Atlantic crowded the harbors and whistled their greetings from all the oceans of the world. Spring had thawed out half a continent and set Canada in full motion again.

But here in Bauline there was no sign of spring. The fishermen huddled about their smoky stove and watched their old enemy, the ice. Then I remembered that Newfoundland was not Canada, except by yesterday's legal marriage of convenience, that in every other sense this remained foreign soil and its people strangers to us; remembered, too, that the union with Canada had been a shotgun marriage, with the United States as a silent spectator, perhaps a disappointed suitor in the long struggle to divide the continent.

Well, here I was in Bauline beginning, after a lapse of a dozen years, the rediscovery of my people. It was a good place, a detached and almost neutral ground, to consider the old question of that people's survival. Before I had finished my journey the question would be answered in my mind, but the end of the road lay forty-three hundred miles, and several months, distant.

Today I could see only the idle boats and, in the twine loft, the latest ingredients of a race little known to itself, known to its American neighbors only in caricature. Over this frozen shoreline, as over the whole nation from the 49th parallel to the pole, hung the historic question mark: could a nation conceived in anger against its neighbor, born in defiance of American power, of geography and economics, dedicated to the proposition that the continent must hold two great powers, friendly but forever separate—could such a nation long endure?

The captain, interrupting my speculations, climbed up on a pile of nets and took from the rafters a rusty weapon, eight feet long. It was not likely, he supposed, that I had ever seen in Canada the like of this sealing gun used by his grandfather.

No one bothered to carry guns these days. It was easier, he said, and saved ammunition, to walk out on the shifting ice and club the seal pups with a boathook. Yesterday the captain had killed five, one mile from land. Their pelts wouldn't bring much, but every dollar helped when you couldn't launch a boat or spread a trap, though the cod were "eatin' the rocks."

Few Canadians, I agreed, had ever seen a gun of this sort, and I seized this opening to ask the local question within the national question which had brought me here: what did he think of Canada? This seemed to stir something deep in all the men of Bauline. They were reacting not as Canadians, but as Newfoundlanders. The retired net-maker grunted again, the eyes of the Chinese idol squinted knowingly, and the needle of the youngster paused in mid-air.

"I'll tell you," the captain said like a man announcing a weighty judgment. "Canada's a very rich country, so dey say. Yes, an' it might be a very good country and good folk, fer all of dat."

Had he ever seen it? No, he had never seen it, and didn't expect to. Canada was far away. A man heard little from over there.

What did he think of Newfoundland's political union with Canada in 1949? For all he knew, it might be a good thing, and it had provided Newfoundland with a lot of money, he'd been told. But with the invariable courtesy of his kind he let me understand that he felt no interest in Canada.

Why should he? And how could he guess that this desolate village far out in the Atlantic—an immeasurable distance, in miles and memory, from the center of Canada—represented the Canadian method from the beginning?

It represented the slow amalgamation of many diverse elements in a single substance. By a time lag of some hundred years Newfoundland had become the final element in the amalgam. This twine loft was a microcosm of a process that began when the first Frenchman set foot on the mainland.

Here it was in its first phase. Throughout the nation, in later phases, it still flowed with ever increasing momentum to its completion. Primarily it was a Canadian process, the true meaning and secret of the nation, but it was more than that. It was quietly changing the whole process of the continent, though the continent had hardly suspected the change or the greater changes ahead.

Only a handful of people own the land of Canada and these sixteen millions are perhaps the most fortunate people in human history. No people of their numbers have ever owned so much wealth, enjoyed more freedom, or faced a happier future. Yesterday Canada was a frontier, living mainly on the export of a few raw products. Today it is the world's fourth international trader and one of its major industrial areas. It is probably growing faster proportionately, in population and in wealth, than any other nation of these times.

Such statistical facts are known to foreign experts, but not to the world at large nor even to most Canadians. They are not the important facts. They only try and fail to measure the important facts.

A new race is forming here organically, cell by cell. A new world power is taking shape on the northern slope of the planet. In a half-century at most it will be more powerful, with its resources, than any nation in contemporary Europe. It will confront the United States with a new continental situation. Soon, for the first time, the United States will find a great nation on its flank, midway between it and Russia on the strategic map of the air age.

Already Canada stands midway between the United States and Britain—the honest broker, one foot in the old world and one in the new, the only Commonwealth nation in America and, as Churchill once called it, the "linchpin of peace." Such phrases may be exaggerated and do not greatly impress Canadians. But it is true that through such agents as Lester B. Pearson, a Canadian and a great citizen of the world, this country has often unobtrusively interpreted the old and new worlds to each other and sometimes prevented grave collisions.

In short, by no merit of its own but by circumstances of history and geography, Canada must be accounted a highly strategic area in military, political, and economic terms. A single fact is enough to show its vital importance to its neighbors: the United States cannot defend itself without the full use of Canada's northern territory and cannot fight a war without Canada's mineral resources.

What kind of men inhabit this half-continent behind the caricature of the tourist advertisements and the legend of a simple, competent, successful, and rather dull folk? What kind of race and power will Canada ultimately produce? The purpose of my journey was to find some answer to these imponderables, but I knew already that most of the current answers were false.

I knew that if my people were outwardly simple and dull, they nourished a hot inward pride and a gnawing discontent; that despite their loneliness and remoteness from one another, in their isolated pockets and shifting bivouacs of civilization, in their two basic racial strains, in a nation of at least six distinct compartments, they were curiously united by a fierce possession of their land, by a single idea which has no name but Canada.

I knew that my people, unlike their neighbors, were ambivalent and perpetually torn between geography and history by the old pull of their ancestral homelands overseas and the stronger pull of their home in America. I knew, too, that though they were rich, hard-working, and successful in all practical things, they were puzzled and uncertain.

For all their wealth and outer look of smugness, they were deeply disappointed with some vital aspects of their life; were clinging to the thoughtways of their ancestors, imitating their American neighbors, yet striving to create something different and unique—a homemade dream. They were young, as peoples go, but their bent of spirit had long been shaped by a mixture of memory and environment. That bent resembled only on the surface the spirit of their American neighbors or any other people.

The Canadian problem, in short, was to adjust these well-established instincts to an almost overpowering new fact—the fact of a sudden material revolution.

The men in the twine loft would be the last to suspect these things. Throughout its four centuries of separate life—the oldest white man's life in America north of the Spanish colonies—Newfoundland has felt little contact with Canada. Until a few years ago it found little welcome among Canadians. Its business was concentrated in Britain, the United States, the Mediterranean, the Caribbean, and South America. Its mind was concentrated on its own island, that oddly shaped doorknocker hanging from the eastern gateway of the continent.

When Newfoundland knocked on Canada's door for admission sixty years ago it was rebuffed and, as it thought, humiliated. Therefore its loyalty beyond its native coast extended only to Britain. Its final entry into the Canadian Confederation was barely accomplished by a combination of accident, two men's genius, some pretty fancy back-room politics, and a narrow public vote. "Come here at your peril, Canadian wolf," is the best-remembered line in Newfoundland's balladry. It tells a long and tragic tale.

The captain, being a Newfoundlander and one of nature's gentlemen, did not remind me of those facts and, in any case, had little time to brood on them. He and every man like him on the island was grappling not only with the weather but with a local revolution inside the larger revolution of Canada that threatens the life of the ancient inshore fishery but promises to make a richer life for all Newfoundlanders.

The machine age is outdating the crude trap spread close to shore by hand. The big boats known as draggers are dredging the distant sea floor with power scoops. The drying flakes which used to cure the entire hand-made catch in the sun are being replaced by factories, salt cod by processed fish sticks to suit the modern housewife. Behind the shoreline, in the forests, the mines and larger towns, half a million Newfoundlanders, owning vast, undeveloped riches, are beginning at last to exploit them in modern industries of many sorts. Still, the inshore fishermen, the eighteenth generation in their craft, cling to the only skills they know.

On the beach of Bauline the captain showed me the last two boats left in a port which once supported fifty, a crude winch to drag them from the water, and the eight-hundred-pound killicks of long, thin stones tied to wooden crosses that serve as anchors.

These men had everything they needed and asked only a few hundred dollars of annual income. They seemed unaware that their living standard, as reckoned by economists, was about one third of the North American average. What economist could reckon the true standard of their life? It is to be reckoned only in contentment, memories, adventures, laughter, and the lonely freedom of the sea.

Concerning these things the captain had definite opinions. He and his people had been happy here a long, long time, and here they would live and die. If I wanted to know about politics, business, and suchlike, he said, I had better talk to Joey.

I promised to do so, and followed the narrow road along the cliff edge, where, by lucky chance, I found the Honorable Joseph Smallwood. He was standing on a hill outside his capital of St. John's, leaning against a bitter wind and entertaining a vision.

The bespectacled, owlish face and sparrow's figure beside the road might not look prophetic, but this little man was gripped by almost apocalyptic revelation. I paused to talk with him not because he happened at the moment to be the first premier of the new Canadian province, but because this tramp newspaperman, pig farmer, radio announcer, amateur politician, and improbable articulator of a mighty dream had somehow stumbled into the history of America and sharply altered its course.

Lacking Smallwood's vision, his oratory, and his organizing talents, Newfoundland would not have voted by a hair-thin margin to join Canada. In his judgment, and in the judgment of the late Prime Minister W. L. Mackenzie King, of Canada, who was his silent partner in this enterprise, Newfoundland eventually would have joined the United States.

Both men believed that an area so vital to North American defense, and already defended by American military bases, could not long endure as a separate and weak political entity in an era of clashing international power; and if Canada's eastern gateway were in foreign hands, however friendly, the effect on the Canadian state, King feared, would be disastrous, perhaps eventually fatal. For, as he told his confidants, a transcontinental nation which could not hold the strategic key to the St. Lawrence Gulf probably would prove non-viable in the long run. Therefore, in King's opinion, Newfoundland's adherence to Canada was not primarily a matter of economics but an essential factor in Canada's nationhood.

But Smallwood, the small-town politician, dreamer, and ceaseless talker, seemed to me, as he stood on a hillside surveying his private kingdom, the most improbable agent of these continental forces. Nevertheless, he was their local agent and will be so remembered long after his political adventures are forgotten.

We were to talk of these things later. Meanwhile Joey advised me to see what was happening among the ordinary people before I attempted to study Newfoundland's economic revolution at his headquarters in St. John's. He dashed off in his mud-spattered Cadillac (a shovel in the trunk against emergencies), and I soon found myself far away at Petty Harbor, whose elders were assembled to consider the ruin of their village.

The parliament of Petty Harbor appeared to consist of three men, in gum boots, overalls, and tattered cloth caps. They loitered on the beach and blinked gloomily at the ice, the broken stages, the ragged cluster of houses, and the prospects of a barren year.

These men were not hostile—no Newfoundlander is hostile—but they were shy, and skeptical of an obvious stranger from Canada. At first they answered my questions in glum monosyllables and in an accent so queer that I could hardly translate it. Having sized me up as harmless, they evidently relished the chance of leisurely conversation.

The leader of this dismal triumvirate—a massive fellow who had distended his moon face with a formidable plug of tobacco—called it a bad year, the worst he remembered. But, then, it had always been a hard life hereabouts.

"I t'inks," he said, " 'tis de hardest work dere is, haulin' traps, but 'tis no matter if dere's fish and proper prices. Last year de fish was good."

He shifted his tobacco thoughtfully, groping for an adequate description of the catch, and finally hit on an unlikely word. "De fish," he said, "was numerous, very numerous. But de price no good a-tall." After a long moment of cogitation he stated a basic fact of Newfoundland's life. "Ah, if we only had land to farm!"

Around this barren inlet of stone, though it would excite the artist, there was hardly land enough to nourish half a dozen cows, or even to hold the cod flakes.

A wizened little man, his eyes blurred by thick glasses, intervened to tell me that a hundred and fifty boats used to fish out of Petty Harbor, and that now there were only thirty-six.

"She's goin' under," he said and peered hopelessly at the stages on their rotting lime-green piles like legs encased in seaweed stockings. "Nawthin' can save her. She's finished."

The third man said nothing. He was incapable of speech, a flimsy, bewhiskered scarecrow who suddenly shook with a wrenching ague as if he would fall to pieces.

I repeated the question I had asked at Bauline—why did they stay with the unprofitable shore fishery? The leader's reply was prompt, decisive, and heartbroken: "Too old."

Yes, too old to change the ways of four centuries, too old to accept the revolution, too old to leave the only home they had ever known. It might be deserted by the young, it might collapse under rain, wind, and ice, but they would die in Petty Harbor like their fathers.

"Too old"—and all the upheaval, the misery, and yet the fair hopes of the revolution were compressed in those two words. "Too old"—and the moon-faced man searched my eyes for a ray of understanding, the little man behind the spectacles muttered to himself, and the ancient mariner was shaken bodily by an unseen hand. "Too old"—what more was there to say?

That point established, the parliament of Petty Harbor fell into silence and stared at its enemy, the ice of May. While we stood there in the cutting cold, our communications severed, a fourth man joined us and quickly revealed himself as the leader of the opposition. He was a tall, rugged man of bulging frame, his face lined but unconquered by toil and adversity.

All this talk of fish, he said, was irrelevant. The fish would soon be swarming in the traps, the country was all right, but Newfoundland would be ruined by its union with Canada.

"Confederation!" he shouted above the wind. "Why, Confederation was the bloodiest fool thing we ever did. The new industries? They'll all go broke, you'll see, and when de Americans finish spendin' money on de airfields, Newf'nland'll be finished, too." He laughed bitterly and added for my benefit: "Then Canada can take care of us."

Pulling a crumpled package of Camels from his pocket (the cigarette introduced by the American troops along with other folkways), he struck a match on his thumbnail and drew the smoke deep into his lungs. Nicotine stimulated his anger.

"Confederation? Wot about Confederation? I'll tell you wot about Confederation. Everybody wants a job from de gover'ment, dat's all dere is to Confederation. Me, I'll starve before I take a gover'ment job."

What of Canada's new social services, the monthly government check for every child, the old-age pensions?

"Oh," said he, " 'tis all very well, de baby bonus and de like o' dat, and very nice fer de wife to buy a bar of soap or a bit of beef, fer ye can't live solid on fish and keep up yer stren'th. But de trouble is in de world today every lad expects de gover'ment to look after him. Dey won't fish, dey go to town and get unemployment insurance in the winter and raise hell wid drinkin' and all."

He pointed to his youngest son, a handsome boy of some fifteen years, who waited silently on the beach.

"Will dat lad fish? Not he, sir! He'll go to town and get a job like all his brudders. I've no schoolin', but I can read and I've a mind of me own and I tell you straight Confederation and all dis gover'ment carry-on is de finish of Newf'nland and no mistake."

There spoke the voice of Newfoundland's native nationality yet to be merged with the nationality of Canada, the racial voice of a proud, indestructible breed. Well, if I didn't believe him, I could drive down the bay to Maddox Cove, his birthplace, and see for myself.

A zigzag path between an avalanche of pink boulders and some flakes still bearing the unsold remains of last year's cod led me to the Cove. There I found only one human being. He was such a man as Rembrandt would have painted and Shakespeare might have taken as a model for Falstaff in his days of ruin—a squat, barrel-shaped man, his swollen face as purple as old claret—and his job was to fix the track called a road.

In a dump cart his shaggy horse hauled a few handfuls of gravel which the driver applied, with a miser's economy, to the potholes. He worked conscientiously for the government and seemed to begrudge even a moment for a chat. Few words were needed to tell the story of Maddox Cove, casualty of the revolution.

Not long ago it was a thriving village. Its men fished for cod a mile down the bay. Its women somehow made vegetables and flowers grow between the boulders, milked a cow or two, and knitted the wool of their own sheep. Now the wharf lay smashed on the rocks, the flakes scattered like toothpicks. Most of the houses were empty, fences down, gardens overgrown by rank grasses.

What had happened to Maddox Cove? The wine-faced roadman replied in two words, each emerging as a separate and hoarse agony. "All gone," he said.

His cheeks turned a deeper purple as he thought of it, and he uttered a final verdict: "Nobody's happy any more.

Nowheres." Dragging his thoughts from a bottomless despair, he pronounced his sentence on life: "Let 'em drop de bomb. 'Twon't make any difference."

That was the voice of age in a land much older than Canada or the United States. The voice of youth, the undying voice of Newfoundland's hope and humor, could be heard that day at Bay Bulls, which crouches in a pleasant valley dappled with newly shorn sheep.

The restaurant of this hamlet has been equipped with civilization's masterpiece, a jukebox. Because his freight schooner was fast in the ice, a skipper had hoisted too many beers and was now pouring nickels into the musical monster. We had never met before, but he instantly recognized me as an old friend, recalled a riotous party we had enjoyed together last winter down in Placentia, and promised, with a solemn wink, to keep that affair dark. He was having a bit of fun, he confessed, but when the ice went out and his ship could move, there'd be no more drinking and no liquor aboard. I believed him. The sea and the mastery of it were legible in that man's jagged, salt-cured face.

Then, for my benefit, he started the jukebox playing a lively air and danced a Newfoundland jig until he slumped down, winded. The newfangled Yankee music, he gasped, wasn't like the good old native tunes. So they have danced and sung and been happy here, in the face of weather and calamity, these four centuries.

On the beach near by a plump youngster, Irish by descent, face, and impudent blue eyes, was painting his boat and singing to himself. He greeted me as a stranger and a friend.

"Why, sure," said he in an opulent brogue, "you'll hear 'em complainin' at Petty Harbor. Always they complain at Petty Harbor. Pay no attention. Mark you, sir, I've bin about in my time, all 'round the world in ships, and there's nothin' as good as right here. Leave me alone to fish, me and five brudders, and that's all I ask. Ah, it's a grand thing fer a man! Why, sure the young lads go to Canada or the States. They make a pile of money, all right, but they always come back here to fish."

He looked across the icy bay and laughed aloud at some private discovery. "I'll tell you what it is," he said. "The fish gets into your blood and you can't get 'em out. And what a grand life it is altogether!"

His family, the O'Briens, have been living this life for something like two hundred years. They may have been here when Iberville LeMoyne, the blond warrior of New France and scourge of America, executed his incredible winter march along the Newfoundland coast, burning every village on the way. Even Iberville could not drive the Irish out of Bay Bulls. Their title deed to this place is proclaimed by their own peculiar monuments. Four up-ended cannon topped by bronze saints form the gateposts of their churchyard. Life is still good for young O'Brien, and there are many like him.

Not far off, on Witless Bay, a youth hardly out of his teens was building his first boat and his unconscious testament to the future. It could be built for $150, he told me, if you cut the keel and ribs out of the forest, and it would soon pay for itself in these good times. Move to town? Get an easy job? Not he, so long as Witless Bay was full of cod and he was his own boss, with his own boat. In him the eighteenth successive generation of Newfoundland fishermen was putting out to sea.

Three aged characters huddled over a beach fire close to Tor's Cove. The salmon were swimming out there under the ice, worth seventy cents a pound, a fortune to these men, and already they had lost half the brief season's catch.

"Still and all," said the oldest of the three, "It'll be a good year." Why, a man might make two or three hundred dollars in a few weeks if the salmon were running good. So they squatted by their fire and waited confidently for the sea's unfailing crop.

Outside Portugal Cove two small boys of ruddy complexion were walking four miles home from school. They climbed eagerly into my car, speechless with excitement at this chance of a ride. Under close questioning they informed me shyly that they had learned the words of "O Canada" and had seen photographs of Ottawa. The slow process of Canadianism was beginning here.

Farther along that lonely road by the sea rocks I picked up a farmer whose gnarled body and rough hands told his story. He had a nice farm, he said, nearly seven cleared acres, four cows, and a fine flock of chickens. He combined farming with a bit of lobster fishing and did very well. Moreover, he and his wife were getting Canada's old-age pension. That was a grand thing. Canada must be a rich country to pay old folks forty dollars regularly every month. He pointed inland to the black horizon of spruce and stone. In there, he said, millions of acres could be plowed, once the vast moors were drained.

As I set him down at the gate, he raised his cap in farewell. The four cows, his major capital assets, stood in a muddy yard with the chickens. His wife planted potatoes between two crooked lines of fieldstones, her skirts flapping in the wind.

Such men and women on every inhabited curve of the coast might be poor, but to me, a stranger, they never appeared pathetic. They were too intelligent, polite, and proud to be patronized; too strong to need anyone's sympathy; too independent, roughcast, and deeply grained to lose their character in a world of smooth conformity; too settled in their own ways to change them by mere constitutional act of union with Canada.

If they are not yet Canadian by any compulsion outside the statute books, and are, indeed, quite different from any other people in America, they are the material of a stronger, richer Canada. They have added to the nation a new strain (or, rather, America's oldest white strain north of the first Spanish settlements) by committing their future to this continent. They have brought us an outlook and temperament distinct from ours, a certain extra chuckle, and all those qualities which come only out of hardship, endurance, and the cold mandate of the sea.

Their lean faces and shrewd eyes, their soft speech and never failing laughter, their dumb love of these native rocks, forests, villages, and lonely waters have been shaped by a ferocious and little-known history. Nowhere else in America have white people suffered so much from geography, climate, poverty, disaster, and human stupidity. From the beginning every policy that government in London could contrive, every obstacle that avarice could imagine, every misfortune that war and weather could invent have combined to suppress this race of men. But nothing could suppress them.

The wonder, after such an experience, is not that Newfoundland remains poor, but that its civilization refused to perish long ago. In the mere act of endurance it has hatched a miracle.

Once Cabot had dropped a basket off this coast in 1497, hauled up a bushel of cod, and reported the wealth of a "New-founde-lande," the great island became a prize of war, commerce, and conspiracy, a victim of conqueror, exploiter, and bungling politician, a pawn in Europe's quarrels. It was a place where settlers were forbidden to live lest they interrupt the world's richest fishery, and yet settled in unknown coves and distant uplands, flourished in secret, and finally possessed their harsh, beloved soil with all the waters around it.

Traveling about these shores, I tried to imagine the parade of men and events that marched here a century before the white man's landfalls at Quebec and Jamestown.

Cabot and then the first fishermen from Europe in the early sixteenth century; Humphrey Gilbert, proclaiming England's first colony to a band of foreign sailors in the crowded harbor of St. John's and soon drowning in mid-Atlantic with his famous shout—"Cheer up, lads, we're as near heaven on sea as on land"; the "admirals" from Bristol who became legal governors, tyrants, and usually rascals by reaching St. John's ahead of their fellows every spring; the first English tax-collector, who discovered that "ye fishermen be stuberne fellows" nourishing a rooted aversion to taxes; Dutch raiders, French in lawful war, and uncounted pirates in casual pillage through the seventeenth and eighteenth centuries; settlers, now legally established, struggling for responsible government and winning it; shipwreck, fire, disease, hunger, and religious riot among the poor; commercial feudalism, sudden fortune, sudden ruin, revelry, routs, scandals, and stuffy Victorian pomp among the rich; abundant fish harvests, lean seasons, lost markets, boom, depression, and bankruptcy; fifteen years of government under an appointed commission; and then, at midnight, March 31, 1949, the birth of the tenth Canadian province and the geographical fulfillment of the nation from sea to sea—such is the record of men's heroism and folly in Newfoundland and Canada.

How can we expect that such a people, nurtured in such a region, distant from us in space and much farther away in experience, should be like that imaginary creature, the average North American? Why should the Canadian expect the Newfoundlander to be like him merely because both have long accepted a common Crown in London? The Newfoundlander is himself in a hundred ways too subtle to be identified but instantly felt by the stranger.

As a stranger from Canada I thought I perceived that Newfoundlanders were more simple, in the literal meaning of the word, than most Canadians and far less sophisticated than most Americans. They have yet to feel the smartness, speed, tension, and fury of the mainland. They have not yet received the doubtful glories of a high living standard, nor the North American disillusionment which accompanies it. They therefore possess a patience, a dogged outward cheerfulness, and, I suspect, an inner contentment deeper than ours.

United by poverty and common peril, they have amassed their own philosophy of endurance, devised their own amusements, thought their own thoughts, written their own robust folklore, sung their own songs, and shared a kind of family jest.

If they have yet to see the full rewards of the machine age, now dawning, they have not suffered the North American blight of uniformity. Almost every native of Newfoundland remains a character, often an eccentric, Dickensian character, unpolished and untamable.

Though less educated, these people are more articulate than

any Canadian outside Quebec; as articulate, indeed, as Americans, because lonely men must talk, and they talk ceaselessly.

More religious than most of us, they still affirm superstitions, ghosts, and legends that we lost long ago.

Their interests have always stretched abroad, but they remain the most provincial folk in Canada, their minds centered on the only land they know.

In short, four and a half centuries of separation and a century without immigration have made them Newfoundlanders and nothing else, a cohesive and recognizable race, a true nationality, and, by every definition, a people.

To me it seemed that, in acquiring Newfoundland, Canada had acquired in these people an asset far more important than the strategic northern gateway to the continent or certain raw resources. Still, these resources, larger than we yet realize, were worth even a vagrant traveler's consideration. I therefore put myself in the hands of a curious person who was a Newfoundlander by birth, blood, and instinct, but became a Canadian by conviction.

Gregory Power is a tall, gangling, soft-spoken, and sad-looking man of large views, a warm heart, and an elfin strain of humor. These qualities had made him, at the time of our meeting, the island's public treasurer, its leading poet, and its largest producer of commercial poultry.

Such a combination, I fancy, would be impossible in any other place, but Power seemed to bear the threefold burdens of politics, poetry, and poultry quite cheerfully and impartially. Over a single glass of rum—he is little addicted to the Island's national drink called "Screech"—he talked all night about government and the natural wealth of his native land, interspersing his statistics with hints on chicken farming, snatches of Newfoundland's folk rhymes and his own, memories of storm and shipwreck, tales of murders, ghosts, and battles long ago.

Such a man and many like him have deeper roots in Newfoundland than most of us have in Canada or the United States. His French ancestors (their name distorted by the centuries) first settled near Placentia when France still hoped to

clutch the whole island. His grandfather was one of the chief
advocates of union with Canada in the Confederation of 1867.
His older cousins once rescued a Confederation candidate from
an angry mob, smuggled him into a whaleboat, and hid him
under the skirts of Power's formidable aunt. His grandmother
captained a crew of seven brothers on eleven fishing voyages
to Labrador. He had seen some strange sights himself—
among them the famous wreck of the *Big Annie* and a
steersman gripping the wheel so tightly in death that his hands
had to be sawed off before he could be buried.

After all this experience the poet in Power naturally produced a vivid omnibus phrase to invoke the destiny of his
province. It now confronted, he told me, its Historic Moment.
Since it was nearly dawn before he isolated that Moment from
the torrent of his speech, I suggested that we postpone it until later in the day. He agreed reluctantly, having many more
tales to tell, and several hours later we started out to survey
his chilly homeland.

The Historic Moment was not apparent to the naked eye
as we passed the huge American base of Pepperell, a town in
itself outside St. John's, and soon were bumping over a maze
of narrow side roads.

Forest and bare hillside revealed here and there a few
pinched yards of cultivation, a dump cart hauling firewood or
manure, a man cutting poles for his fish flakes, three men
guiding a single horse along an almost vertical field not much
larger than a city lot, or a woman feeding a dozen chickens,
far from any neighbor.

The rusty whaling fleet was locked in the ice of Harbor
Grace. The little town of Carbonear told us nothing of that
memorable day when Iberville drove its inhabitants to an
island near by, could not make them surrender, and retreated
from the only failure of his brutal winter march. At Clark's
Beach a kitchen chair was fastened to a roof by the shore as a
humble reminder of the woman who waited there so long for
her drowned sailorman. Then on the horizon loomed the
whale's back of Bell Island and great ships loading iron ore
from shafts miles under the sea.

That iron was a Canadian treasure, to be sure, but I still looked in vain for any portent of the Historic Moment. At length Power led me past a jungle of stages and flakes named Pouch Cove, up through drifts of snow to a moorland as empty, cold, and silent as the Arctic, and out upon a cliff high above a pounding surf.

There the politician, the poultryman, and the poet halted to survey a range of hills unchanged since the early hours of creation. The last ice age had shaved them clean and left a surface of burnished glass. No tree, no flower, no single blade of grass had ever taken root on this appalling desolation.

"The mountains of the moon," said the poet, shouting into my ear above the gale. "Look at them! They make you think."

At any rate they made him think, though I was too cold for thought. That scene, said the politician, represented most foreigners' notion of Newfoundland. I looked up at the leering rock face above, the dim cliffs, the frozen sea below, and, near us, among a cascade of rounded pebbles, a man who was digging twenty square feet of earth to plant a handful of potatoes.

Having accomplished his purpose, Power regarded me with a sly grin and spoke as a practical businessman, the master of poultry. This, he said, was not the real Newfoundland at all. It was only an aberration of the landscape, a freak, a parody.

The real Newfoundland, he assured me, owned the world's richest fishery, probably the most valuable forest in Canada, and, in its mainland territory of Labrador, some of the most valuable iron deposits discovered anywhere, adjoining the largest undeveloped sources of hydro power in America. All these things would soon be needed in a world hungry for food, wood, minerals, and electricity. Whereupon, he announced in the voice of the poet, the Historic Moment would arrive.

I confess I saw it dimly at that unhistoric moment. However, clear intimations of the great change were visible later in some newly built factories incongruously planted among the changeless fishing villages to make such things as plywood, gum boots, gloves, leather, textiles, storage batteries, cement, machinery, electronic devices, chocolates, and, of all things, movie films. These industries were built on government loans, some of them were undoubtedly unsound and already had produced grave problems of finance, but for Power they indicated that the Historic Moment lay not far distant. They were the first installments of the industrial revolution leaping from the mainland to the island.

To see the raw materials of the larger installments ahead a stranger must penetrate the island's interior. As the new highway across the island was still incomplete, I reached the interior on America's most remarkable railway—a journey of some physical discomfort but indelible memories.

It is quicker, of course, and easier to fly, but it is more instructive to go by ship and train.

My wife and I began our journey at North Sydney, Nova Scotia. When the crowded and suffocating little ferryboat (it was to be replaced the next month by a fine modern vessel) wallowed into Cabot Straight, a Newfoundlander of many voyages invited me to the bar for a mild rum nightcap and declared, with the invariable optimism of his race, that the crossing would be smooth.

The words had barely left his lips before the ship answered by a lurch of derision and he found himself flat on the floor, a table on his chest and an empty glass clutched thriftily in his hand. Being a Canadian outlander, distrustful of this foreign weather, I had braced myself in advance and, alone in that company, retained my chair and drink in vertical position. Every other man in the barroom was horizontal. My proud moment proved fleeting.

All that night the ship slid up and down an invisible corkscrew. The cardboard containers affixed to every bunk were all put to use. The passengers arose sick and bruised. And at dawn we crawled into a gloomy cove a few yards wide called Port aux Basques at the southwest corner of Newfoundland.

That name held a faint flavor of the old French days, but no one seemed to notice it. We climbed hastily into a narrow-gauge train of two locomotives, two diners, and five crowded sleepers which awaited us on the wharf and soon moved off, clanking and snorting, in a rough trot. The natives have mastered this violent gait by long practice. A mainland horse-man resorts instinctively to that rhythmical equestrian motion known as posting.

Though the natives always jeer at their railway, they love it as a friend, they remember it as a feat of wilder enterprise than any transcontinental line, considering the builders' resources, and they have made the trip across their island a family party, a festival, and a lark.

Peering through the window as on a foreign land—which, indeed, it was for us—we realized at once that everything we had read or heard of Newfoundland was absurd.

We had imagined endless flat muskeg, and saw the Rockies in blue miniature, flecked with snow. We had expected a bare horizon of rock, and were soon moving past noble forests, myriads of winking lakes, spacious green valleys, and some fat farmland beside rivers of clean, dark water. We had pictured only mean fishing hamlets, and presently were in the thriving little city of Corner Brook, beside a mountain of pulp logs and one of the world's largest paper mills. We had dreaded the monotony of the interior barrens, and found them as brilliantly colored as the moors of Hardy's England, as mysterious and haunting as Wuthering Heights. We had studied the map of a twisted coastline drawn by a nervous hand, had supposed that every mile would be the same, and now looked out on sea vistas of Norway, Cornwall, Spain, and British Columbia.

All day we watched that montage of changing landscape, and at daybreak next morning beheld the glitter of Conception Bay, where huge swans of sculptured ice floated in a jewel case of sapphires and emeralds. Some day, we thought, that ubiquitous explorer, the North American tourist, would discover this scenery, and especially the fish in Newfoundland's lakes and rivers. Then there will be an annual stampede across Cabot Strait.

Like a horse in sight of barn and manger, the train shifted from trot to gallop and scampered down a winding grade into the foreign metropolis of St. John's.

No city could have looked more foreign to a mainland

Canadian than this dark lichen growth crawling up the sea rocks; no spectacle more unlikely than the ice-coated harbor, a shiny bathtub of white porcelain, full of a child's toy ships.

St. John's is foreign to all mainlanders in history, architecture, and spirit, and far older than any white man's habitation in Canada or the United States. Foreign and unique.

There may be touches of an English port along its busy wharves, memories of Devon in its tangled rigging, a whiff of London in some walled garden, a crooked street, or the Gothic cathedral. Yet this agglomerate of sea, stone, and wood is not derivative. It is original and indigenous, built by native craftsmen to a native design as the authentic capital of an authentic nationality, the ancient fortress of a seagoing race. The sea more than the land has shaped and colored it, has penetrated every cranny and aching bone of the town with storm, fog, salt, fish smell, and memories.

This place is bleak and ugly, I suppose, by the usual definition. Its tiers of square wooden houses (built overnight after the last of three total conflagrations) have been packed together cheek by jowl. Most of them are antiquated, shabby, and identical in every line. The business streets, for all their bustling traffic and modern goods, have still a dingy Victorian look.

But stand off a little way, stand on Signal Hill above the narrow canyon of the harbor gate, and observe St. John's whole. Its ugliness, like the ugly face of an old friend, turns into a wrinkled, scarred, and timeless beauty, the beauty of character, suffering, toil, and human adventure beside the calm and awful beauty of the sea.

On this May morning St. John's waited, in a murk of fog and coal smoke, for a northeast wind to change and clear the harbor. Newfoundland's genial summer could not be many days off.

The skipper of a chunky schooner, heavily laden with gasoline drums, lumber, and two automobiles for the outports, stared at the swirling haze and cursed the "damn hice." Two big freighters lay helpless at their iron buoys. A crowd of longshoremen, garbed like the longshoremen of Liverpool or

Southampton in long, clumsy overcoats, shivered idly in the lee of a brick wall.

Near by, her bow thrust almost into the main street, the white Portuguese ship *Maria Celeste* glistened by an alien shore like an exiled ray of Mediterranean sun. Her decks sprouted a gay flower bed of crimson, brown, and yellow sails on her fifty dories. The squat sailors, in berets, sweaters, and wooden-soled sea boots, mended their nets on the wharf, spoke only among themselves, and hummed some song from home. Their ship, like countless European ships through the centuries, had been fishing on the Grand Banks and had found sanctuary in the old haven of the North Atlantic.

Water Street, only a few yards away—a fisherman's trail long before the feet of Canadians or Americans touched the soil of the mainland—ignored the Portuguese. It had grown used to foreigners, and seemed to have pressing affairs.

It was absurd, of course, to expect that any business street in America would be different from another. Still, Water Street, bursting with traffic and crowded with businessmen in the universal business uniform, rather disappointed us at first. After we had walked its full length, the smell of ships and cod, the cold sniff of ice, the clutching fingers of the fog, assured us that St. John's did not belong to the mainland. It stood alone on its island, lost that day in Atlantic cloud banks. No ship could enter or leave its harbor. No plane could reach its airport. The people bustled about their business, but essentially they were marooned in mid-ocean like the original Newfoundlanders who awaited here the first sail of springtime, long ago.

Only a mainlander could feel the loneliness and piercing cold of St. John's. The natives knew that a belated spring would arrive tomorrow or next day, sweep the ice from the harbor overnight, free the fishing fleet, and open the Atlantic gate. The town was cheerful in anticipation of that annual release. Business was booming. The businessman's club on Water Street was crowded with a gay company of merchant princes, survivors of a lost age. I found them lounging in a room which must have been taken straight from London, and playing billiards or fortifying themselves on good West Indies rum.

The inmates of that club represented a dying civilization, and they knew it. Most of them deplored the union with Canada, one scholarly gentleman described himself as "a British subject resident in Newfoundland," and all of them predicted that the economic revolution, pressed ahead too fast, would end in financial ruin.

Well, the superannuated feudal barons of the great days had grown used to alternating ruin and prosperity. They were philosophical about the new age, they had no doubt of Newfoundland's long future, and they entertained me on crusty humor, rousing sea tales, and native folk songs.

Men of that sort, as able, educated, and widely traveled as any of their contemporaries in mainland Canada, have watched the harbor for a long time. They were here three hundred years ago when Sir Richard Whitbourne repelled a boarding party of amorous mermaids, their flesh rosy, their hair bright blue; when pirates were barred from the harbor mouth by iron chains; when the sealing fleet of the nineteenth century set out on its spring voyage amid cannon fire and cheers from the shore; when ladies of fashion, their virtue questioned by an English governor, "did hamstring him, making him a cripple for life"; when fire, storm, plague, riot, and foreign enemy engulfed, but could never destroy, a town that knew not how to die.

A system of business, centralized, all-powerful, almost feudalistic, had always been defended by its managers as benevolent, and attacked by the poor as the agent of enforced poverty. Good or bad, it was finished. In the little legislative building, a neat cube of gray stone set on the hill, democracy, the Canadian system, and politics of a boisterous, shrill sort had taken over from the quiet businessmen. Government had launched its revolution without violence, without any significant opposition, without any real knowledge of Canada, but not without sound, confusion, and mistakes.

I sought out the headquarters of the revolution in a vast wooden house, inhabited as home and office by Smallwood and guarded by a faithful sentinel. He puffed a rank cigar, observed me suspiciously out of his knowing old seaman's eyes, and grudged even the admission that spring was late. The two of us sat mute in an anteroom which had once been a kitchen, as a sink in the corner attested, while cabinet ministers, officials, and humble constituents poured through the inner door as pilgrims enter a shrine, and poured out again, obviously elated by their glimpse of the prophet.

Among those visitors I met a women who unconsciously proclaimed the future of Newfoundland and the larger future of Canada. She was of middle age, a housewife from a poor home in some distant outport, and she had dressed for the great occasion in a new frock.

Now she sat upright on the edge of her chair, nervous at the prospect of meeting her hero. The whole story of her people, the four and a half centuries of struggle, poverty, and endurance, could be read in that woman's look. But she said nothing until I ventured to remark on the unseasonable weather. Whereupon, as my accent doubtless betrayed me as a mainlander, the floodgates of her life opened to release its contents of suffering, hope, and discovery.

The suffering was written on her lined cheeks, the hope in her eager eyes, and the discovery, oddly enough, on some colored postcards.

These frayed exhibits from her handbag, more profound in their meaning than any government document, pictured in crude hues the cities of Canada, Niagara Falls, the prairies, the forest of the Pacific Coast. Had I actually seen these things? I said I had often seen them. She looked at me as at a visitor from Mars.

Someday, she added timidly, after her five sons had grown up, she would save a little money and see the mainland before she died. Then, uttering her discovery, she touched my hand and whispered: "We're all Canadians now, you know. It's our own country, every bit of it. Yes, it belongs to every last one of us. My, what a thing to think about!"

A thing to think about. How the presence of Canada had touched the mind of this woman, what improbable chemistry had been at work in some grubby outport, by what accident she had perceived the nation and accepted it as her own, I could not guess. Yet here and nowhere else on the island I thought I had encountered that inward spark and fragment of a dream which alone made Canada from the beginning and someday will join Newfoundland to it.

In Smallwood's office—once the parlor of the spacious house, and now a museum crowded by the trophies of his long political chase—I heard this man's vision of Newfoundland's future in such a wealth of statistics, oratory, wit, and passion that I reeled out, exhausted.

My wife was awaiting me at the Torbay airport, and so was a plane, grounded like a helpless bird in the fog. We sat there beside the plane for three days, and finally escaped by train.

After a night in a narrow upper berth, which I was exceedingly fortunate to get, I beheld next morning the first blazing day of spring on a lonely moor. And suddenly I remembered that woman with her picture postcards, her valid Canadian passports. She at least, and perhaps many other unknown Newfoundlanders, had perceived Canada through the mist of the Atlantic and the centuries. Like all her people, like the fishermen in the twine loft, she was just entering the slow racial experience of Canadians from the beginning.

LANDSMEN BY THE SEA

✧

*T*hree oceans wash the shores of Canada, grind the coastal rock, break on the indestructible sand, and hurl the gales of Atlantic, Arctic, and Pacific to the center of the continent.

The perimeter of the Canadian mainland stretches eighteen thousand miles. The offshore islands add forty-two thousand miles of coast. Hudson Bay almost bisects the nation from north to south. Ships move almost halfway across it by the gaping slit of the St. Lawrence to the inland seas of the Great Lakes. The Pacific, with its Japan Current, warms the western shore but bores its fiords through the Coast Range to the base of the inland plateau.

The sea brought all men here in the beginning. Indians, Eskimos, and prehistoric races before them came by the Arctic in remote ages. The junks of China were blown across the Pacific, and their sailors saw the coastline of a future nation long before any white man had heard the name of Canada. Only a moment ago, by the measurement of men's life upon the earth, the mixed white races who call themselves Canadians crossed the Atlantic in tiny sailing ships.

Like life itself, the nation emerged from the sea. Though Canadians became a land people of farm, forest, mine, and town once the French ships had anchored in the St. Lawrence, they could never escape water, for it covered much of their land.

The eastern Indians taught them to make canoes of birchbark, and in those flimsy craft they crossed the bulk of the continent in advance of any other white men. On the Pacific they learned to make a salt-water canoe of hollowed cedar. Always they have been building vessels of some sort since Jean Talon launched his first little ship at Quebec.

In the days of sail they built and sailed from the Maritime ports one of the largest fleets afloat. They were among the first to cross the Atlantic by steam. Their sternwheelers carried them from the lakes to the mountains on the prairie rivers, down to the Arctic on the Mackenzie, and between the walls of the Rockies on the Fraser and Columbia.

Their modern coastwise ships penetrate every inlet, even through the Arctic icefloes. Their liners and freighters, though few in number, ply all the seas of the world. Their growing navy has been blooded in two world wars.

Some Canadians, a small minority, have never left the sea. Only seamen of lifelong skill and a born sea sense could navigate the seagoing draggers, the whalers, and the inshore cockleshells of the Atlantic fisheries, in storm, mist, and ice, or the seiners and trollers bobbing a hundred miles off the Pacific coast. And in war, Canadian boys from the inland plains who have never seen the coast suddenly feel an inherited instinct, take to sea, and make the nation's best sailors.

In war and peace Canadians are sucked back across the sea to the lands of their ancestors. Salt water still bounds them on three sides within the island of North America, but it joins them to the world, takes their goods to market, supplies their teeming fisheries, and subtly colors their lives.

The landsmen look out from the wrinkled Maritime shore, from the wooded cliffs of British Columbia or the Arctic barrens, and remember whence they came.

CHAPTER TWO

◆—

The Kingdom of
Joe Howe

THE sun, announcing its first landfall on the North American mainland, blazed across Bedford Basin as down a burnished gun barrel. It glinted on the domes and spires that rise from a jungle of foliage to cover Halifax beneath a higher jungle of stone. It set the fat old Citadel agrin, checked the time on the Duke of Kent's leering town clock, and rouged the round toadstool of his bandstand. It warmed up the stiff wooden bones of St. Paul's Cathedral, re-painted the blossom of the public gardens, re-glazed the bronze face of Governor Cornwallis, re-etched the wrinkles of Barrington Street, and re-polished the carved marble seashells on the mantle of Joseph Howe's office. These chores completed, it peered through the fanlight windows of a thousand ancient houses, sparkled on their littered family heirlooms of glass and mahogany, and brought another day to a people who had lived through many days, good and bad, since 1749.

After this hopeful beginning, it was to be a bad day. The sun withdrew by noon, the sea turned sullen, a rack of fog rolled into the Basin, the ships moaned at their moorings, the gulls screeched, and spray from the eastward settled on a man's lips with a salty flavor.

But I didn't care. This was the way it had always been in Halifax, child of the sea, southern bastion of the continental gate and eastern anchor of the Canadian boundary. No storm could ruffle it. No army or navy had ever captured it, though many had tried. The great explosion of 1917 could flatten it only for a year or so. In two world wars its harbor was crammed with the convoys of the North Atlantic. In peace it loads and ships much of Canada's overseas exports when winter closes the St. Lawrence. Today even the dullest land-lubber could scent on the sea wind the whiff of high adventure and the memories of a separate race within the race of Canada.

So, abandoning my car, I set out to inspect this eccentric and misunderstood town on foot. I had not walked long before I began to realize, as I had never realized on former visits, that here, in this unlikely place, the civilization of Canada had built a civic masterpiece.

Only the peculiar virtues, crotchets, and glorious lunacy of the British Isles, above all, the granitic instinct and stern whimsy of Scotland, could conceive this museum piece of square Georgian architecture, combine it with the soaring Gothic of Edinburgh, use it to house Canada's first responsible government, and go on to invent a private myth more durable than any public institution.

The outside of Halifax is deceptive, and more deceptive still the outside of its people.

An antique and pompous look was impressed on the town by Cornwallis, its founder; then by the future King William IV of England, who conducted here his gaudy love affair with a Mrs. Wentworth and later carried her off to London; finally by William's brother, the Duke of Kent, and the Gallic fancy of that royal governor's mistress, Julie St. Laurent, before he was called home to beget Queen Victoria as an urgent duty of state.

The Georgian look is only stone-deep. I had just begun to penetrate it, after walking three blocks through the jumble of Barrington Street, when, by a minor transcontinental accident, I encountered a youth of my acquaintance from Vancouver. He was gazing at the tower of St. Paul's—cunningly painted in 1750 to look like stone because the new hamlet could afford nothing better than wooden boards cut in New England—and he was catching his own vision of an unknown country.

This boy from the Pacific coast had been bred in a prodigal society of brash and perpetual boom. In the quiet of the Dalhousie law school he had found a new kind of life. It had amazed him, as it amazes all western visitors to the Maritime provinces. The people of Halifax, he said, had first asked his politics and religion (still matters of importance in the Maritimes) and then, careless of his heresies and ignorance, had taken him to their homes and hearts.

He tried to explain his discovery, found no words to fit it, and could only say: "These are the best people in Canada. They've got something we never had—what, exactly, I don't know, but it makes you warm. You hear that everybody wants to leave this town and go west and get rich. Me, I'm going to stay. You can really live here."

I left that boy to ponder his first glimpse of a nation infinitely diverse, and walked on to the Provincial Building, a chaste jewelbox of gray granite with shiny white lining. There I found a profane, sentimental character, the essence of the Maritimes, double-distilled.

With a seaman's oaths, a historian's knowledge, and a bawdy wit, he introduced me to the glistening legislative chamber where Canada's first responsible government was born before the nation itself had been conceived. He rejoiced in this early triumph for democracy, but, winking slyly, paused to enter a few caveats.

His tales of the highly practical politics long practiced in these premises were designed to shock me, but nothing could shock a westerner accustomed to methods still more robust. I was beginning to realize, however, that politics in the Maritime and the west differed not only in their degrees of practicality but also in kind.

Most Canadians are not deeply interested in government except at election time, and few are permanently attached to any party. Every Nova Scotian is an amateur of politics every day in the year, and usually a hereditary partisan of one of the old parties. The political principles that once divided our grandfathers, even our fathers, are almost forgotten in most of the nation. They live on in the Maritimes with passionate conviction for reasons I had yet to discover.

When I asked my guide about it, he said I would find out soon enough if I explored the grass roots. Having dropped this hint of an abiding mystery, he took me to see the huge ship's table on which Cornwallis's secret instructions were opened before he landed to found Halifax.

Those instructions, he remarked, had been fully carried out. In Halifax, Britain had established its northern base of power, well in advance of the final struggle for the continent, an impregnable base against France, and then, contrary to all calculation, a base against the American Revolution, and finally against the American Republic in 1812.

That, said my guide, was quite a story, and he chuckled as if he had lived through it, or even planned it, from the beginning. His mirth mystified me then, but I understood it later on—it represented that separate Nova Scotian mind which, more than any other mind in Canada (outside Quebec, at any rate) is steeped in history and myths, like the sovereign myth of Joe Howe.

We now entered the sanctum of Nova Scotia's greatest son. In this fine old Georgian room Howe had come to power over the colony and his private kingdom. He had arrived here after an apprenticeship of journalism, oratory, libel, riot, and duel, and he had brought with him a mixed equipment of talents and defects, a passion for liberty, a powerful thirst for liquor, and a weakness for women—all the makings of a myth. There were the makings of tragedy, too, and of final triumph.

The old Nova Scotian pointed to the well-charred fireplace before which Howe had often warmed himself after a night in the saddle and perhaps had brooded on that tragedy without foreseeing the triumph.

"Why, you can see him standing there," exclaimed my guide, "as clear as day!"

I tried to imagine the square, massive body, the head carved roughly out of local granite, the ceaseless flow of speech, the scandalous jest. Not being a Nova Scotian, I failed to see Howe. To me he was only a name in the history books of the nineteenth century, a man who had ruined himself by attempting to prevent the union of the Canadian colonies into a single state, and who redeemed himself in his old age, with repentance and agony, by accepting that union and quarreling with his lifelong friends. To his people, to men like the old Nova Scotian beside me, he remained a native giant, father image and supreme product of the Maritime race.

"Sometimes when I'm working alone at night," said Howe's aged worshipper as he ushered me to the street, "I can hear old Joe's footsteps in the hall, chasing some silk petticoat. Yes, and he usually caught it."

I bowed to the giant's statue on the lawn, but absent-mindedly. For these fragmentary rumors from the past had started me thinking of the present—specifically of Professor Arnold Toynbee, the eminent English historian, who, disposing of the world's various civilizations like a man judging handicrafts, prize cattle, or pickles at a country fair, cites Nova Scotia as a classic example of inevitable defeat.

The Challenge of environment, in Toynbee's celebrated phrase, has proved too much for Nova Scotia's Response, and hence this province, like the northern New England states, must remain one of the "least prosperous and progressive areas in America," its civilization arrested, stunted, and forever doomed to inferiority by a niggard land and a misplaced people.

Was there anything, I wondered, in Toynbee's Olympian dictum? Before the day was finished, I concluded, with respect, that there was little or nothing in it.

To be sure, as the businessmen, politicians, and economists agreed, Nova Scotia must always live on a relatively poor land. As if that were not handicap enough, it has been detached by a purely political arrangement, the Confederation of Canada, from its natural market and source of supply in the adjoining American states. It must haul its products all the way to

central Canada and buy what it needs there at prices raised
by the nation's protective tariff. Its economic affairs are distorted for national reasons, by national policies. Therefore
it remains a relatively poor province.

Yet I was already discovering certain exhibits against
Toynbee's case, and would discover more in my travels. What
had the Professor to say, for example, about Dalhousie University, a treat national seat of learning, set around an ivy-
clustered quad like a corner of Oxford; about a total population in Nova Scotia half that of Toronto which nevertheless
maintains seven universities, has produced more statesmen of
stature than any comparable segment of the nation, and still
can export enough surplus talent to carry the odd quality of
this land to every other province?

Inevitably, Nova Scotia has lagged behind richer provinces
in what we are pleased to call our standard of living, but what
about its standard of life, especially its standard of thought?

I wished that Professor Toynbee could have been with me
in the streets, offices, and homes of Halifax while I explored
this question. He would have found here more ideas, more
argument, more learning and clear thinking in one day than
most Canadian cities can supply in a month. These people,
as I should have known but didn't, as the Toynbees of the
world have yet to understand, were always compelled to
think hard if they were to survive. Their thoughts emerged
in an illustrious role of national leaders, in perpetual civic
debate, in the Howe legend, in the earthy wisdom of Judge
Haliburton's immortal Sam Slick, and—let us never forget it
—in the essential Atlantic ingredient of Confederation.

If these exhibits do not impress him, let the theorist of
historic Challenge and Response sit for one evening under
the fluted ceilings and molded cornices of some old Halifax
home, let him listen to the casual talk of the dinner table,
and he will encounter minds as up-to-date, active, and practical
as any that made the great Canadian boom out of easy materials to the westward, together with a certain serenity, balance, and reverence for good things, good men, and good
living that most Canadians have yet to learn.

He will find a sense of past time providing a sense of proportion in a hurried, disordered present. The standard of living, as measured by the Dominion Bureau of Statistics, may be relatively low. I suspected, after a few days in Nova Scotia, that the standard of life was perhaps the highest in Canada. In those terms, at least, Response was meeting Challenge.

The long struggle has left its mark. It has created a folk instantly distinguishable among the Canadian creaturehood. What most distinguished these people, it seemed to me, was their awareness of living in a poor land, of being the family's poor relation, of knowing, as few Canadians know, that life must be hard.

This makes a thrifty, unpretentious, but—because all of them must struggle together—a kindly and generous folk. They have a family feeling and next-door neighborliness almost lost in our richer communities. They resist better than most of us the conformity of the mass age. They are filled with a quiet pride and a pawky humor, the gift of Scotland, emerging in the silent chuckle, the mad tale, and the Scottish crack too wise to be called a wisecrack. They hate ostentation, support no Cadillac set, and, in the original meaning of that corrupted word, are well-bred.

These were only a stranger's first random impressions of Halifax, but my wife and I came to believe them by the time we had driven westward over the narrow neck of Nova Scotia to follow every curve in its serrated coast.

Crossing an upland moor, we soon entered the Annapolis Valley and saw it rolling before us as fair as King Arthur's Avilion in orchard-lawns and bowery hollows crowned with summer seas. Immaculate villages snuggled in every hollow. White church spires pierced the rounded English skyline. Fruit trees and fat cattle dozed on every hill. Here, we thought, was the outward sign of an instinctive order that the progressive provinces of the west have abandoned or not yet discerned. And here, outside Wolfeville, we stumbled on an inn designed for a tale by Stevenson or Conrad.

It had been built in the days of sail by some retired sea captain of wealth and wild originality. His fancies included

arched windows of crimson glass, a stairway of some exotic
timber brought from the South Seas, a striped floor of alter-
nate black mahogany and white pine, a carved and monstrous
bed measured to hold a sultan and his entire harem.

In the dining-room a character perhaps drawn by Stevenson
and certainly fictional—he had a mane of rusty hair, a face
cured in rum, and the soft, disarming voice of a reformed
pirate—was titillating a table of schoolteachers from New
York with stories of shipwreck, Spanish gold, bleached corpses,
and banana revolutions in South America. Anyone could
identify him. He was Captain John Silver in disguise.

The sure homing impulse of the Nova Scotian had brought
him back from his last voyage. The sea? He hated the very
thought of it. He was through with the sea. How, asked the
maiden ladies from New York, would he spend his declining
years? Well (he confessed it rather sheepishly for a pirate),
he was building a boat, just a tiny bit of a boat, and would poke
about Fundy.

Fundy, as I had heard, is accounted some of the world's
worst water, but it lay quiet that night. Its tide had sunk
forty-seven feet since noon. Minas Basin lay in a vast smear
of brown mud as if some careless titan had spilled a few
billion gallons of sticky cocoa and imprisoned a score of
little ships now lying, helpless, on their beam ends, miles from
sea. To the west the unshaven chin of Cape Blomidon, one
of the continent's major landmarks, jutted grimly across a
watery sunset.

This scene suddenly reminded me that we were now in
the original home of the Acadians whose Expulsion was
one of early America's most celebrated crimes. As every
schoolboy knows, the crime produced an equally celebrated
poem. It was here that Longfellow placed his heroine,
Evangeline, by a remarkable feat of remote control, from
Boston, and minutely described her surroundings without
bothering to inspect them for himself.

In deference to the poet and his brain child, we trudged
by twilight across the marshy acres diked by the French
settlers, admired the reproduction of Evangeline's little stone

church, and stood for a moment in tribute before the statue
of the girl who never was but should have been.

This duty performed, we return to the inn and encountered
there an old man musing on a splendid secret. He had devoted his life to the Evangeline myth in an innocent posthu-
mous love affair. We found it quite moving. As he warmed
to the subject, he told us, somewhat crustily, that Evangeline
was not a myth at all. She was a fact, or part of a fact. True
enough, Longfellow had heard rumors of her third-hand
from a Boston minister, who had talked to a native of Minas
Basin, but the indisputable stuff of truth was in the story just
the same.

Sometimes, he said, he could sit here on the marshland
and hear the waves gurgling in the caverns of Blomidon, far
away, precisely as Longfellow had described that eerie sound.

Moreover, how could we explain another strange fact care-
fully recorded by the poet? The mist piled up in Fundy,
overtopped the Cape, but never descended on its eastern
flank—undeniable testimony in Longfellow's defense, said
Evangeline's steadfast lover. Finally, he had heard with his
own ears, many a time, the murmuring pines and the hemlocks
in the Forest Primeval; though he added, being a truthful
man, that the hemlocks seemed to have disappeared from
the neighborhood. But there were still plenty of pines.

On this evidence there must have been, there had to be,
a real Evangeline. If we would stay here a few days, until the
wind changed, we might hear the voice of Blomidon and
sense, if we could not actually see, the spirit of the Acadian
maid. Unfortunately we had to move on next morning to
Annapolis Royal and an appointment with factual history.

We found there the long inlet from Fundy lying like a pool
of quicksilver under the noonday sun—" a thing so marvellous
to see, the fair distances and the largeness of it," as Marc
Lescarbot, the French diarist, first reported. Fort Anne
drowsed on its greensward after so many sieges, battles,
capitulations, and changes of ownership that only a historian
can sort them out. And from their crowded parlor the Misses

Perkins observed, as they had observed for more than three-score years, the life of the most eventful town in Canada.

Their family came to Annapolis long before the United Empire Loyalists reached here in flight from the American Revolution. The present and, I suppose, the last Perkins generation had traveled widely, but found no place as good as this. Well satisfied with home, the two spinster ladies have spent their lives chronicling in modest footnotes a civilization which began three and a half centuries ago as one of the first French settlements on the American mainland.

The elder of the two, an apple-faced person shaking with merriment, protested that she had no mind for facts, but her memory was good, she had a keen eye for the human comedy, and her sister, Miss Charlotte Isabella, had put their joint recollections and diligent research into a little book. Miss Charlotte diffidently offered me a copy of her work, illustrated with her own lively ink sketches. I shall keep it in memory of a spring day in Annapolis, such a day as the Frenchmen beheld on entering the refuge of Port Royal.

We sat for an hour or two in that parlor of tinkling bric-a-brac while our hostesses, quite unconsciously, paraded the mighty ghosts of Champlain, DeMonts, and Lescarbot; the lesser ghosts of Argall, pirate from Jamestown, Judge Haliburton, jurist and humorist, Mme Freneuse, *femme fatale* of Annapolis; and the nameless ghosts of those hoop-skirted ladies who, on a stormy Sabbath, dropped their metal hoops and bustles outside the church lest they attract lightning.

The Perkins sisters laughed and then quickly blushed at the memory of those worshippers disrobing in the public streets, but, to tell the truth, I was more interested in the scandalous Mme Freneuse. Her trail led me to the remains of old Fort Anne and the sunny museum, once the officers' quarters, where I found Miss Laura Hardy, the librarian. She calls herself an amateur of history, but doubtless knows more about Annapolis Royal than anyone else alive.

If Joe Howe was right in saying that "a wise nation preserves its records and gathers up its muniments," Miss Hardy was doing a work of national importance. She was collecting and polishing the stuff of Canadian civilization. But what of Mme Freneuse?

Though Miss Hardy was surprised, perhaps a little shocked by my interest in Governor Bonaventure's notorious mistress, we spent a full hour reading the chronicles of the French occupation. They didn't tell us much, but revealed enough to show that Mme Freneuse must have been a remarkable woman, a kind of early Canadian Mata Hari.

As Miss Hardy reconstructed the tale from faded and rather cryptic diaries, the English, on taking the fort from the French, had instantly exiled the seductive agent of the Quebec government, banishing her to the wilderness across Fundy. Thence, in an almost unbelievable adventure, she returned by canoe in midwinter with only an Indian boy to help her paddle—unbelievable, but set down in the brief, tantalizing records of the fort.

What had happened to her then? Alas, the records told us no more. So we spent another hour tracing down the pedigree of Gregoria Ramona Antonia de Reiez, a lady of Spain and one of Wellington's discarded flames, who became the respectable Mrs. Joseph Norman, wife of Fort Anne's barrack-master, about the time of Waterloo.

Few spots in America can have spawned so many improbable characters as the vivid company of Annapolis Royal. It seemed to me, however, that Miss Hardy, the modest librarian, represented the most significant fact in all this strange assembly—the fact that a local civilization was guarding its legacy. Any Philistine who calls this work of history merely sentimental and irrelevant to our time should have walked with me a few yards from the fort to the old courthouse.

They were trying a young man for manslaughter in a hot little room. It was a routine case, the result of a traffic accident, but in this same room the saturnine Judge Haliburton had administered justice while inventing the genial crimes of Sam Slick. On this same site the English Common Law had first entered the life of Canada and begun to tame it. That law still lived because men had learned and treasured the lessons of the past. Annapolis Royal looked like a sleepy hamlet, one of many in Nova Scotia. It was in fact a national treasury, the home of a myth even more durable than the law.

We left Annapolis Royal to drive down the north shore of the Basin and rediscover the beginnings of a French civilization older than the English. In 1605—two years before Jamestown and three years before Quebec—DeMonts built Port Royal, with Champlain as his geographer, the merry Lescarbot as his secretary and earliest North American playwright. When assorted pirates, invaders, and Indians had snuffed out New France's first brief candle, there was nothing left of Port Royal but a well filled with earth.

This last mark was found, not many years ago, and the plans of the fort, as Champlain drew them, turned up in some Paris pigeonhole. On the original site, inch for inch, the old buildings have risen again in hewed timber, high-pitched roof, yawning fireplaces, and cool wine cellars, accurate to the last beam and wooden peg. Here, as at the English fort, a wise nation was gathering up its muniments.

Only a Philistine can enter this ancient Canadian home, even in replica, without emotion, and he must be a dull man who cannot imagine the little band of Frenchmen enduring here the brutal Canadian winter, their nearest white neighbors the Spanish of Florida and Mexico. It was not difficult to picture DeMonts reckoning up his fur-trading accounts at a rough-hewn desk, Champlain planning his gardens, summerhouse, and fishponds, Lescarbot writing his masque "The Theatre of Neptune"; and then that happy joint invention, the *Ordre de Bon Temps*, with its banquets of moose, caribou, partridge, geese, and beaver tails to cure the boredom of the long exile.

Port Royal's present caretaker, a bespectacled and gently spoken little carpenter, had scanty book learning, but he felt more deeply than any scholar the invisible contents and meaning of this place. A descendant of some forgotten Loyalist family, he lived across the road, and often at night walked about the fort to make sure it was safe. He told me shyly, but without shame, that when the moon was shining, the snow thick in the courtyard, the lights glowing from the windows of scraped rawhide, he could almost see the old inhabitants feasting in their Order of Good Cheer.

"Sir," he said, his eyes illuminated by private revelation, "those were big men!" Their fame, I thought, was safe in his hands. Unlike most parts of Canada, Nova Scotia does not forget.

The road from Annapolis Royal follows the long Basin down to Digby, a fine old weather-beaten town pungent with the smell of fish, and skirts the barren shore to the southward where the Acadians crept home, a family at a time, after their dispersal. Dark Norman faces, wind-swept villages, huge churches, plodding oxteams, and multitudes of children by the roadside tell that heroic tale.

Twelve years before, I had stopped at Belliveau's Cove, in a house that trembled under Fundy's bluster, and had heard from a terrifying old sea captain the story of Jerome, another Nova Scotia myth or fact.

Toward the end of the last century, as I recalled the captain's tale, the fishermen hereabouts had seen a four-masted ship disappearing into the evening mist. Next morning they found on the beach a young man, both his legs amputated and bandaged, evidently by a skilled surgeon. What secret lay behind that awful discovery no one ever knew, for the ship did not return and the legless man, known only as Jerome, uttered no word but that name until he died long afterwards in silence as he had lived.

Now I could not find the house at Belliveau's Cove or its owner who remembered Jerome. My inquiries elicited from a grizzled man behind a team of black oxen only a skeptical grin, a shake of the head, and a torrent of Acadian French. So we drove on to Yarmouth, which had another story to tell, and a sad one.

It was told to me in disjointed snatches by a fisherman of leather face and truculent speech as he stood up to the knees of his gumboots in a tone of gaspereau. These fish, his night's catch, he admitted grudgingly, should be worth fifty dollars, and he evidently considered that sum a minor fortune.

Half a dozen other fishermen watched his heavy-laden boat in envy while he ripped the fish out of his net with a rhythmic sound of torn gills.

We had talked some time before I established contact with this man, who unknowingly represented the calamity of Yarmouth. When I suggested that fishing from so small a boat out there in the opaque fog, must be dangerous work, he stopped suddenly, a fish in his hand, and gave me a fierce look.

"Sure," he said, "it's dangerous, all right. But you go when your time comes, no matter where you are." He paused, staring at me with mixed anger and interrogation. "What of it?" he added. "I believe in God, see? Don't you?"

That question was startling and embarrassing to a westerner. No Pacific-coast fisherman, or any stranger, had ever spoken to me with such candor. Realizing how far I was from home and the common thought of Canada, I evaded the man's eye and glanced about me at the extraordinary shape of his town.

Its main street was long and wide enough for a metropolis. The Grand Hotel stood like a gigantic monument to Yarmouth's lost hopes. The side streets of clapboard mansions, domes, towers, and crazy gimcrackery had been built by the rich captains of sail, and some were still inhabited by their immortal widows, rocking behind curtains of smuggled foreign lace. Now, beside these relics of a splendid, sinful youth, the wharves, once crowded with great ships from all the ports of the world, were idle and silent. A knot of fishermen watched a lucky comrade who had made fifty dollars and believed in God.

To a traveler from a land still in its crude youth, dizzy with success and believing in little but its own opulence, that scene was difficult to believe. It could not, surely, belong to contemporary Canada.

In fact it was more Canadian, by the measurement of time and the oldest instincts of the race, than any scene remembered by the furious, forgetful west. But only a few of Yarmouth's old sailormen, in black suits of square Victorian cut, can still recall this town's fleet of sail as the third largest afloat.

These survivors of the great days are usually to be found beside the Grand Hotel's coal fire (it never goes out, winter or summer), and the life of every man there would make a book. But they never talk, and will soon be gone. They know that no landsman can comprehend or any book convey what they have seen in all the seas of the world.

Fortunately one man in Yarmouth has undertaken, single-handed, to rescue the native history. George MacInnes, who works by day in a grocery store, welcomed me at night to his personal museum of ships' logs, diaries, maps, and marine relics, and there held me with curious legends until dawn.

Among them I liked best the true story of the Yarmouth ship *Lennie*, whose sailors locked Captain Hatfield in the hold and sailed out of the English Channel for South America, but neglected the cabin boy. This enterprising fellow wrote pleas for rescue and consigned them to the sea in bottles that floated eventually to the shore of France. The *Lennie* was overtaken, its mutineers were hanged in London, and MacInnes, in a Yarmouth grocery store, was now preparing to write another chapter of Yarmouth's Odyssey.

We left the sedulous scholar and a few hours later were standing on the sea rocks of Shelburne, where ten thousand Loyalist refugees from the Revolution landed in 1783 with their carriages, family plate, silk gowns, and Negro slaves to found a second Philadelphia. Today nothing was left to mark that brave beginning but a few overgrown wells and some good Canadian citizens of Negroid skin.

The man talking to us in his shipyard bore the name of McKay, a famous name around Shelburne. His father had built some of the largest sailing ships ever launched in Nova Scotia, and once launched two on the same tide. The son was seventy-five years old, a bent and gnarled man who grinned in secret mirth after every sentence.

Crouched beside the wood skeleton of his latest vessel—a sixty-foot fish boat and successor to one hundred and fifty much larger craft before her—McKay allowed that the fourth generation of his family was now working in this shipyard.

He laughed and wriggled at the thought of it. His sons and grandsons swarmed over the skeleton with a jolly click of hammer and chisel.

Yes, he had been building ships for fifty-eight years. "I say," he chuckled, "it's been a good life. None better."

The recollection set him heaving again, but when I asked him if his new ship was made of Nova Scotia timber, he scowled as if I had insulted him. "I say," he retorted, "of course it's Nova Scotia timber. Oak ribs. You can't beat 'em." And the keel? "I say it's rock maple. Nothing else, you bet. Lloyd's rate it the best in the world. Yes, sir, rock maple."

As we left the shipyard, he was climbing like an aged cat about the framework of oak and rock maple. By the methods of his grandfather and father before him, he would flesh it and bring the skeleton to life.

In the schoolyard of Shelburne we noticed an odd little scene which symbolized, though no one seemed to notice it, a deep and often tragic process in North American life.

Some boys were playing baseball, and evidently worshipped the catcher and the pitcher as acknowledged champions. Those two were descendants of Negro slaves. Shelburne had solved the problem of desegregation, but the Loyalist aristocrats, I suspected, whould have been somewhat shocked if they could have seen their own descendants playing on equal terms with boys of inky black. The dream of an imitation Philadelphia had died. Something indigenous had grown up here in its place—humble, poor, but Canadian.

A smooth road (Nova Scotia has some of the best highways in Canada, all the better for their wayward curves and wild eccentricities) swung around a jagged shore, through forests of black spruce and maples dripping the Burgundy of spring buds, over cliffs of mustard-stained seaweed, past villages cuddled in some cosy inlet, and at last into an imaginary town called Lunenburg.

I call Lunenburg imaginary because it is not really a town at all. It is a picture by some vagrant artist arriving several centuries late and dreaming of the past in paint; a German artist, as it happened, one of those first Germans who founded Lunenburg long before Teutonic imagination had turned into Hitler's nightmare.

From a green hill we beheld, that evening, the downs of southern England, a Cornish harbor, and a black schooner that must have dropped anchor here after a voyage from Treasure Island. The setting sun washed the white houses with rosy pink. The moon turned them into glowing silver. A frog chorus broke into a moonlight sonata, a lighthouse winked a red eye far out to sea, and the salt smell rode in on the sea breeze.

Then, lifted out of this age and set down gently in another, we retired to Boscawen Manor, supposedly a hotel but actually a mirage, a delayed emanation of Victorian times likely to melt and disappear at any moment with all its indescribable furniture, Oriental rugs, candelabra, brassware, and tilted fireplaces.

Happily, the forgotten shipmaster's house did not melt that night. It was built to last. So, as we learned next morning, was Captain Angus Walters, the most famous seaman left in Nova Scotia and once skipper of the peerless *Bluenose*, a name to set the Canadian fancy tingling.

Strangely enough, we found Captain Walters in the steam and tin clatter of a dairy. He was hurling milk cans around, answering customers on the telephone, and talking in an accent compounded of England, Scotland, and Germany. The spirit of old Lunenburg seemed incarnate in a squat, powerful figure and a face grooved deep by Atlantic weather. Home was the sailor, home from sea, and right glad of it, he told me. This agile little man had mastered the sea, but, as he thought, the sea had turned against him and all his kind. How was that?

"Well, I'll tell you," said the Captain, his stumpy legs spread wide as on a heaving deck, "the sea life was fine in my time. A shipmaster was the master, by God, and no mistake. If I sailed at three o'clock and any man wasn't there, he could stay ashore and be damned to him. That was the story of it. But not any more. The crew's the master, even if they don't know a halibut from a lobster, and most of 'em don't. That's the story of it."

The day of the schooner, the dory, and the net was passing, and Captain Walters wanted none of the new day. "Why," he shouted in sudden fury, "the big draggers drag and rile the bottom like harrows, churnin' up the fishin' grounds and ruinin' the fish of all the sea. That's the story of it."

His fierce old eyes peered from under the dairyman's incongruous peaked cap to make sure I understood his larger meaning. After a pause the seaman who had penetrated the ultimate mystery unknown to any landsman said a curious thing: "There's in the sea everything there is on land—ah, more, far more than you can imagine. What is it? It's life, that's what. And now we're spoilin' it all. That's the story of it."

Why had he chosen, of all things, a dairy in his old age? Because without work he would die in six months. And, uttering the old faith of Lunenburg, he added: "We're a strivin' people."

A striving people. It occurred to me that the life of Nova Scotia needed no better definition.

Yet there was something rather sad in the Captain's confession that he never went near the wharves any more, this master of shipmasters. All the ships and the sails and the men he knew were gone. The intimate partnership of man, weather, ship, and fish had ended in an age of engines, factories, and processed fish sticks. A great thing had perished, or at least had changed beyond this man's recognition. Yes, but he had seen the mystery. He had mastered the sea, and he was still striving. That was the story of it.

From Lunenburg we set out in search of Peggy's Cove, which everyone has seen in a hundred familiar paintings and photographs. It was a long search in a maze of twisting roads designed by a mad engineer, and, at first sight, the famous Cove was hardly worth our trouble.

The painted glimpse of Arcady and the photographer's deceptive angle shots turned out to be nothing more than a narrow gash in a shore of solid stone, not much larger than a good-sized washtub, a surrounding chaos of boulders strewn broadcast like a giant's dice, a dozen listing houses, some wharves on rotted stilts, and a few battered fish boats. But we soon discovered something more important than scenery at Peggy's Cove.

A boy of some sixteen years was standing at the head of the cramped harbor, and his legs could almost span it. He had been grappling since dawn with his native environment, offering his own unconscious Response to Toynbee's brutal Challenge, and he had come home bearing one lobster from his homemade pot. With a man's pride the boy showed us his catch and said hopefully that he might get two or three more lobsters on the evening tide.

Oh, yes, things were mighty good at Peggy's Cove these days. Why, his grandmother could remember when only three houses stood here, and now his brother owned a truck, second-hand but still running fine. The land was thin and poor, but you could grow potatoes on beds of seaweed if you knew how. His father had a cow and moved it inland if the weather turned bad. "Oh, it's pretty, sir," he ventured, "when the waves come in a good fifty feet high over the rocks."

The lank figure in oilskins, the grinning young face against the rim of that stone inferno, and the pounding surf behind him would have made a picture for any painter. It seemed to me the humble portrait of a race. Yet all the thousand painters and photographers who have captured the mere outer quaintness of Peggy's Cove have somehow missed its meaning. So, perhaps, has Toynbee, the historian.

We had lingered too long on this south shore. The north shore and, beyond it, the half-continent and another ocean lay before us. So we cut across the peninsula again and, after much wandering, discovered Antigonish between its lazy river and its gentle hill. A town of some sort must have stood here, near the southern rim of the St. Lawrence Gulf, for a long time, since its name, in the Indian tongue, means The Place Where Bears Break Branches to Gather Hazel Nuts, or something like that. Antigonish is now more than a town. It is an idea.

We began to guess the idea as soon as we entered the halls of St. Francis Xavier University. This deceptive institution seems to slumber on its hillside, but, dining with its professors and priests on lobster fresh from the sea, we realized that the nation holds no livelier center of learning, none other perhaps with so clear a vision. Certainly none has produced a more practical or a nobler achievement than the Antigonish Movement.

A swelling library of books records this strange local prodigy. The network of co-operatives built by farmers, fishermen, and consumers throughout the Maritimes, but inspired by the scholars of St. Francis Xavier, and the university's course of social studies, have brought investigators from all over the world. The advice of obscure men in a Nova Scotia village has been sought by many backward countries, and that night Father M. J. MacKinnon, once a coal-miner, had just flown home from conferences in Asia and the West Indies. As we drove away next morning, he passed us in his car, at the legal speed limit or better, bound for some kitchen meeting on Cape Breton Island to advise his own folk on their problems.

We intended to follow him, but meanwhile paused for an hour beside the shore of Northumberland Strait to inspect one visible result of the Antigonish Movement. Here a fisherman, too old for the sea, was tending eight thousand live lobsters in salt-water tanks and preparing them for shipment to Boston. He picked up a lobster reverently in his fingers as if it were one of nature's masterpieces, as doubtless it was. Eying it with wonder, he assured us that "a lobster, sir, is a lovely thing, a very lovely thing. Why, look, the color's better than a flower, and it's shaped just right."

We examined those varied opalescent hues before they could be boiled to uniform scarlet in Boston, and watched the fishermen unloading lobsters in thousands upon their wharf. The lobster, however lovely, was not the significant exhibit in this place. Hard by the shore, where their forefathers had always lived in defenseless poverty, the fishermen had built their own co-operative shipping and canning plants, had prospered by their modest standards, and, having been taught to think and plan by the scholars of St. Francis Xavier, spoke of the Antigonish Movement as they might speak of God.

Cape Breton, we began to think, must be quite a place to breed men like Father MacKinnon, the coal-miner, the priest, the mystic, and the practical man of affairs. We were not disappointed.

The first person to greet us as we crossed the long man-made causeway of Canso Strait and reached the huge island which extends the Nova Scotian peninsula far into Cabot Strait toward Newfoundland was a coal-miner with a sickle nose, a Scottish face baked red at Bannockburn, and the un-diluted accent of Robbie Burns.

We found this man beside the inland sea, called Bras d'Or Lake, and offered him a lift to Sydney. Since it was a day of bitter wind, rain, and sleet, we also offered him a distilled tot of purest Scotland. He accepted both offers with thanks but no enthusiasm.

Later on, when he learned that my first name was Bruce, he fell upon me like a long-lost clansman, regretted that I had lost the Gaelic—all the youngsters had lost it nowadays— and, after a second drink, recited, with lunging gesture and contorted features, Burns's immortal ode to haggis, great chieftain of the puddin' race. No, he had never been to Scot-land, nor had his father, but assuredly he and his kind still beheld in dreams the misty Hebrides.

We drove through a land of postage-stamp farms and blurred seascapes while the miner told us the story of his life. It was the story of Cape Breton, of a folk physically separated from Nova Scotia by a narrow strait and spiritually by the unbridgeable chasm that surrounds coal-miners every-where.

The island has bred two peoples, the landmen above ground and the coalmen below it. This miner said he could never leave the mines to till the soil or work in the great steel industry. Though mining was dangerous work and often interrupted, still a man grew to like it and could not be happy far from a mine. Yes, the coal industry might be in trouble, more mines might close, but in the end mankind would have to burn coal. I asked him why, and, after a moment's consideration, he pronounced a personal faith in his craft: "Because coal is natural, it was put there for men to burn, and, mark you, they'll burn it someday."

That was faith only, the faith of a man who had seen some dark mystery beneath the earth as a Lunenburg man had found it beneath the sea, but probably it was as good economics as most of the theories I had heard from the experts.

Farther along the lonely road we picked up a raddled little man in the remains of a flashy, checked suit. He was a retired pugilist now training half a dozen prize fighters in the steel town of Sydney. How, I ventured to inquire, could he hope to make a living from pugilism in Cape Breton? His shattered old face took on a thoughtful look. "Well," he said at last, "I fought all over Canada and the States and I come home. There's something about the Island."

What that something is, apart from the obvious beauty of farmland, forest, and stark cliffs falling straight into the sea, no stranger can guess, but it includes three clear human traits: the nostalgia of the Scots (especially strong if they have never seen Scotland), the carefree, live-for-today philosophy of the coal-miner, and the brittle, half cynical humor that grows out of a poor and perilous life.

> *Down where the sun is about like water,*
> *Ma sold a drop till the Mounties caught her,*
> *And you spent the rest when you hadn't oughter,*
> *Down where the East begins.*

The anonymous troubadours of Cape Breton, survivors of a long line, turn out endless scoffing jingles of that sort, more expressive of their life than any official document.

We were surprised to find at Sydney a luxurious hotel crowded with travelers from everywhere. Cape Breton was once the strategic focus of the North Atlantic in the struggle for the continent, and now Sydney is a natural crossroads of the air age. Its harbor is busy with the ore ships from Newfoundland. Its main street must be the widest in the nation. Black smoke pours from mines and slag dumps. The steel mill looks from the distance like some monstrous ship from hell, steam up, masts and rusty conning towers dwarfing the town.

A bustling, brawling town it is, nourished by coal and steel, the far eastern pivot of the Canadian economy, yet a town of tragic memories. From businessmen, labor-union leaders, and miners idling, off-shift, on the street corners we heard a little of those memories—the depression and the family dole of six dollars a week, the strikes, the communism among hopeless men, the riots, and the killings.

Even though the coal industry was sick here, as everywhere, and Sydney was the apex of Nova Scotia's economic problem, the hopelessness had disappeared. Management and labor, we were assured by both, had united as never before to meet the challenge of this environment. Cape Breton, they said, had rich natural resources, and soon the nation would need and develop them.

This island once faced another sort of challenge; its response failed, and thereby France lost more than half a continent.

Louisbourg, a few miles from Sydney, was the strongest fortress of the New World, a French town of five thousand people, of mansions, theaters, masked balls, intrigue, and corruption, the North American miniature of Versailles and the invulnerable guardian, as Versailles supposed, of the St. Lawrence. A handful of blundering New England farmers took it, Amherst took it a second time, and Wolfe sailed on to Quebec.

Now, on a cold and empty headland nothing remains but a broken arch or two, the grave of the doomed Duc d'Anville, whose fleet sank in Bedford Basin, some children at play in a moldering powder magazine, a few rusty cannon dredged up from the harbor, and a band of sheep grazing on the site of the governor's palace.

But the ruins have something to teach us about the successors to the vanished French. Those thrifty Nova Scotia pioneers shipped Louisbourg's "cursed stones" to Halifax and used them to build a city and house a civilization.

LAND AND PEOPLE

*I*f any stranger would know the Canadian mind, let him look first at the land of Canada.

The land, more than anything else, has shaped the mind. We are too young to be fully shaped by history, too remote from one another to be shaped by any abstract theory. But we hold the land jointly, its beauty, illimitable distance, and healing silence. The land lives for all of us in that hidden, wordless region where nations are darkly fashioned and a people is born.

Our eyes see and our racial mind remembers the mountains, the plains, the forest, the lakes, the rivers, and the seacoast. Our ears are tuned to the sounds of the land, to trees under the wind, grain whispering in summer dawn, the song of birds, the nighttime boom of frogs, the hum of insects, the click of ax, and the crunch of footsteps in the snow. We remember the sound of water as it moves across the land, the brook's gurgle and the river's deeper voice in the darkness, the lap of waves on the inland beach, the pound of surf on the sea rocks, the splash of trout or salmon, the swirl of paddle, and the boy's shout in the swimming hole.

These things enter through the eye and ear, but within the racial mind they are distilled and compacted beyond the measurement of knowledge.

The land can be reckoned in area, topography, and wealth. No man can reckon its power in the Canadian's subconscious. It is ours, won through long struggle, broken, tilled, and reaped through three centuries of toil. Its image—so large, inexpressible, and fair—overtops our divisions and unites us, by a common possession, in the Canadian creaturehood.

So vast is the land, so varied are its images, that no man lives

long enough to see more than the surface of Canada. The cities
we know, the institutions, governments, and all the visible apparatus called civilization. These physical dimensions do not
make a nation. It is made by nameless men and women who,
like all their species, live and die alone in the land that shaped
them.

The people are as varied as their land, in race, occupation,
and thought. A farmer in a square mile of grain planted by his
hands; a woodsman chopping the little trees of the east or the
huge conifers of the west coast; a fisherman gathering the lobster pots of Shediac, hauling the cod traps of Newfoundland,
or laying out the seine nets of the Pacific; a mechanic in a new
mass-production factory; a physicist in an atomic laboratory; a
ragged figure shuffling through some midnight street; a woman
peering from her kitchen window in the wilderness as the train
rolls by; children playing in the city's snow—all these and
many more make Canada.

An old stone house by the St. Lawrence; the buzz and click
of summer in Quebec meadows; a costly farm machine beside
a crumbling barn of poplar logs on the prairies; a ghost town of
the Cariboo gold rush; skyscrapers ranked against Lake Ontario; scarlet autumn in the Laurentians, daffodils among the
Vancouver Island oaks, a blizzard over the Shield—these casual things, disordered as a dream, cling to the traveler's memory after all facts are forgotten. They, and the presence of the
land, tell us more about Canada than any fact.

CHAPTER THREE

$\blacklozenge$

The Toy Continent

A THIN band of dark blue hung just above the sea to the northward. Then I could make out a second band, of a terra-cotta hue. Soon an upper band of green appeared and the three distinct layers of color floated like a fallen rainbow under a cold, mackerel sky.

As I watched from the little ferry steamer, a gaunt figure in clerical clothes joined me on the deck. The ascetic face and tired old eyes were turned fixedly on the triple-hued horizon. When I asked this man if land lay ahead, he replied in the ringing voice of the pulpit: "Sir, that is The Island!" The official name of Prince Edward Island evidently was superfluous. What other island in all the world could interest a sensible explorer?

"Yes, there's The Island, safe and sound," the minister repeated in a tone of relief, as if his home might have sunk since he had left it a fortnight before.

He spoke like a Christian catching his first glimpse of the Promised Land or a prophet announcing a miracle. No miracle was yet apparent to me, but its presence had attracted half a dozen Islanders to the deck. Pitying my ignorance, one of them explained that the blue band was the Island shore, the terra-cotta band marked the soil behind it, and the green reflected the forest.

Some farmers began to argue the superior merits of The Island's hogs. A traveling salesman recommended The Island's lobsters, undoubtedly the best found anywhere. His companion agreed, but insisted that The Island's oysters were even more remarkable. A tiny fellow, with cheeks of pink jelly and an eye glistening at a welcome sight, recited a long personal illness in clinical nicety and boasted that his fifteen gallstones, recently removed, were as large as hens' eggs—Island hens, he added. Everything, I gathered, grew better and bigger on The Island.

It was not until we reached a shore glowing like bronze in the sunset that I began to see the truth of these modest claims and to guess the nature of the miracle. For it is miraculous, all right, this tiny particle of land which seems to have been washed down by the St. Lawrence and anchored precariously in its Gulf—miraculous enough in geography, but still more unlikely in its human content.

The stranger will need a little time to discover why The Island's life is unique among all the regions of America. The reporter will not find here any "angle" for his story, since The Island has been polished smooth by more than three centuries of expert lapidary craftsmanship. But the scholar cannot confuse the Island race with any other. It has contracted out of the world's tumult, has refused to play the noisy charade of these things, and stands, by choice and necessity, alone.

No traveler, however insensitive, can fail to see, as soon as he has landed, that The Island is not merely a speck of soil detached from the mainland by water, but a state of mind detached by a much wider void of thought. This is a Lilliputian continent, physically and spiritually, and it is quite unimpressed by the larger continent beside it.

At first sight The Island denies all its portraits. The photographers and painters have long tried to convey this picture, and all have failed. Where most scenery disappoints your expectations, The Island exceeds them in a certain subtle fashion impossible to fix on film or canvas.

Impossible, I suppose, because the thing lacks all reality, evades the beholder like some shred of childhood memory, and, though inhabited by a thrifty and not very imaginative folk, somehow manages to create the brittle enchantment of a fairy tale.

You can hardly drive half a mile before you are wondering when you will wake up. This surely can be no part of America or of the contemporary world. It must be an optical illusion cunningly arranged to deceive the stranger, a conjurer's genial trick. Actually it is all the result of long and plodding toil by a people who may not have known exactly what they were doing, but have ended with a man-made miracle in miniature.

The terrain, alternately tonsured in cultivation and curled in foliage; the precise mosaic of reddish fields, each geometrically cut by a narrow wood lot of green; the gentle roll of the earth carrying inland the roll of the sea; the high-roofed and gabled houses, all as white, angular, and prim as genteel spinsters in crinoline; the fat crimson barns and overstuffed cattle; even the farmer himself, the boy fishing with his willow stick in some quiet pond, and the lobster boats asleep in a shady cove are arranged like elaborate toys of paint and cardboard.

There is nothing like this anywhere else in America—a valentine of some two thousand square miles. To find an equal orderliness and minute design you must go to England and Europe, where men have long nursed, pampered, and worshipped their earth. Even there you will not find an exact replica. The Islanders imitate no one and defy imitators.

No fence, building, stone, tree, or blade of grass is out of place. Best of all—that is The Island's true secret—no human being is out of place either.

This smallest Canadian province has learned the partnership of man and earth as no other province or State of the Union has yet begun to learn it, undoubtedly because The Island is so small and manageable. If this is not perfection, it is the nearest equivalent that any Canadians have ever attained so far.

Nothing, you would think, could ever happen here, nothing unpleasant anyway, nothing unfit for the nursery. In fact a good deal has happened, some of it shameful and violent, most of it peaceful and dull, all of it useful to Canada and quite unlike the experience of any other place. It could not be otherwise. The Island has always lived alone.

Across the floor of checkered linoleum we caught our first glimpse of the odd little monument built—one should rather say invented or dreamed up—to mark The Island's history and govern its civilization.

Charlottetown, rising on the far side of a placid bay, was obviously no suburb of Canada, of America, or of England. Seen in the distance, it looked purely European, perhaps a port in Normandy, a stray morsel of the Channel coast, a lost fraction of France under the twin towers of a Latin basilica; or it might be a stage setting by a classical designer for some royal masque at Versailles.

That illusion of Europe was rudely broken as soon as we reached the busy streets of Charlottetown on a Saturday evening, an evening of special celebration. Seen up close, the Provincial Building of square Georgian cut, the churches of rusted rock and Gothic line, the gardens behind mossy walls, are a mellow mixture of England and Scotland. The clapboard houses, the modern stores, and the people's accent are unmistakably Canadian. Nevertheless, if not foreign, the town is unreal.

It was particularly unreal that night to us who had just come from the frozen coast of Newfoundland and the smoke of the Cape Breton coal fields. Of course I cannot convey this air of unreality, the sensation of leaving a familiar world and emerging upon the pages of a child's picture book. I only affirm that Charlottetown, swimming in foliage and moonlight, almost incorporeal in the mystery of dark shadows and ancient stone, and suddenly haunted by a faint ghost of music, was no part of the life I had ever seen before, was not a few miles but at least a century from the mainland.

Since I cannot evoke a lost magic, I must stick to the facts. Having just settled down behind the tall pillars of the Charlottetown Hotel, and feeling unworthy of its antique grandeur, we heard bugles sound far off in the darkness. They might have been the horns of elfland, but, as it turned out, were blown by a military band which presently came marching along in a brave show of scarlet and brass, followed by a company of tall lads in khaki.

Some of these men had fought overseas not long before; all of them were ready to fight again. Yet in the queer old street, under a May moon and a fluttering thatch of leafage, the scarlet band and the double rank of militia were transformed into toy soldiers, deftly articulated and moving by clockwork. That band was too wise to play martial music in such a place. It played some jingling tune out of a mechanical music box, and it marched like a nursery rhyme.

The spectators in the street shared a general look of wonderment, wore Canadian clothes, and talked in English, but they should have dressed in some quaint peasant costume, sung in some foreign tongue, and danced around a Maypole.

Unfortunately, the parade moved off. The spangled lights of the fire-hall tower flickered and went out. The hour of magic was over, and the toys returned to the nursery shelf. Somewhere a clock spoke ten times in a grandfatherly tone, and the houses of Charlottetown sank to sleep under their new quilt of spring blossom.

Too hungry for sleep after a long day of travel, and still dizzy from too much magic, we set out in search of nourishment (ambrosia, perhaps, and nectar), and found ourselves, in abrupt descent to reality, before a glorious Chinese mess cooked by a displaced genius.

Chop suey in Charlottetown seemed alien and profane. So did the pictures of Marlon Brando and his brutal *Waterfront* on a movie theater a few yards from a real waterfront of lobster boats dozing innocently in a star-flecked harbor. And so did the election banners on the street. Was it possible, we asked the Oriental genius of the kitchen (a sad-faced young man who would never make an Islander), that The Island was engaged in the worldly business of politics?

He said it was, and a hulking farmer from the country informed us solemnly that the approaching provincial election would be one of the most important since Confederation. What, he demanded, did the rest of Canada think of the vital issues to be settled a few days hence at the polls?

I didn't like to confess that the politics of The Island were less known to the Canadian people than the affairs of Russia, Egypt, or Timbuctoo, so I assured the farmer that the nation was awaiting the election with unbearable suspense.

Well it might, said our informant, and he held us for an hour to denounce the government's scandalous failures, to extoll the glories of The Island's harness races (we really must stay over for a month and see them), to describe the approaching festivities of Old Home Week, and to explain the life cycle of swine.

Politics, however, were the best sport of all, he intimated, and were played with an intensity unknown in any other province. This we could well believe since only here was every last voter classified by name and party, his vote reckoned in advance, and his partisan loyalty never doubted; only here could any citizen of North America reach his legislator at any hour of the day or night and confront the government itself, in person, by driving a few miles.

Canada's Confederation, the farmer reminded us with an air of challenge and truculence—we were merely mainlanders— had been born a hundred yards down the street, and what The Island didn't know about politics wasn't worth knowing. This statement, as we found out later, had the added advantage of being true. Moreover, for reasons unsuspected by the Islanders, a humble and parochial contest of politics had a profound lesson to teach the mainland continent, which unfortunately would never hear of it.

Next morning, when ruthless daylight had turned the capital into a town of sixteen thousand mortal folk going briskly about their business, I began a brief but intensive study of its political system, for already I had begun to suspect that The Island was probably the last primitive, unspoiled democracy left in America, a genuine antique, almost a personal, Athenian democracy.

The specific issues of the election no doubt are forgotten by now, and do not concern the mainland continent, but they leaped nakedly that day from the headlines of *The Guardian*, which modestly admits on the front page that it "Covers Prince Edward Island Like the Dew."

The dew apparently lay at the moment over a troubled and dangerous landscape. In a full-page advertisement the government promised that "What has been promoted to date is only an index of the Tremendous Industrial Expansion program to come." A new filleting plant at Souris was employing one hundred persons, a new poultry plant at Charlottetown would need three thousand chickens a day, the government had supplied four bulldozers for land-clearing, had helped to build two smokehouses at Egmont Bay, and had provided so much employment that The Island's population would show a huge increase of several thousands in the next national census.

The opposition replied in gaudy type that the government had broken all its pledges, had undertaken to build seventy bridges and instead had installed only some "clay-covered culverts." It had failed to erect a new Home for Delinquent Children, and, boasting that it had thus saved $100,000, might just as well promise a causeway to Newfoundland and then, by abandoning it, boast that it had saved billions.

To these grave charges the government offered a crushing rejoinder. Below its black headline announcing "The Opposition Platform" it left a whole page of *The Guardian*'s newsprint completely blank. The primitive democrats of Athens would have appreciated these dialectics of sarcasm. They were rather too simple for a mainlander accustomed to the ponderous logic and higher sophistry of current politics.

I was glad to see, however, that the editor of *The Guardian*, with some effort, had maintained an unruffled editorial dignity in the storm. He remarked that the present warmth of debate was "a good sign" and concluded in this classic dictum of democracy: "Within reason, of course, let it be a case of 'Lay on MacDuff and damned be him who first cries 'Hold, Enough!'" The true democratic process, I felt assured, was still at work with frontier passion among the few surviving grass roots of America.

After this alarming preface to politics, I approached the storm center of the Provincial Building in some trepidation, and was relieved to see no sign of combat in the leafy square, only a moldering cannon or two, a bed of flowers in orderly rows, and some old men blinking in the sun.

All seemed quiet on the front line of the election campaign, but no Canadian could pass the Greek columns of the capitol without sensing a ripe flavor of time and events. The interior was like a cool and soundless vault. The broad flagstones of the hallway were worn into deep depressions by countless feet (and wisely the government has refused to renew them and disturb the antiquity of this fine old pile). My footsteps echoed in the silent corridor, and I found myself instinctively walking on tiptoe.

The legislative chamber upstairs looked no larger than a good-sized living-room furnished by some careless eccentric. Its speaker's dais was hung with appropriate purple drapes of velvet, but a misguided architect had disfigured the carved wooden posts on either side with incongruous pear-shaped electric lights. A narrow public gallery could hold perhaps a few dozen spectators, and the crowded semicircle of desks below would barely accommodate thirty legislators squeezed tight.

There is no other legislative chamber in the western world, I dare say, where the government sits on the left side of the speaker and the opposition on the right—a native oddity, like many others, growing from historic roots. Some colonial government of boisterous pre-Confederation times, it is said, selected a strategic position from which it could disappear discreetly into an adjoining room for the essential stimulants of statecraft without exposing itself to the public gaze in the corridor.

The other end of the corridor opens upon one of the nation's shrines, a sunny room where the whole course of North American history was once suddenly altered. This toy box of white symmetry used to house the upper chamber of the legislature, now abolished, and on September 1, 1864, contained the dubious ingredients of a transcontinental state. If Canada has a place of birth or, at any rate, of conception, it is here.

Twenty-six chairs, upholstered in brown leather, are deployed around a long table exactly as the Fathers of Confederation left them after their first conference. Their figures, all comically dressed in the togas of Roman senators and brandishing various obscure emblems, cling to the wall in metal sculpture (doubtless to the amusement of Sir John A. Macdonald, the first Canadian prime minister and the nation's chief builder, who revisited this scene in old age and described himself in the visitors' book as a "Cabinet Maker").

All the relics of the Charlottetown Conference, counterpart of the first Continental Congress in Philadelphia, are preserved, shined up, and jealously guarded by a Scots commissionaire. He has evidently found The Island as congenial and natural as his native heath. His lean Scottish face lighting up with Canadian pride, he told me in a rich burr that the conference table was unquestionably genuine, despite base rumors to the contrary. Regina, capital of that parvenu western province Saskatchewan, believed that it possessed the original, but it was wrong. Regina's table had been used not at Charlottetown, but at the anticlimax of the subsequent Quebec Conference. The meeting here, he emphasized, had been the real beginning of Canada.

I resisted the temptation to recall that Charlottetown had given a pretty indifferent welcome to the delegates from the colony of Canada—not a soul to meet them at the wharf, no accommodation prepared for them ashore, not even a wagon to carry their luggage, the whole town being engaged in the livelier entertainment of a circus. As the visitors waited glumly on their ship and wondered if The Island would join Confederation, a member of the Charlottetown government discovered their arrival, seized a skiff, and rowed out alone to apologize. The town made up for that churlish reception with such a round of banquets, balls, routs, and champagne that the delegates went reeling off to Halifax in amiable humor, the foundation of the new state well and truly laid.

Nor did I depress the commissionaire and arrest his inspired flow of recollection by pointing out that Charlottetown might have conceived Confederation, but had refused for some years to accept its own child and only joined the nation later on because it had to.

The records of these events and others before them are written by hand in the copperplate penmanship of some old leather-bound volumes three feet square and a good six inches thick. Their custodian opened them at random to show me the entries far back into the eighteenth century.

One notation which tickled his Scots fancy was dated July 19, 1797, and written in a penman's flourish by John Hawkins, sergeant-at-arms of the colonial Assembly. That scrupulous official had just delivered the governor's subpoena to Captain Macdonald, of Tracadie, who "would not receive the letter" but "rode along abusing me and calling me a rascal and would see me hanged." Clearly, as the commissionaire said, this must have been a serious affair. Happily, Captain Macdonald changed his mind in the nick of time, after a few soothing drinks, and capitulated. A crisis in The Island's history had passed.

Confident that the crisis of the current election would also pass and that the Confederation Chamber was safe in the hands of a Scotsman far more aware of its meaning than most native Canadians, I called on some of the leading politicians to see how Confederation was now faring in its birthplace.

These men admitted candidly, but not for publication, that they were at a loss to judge the outcome of the election. The people—they spoke of some hundred thousand Islanders as one might consider the electorate of a first-rate power—remained ominously silent. The public sphinx had never seemed so uncommunicative. What went on in that mysterious mass mind?

This question was asked with the portentous look of men trying to calculate a national election or a world crisis. No one could answer it. The inhabitants of a sovereign province, fewer than the population of many Canadian cities, had yet to indicate their verdict.

A mainlander, ignorant of The Island's past, might smile at the sight of a local election campaign fought among a handful of voters with all the fervor of a great cause, all the horrendous propaganda of politics, and all the paraphernalia of party organization. One might ask why a morsel of land one hundred and forty miles long, four to forty miles wide and occupying 0.1 per cent of Canada's area, was carrying all the load of a separate government, legislature, and judiciary. There is nothing to smile or wonder at in this insular but vehement democracy.

It must be, indeed, the most truly democratic system in the nation, or perhaps anywhere, because it is small and intimate enough to keep government in daily and hourly touch with all the people and well able, as larger units of government are not, to argue, understand, and master its own business strictly by the democratic process. This, I began to see, is the key to The Island's private riddle.

It has mastered its own business. It has accomplished nothing grand but the grandeur of contentment. It has built nothing of note but the quality of its life. It can never be wealthy like some other provinces because it lacks the materials of wealth, and it cannot be poor because it is assured of a steady livelihood. It cannot have more than a moderate portion of what men call progress and cannot lose that tranquillity which most progressive regions have mislaid in their rush. Its only achievement is perfection.

In short, this is a thing long sought by our fathers and now dead, nearly everywhere, of magnitude and dropsy. It is a manageable community, a neighborhood, a fellowship, and it would perish, as those qualities have often perished elsewhere, if The Island suddenly expanded to touch the mainland or even if its population greatly increased.

No wonder, then, that this distinct society insists on maintaining its own government to enforce its own ways. Any government beyond these shores would not know how to maintain them. Any nation with a lick of sense would not wish to change them, for here Canada possesses something rare, priceless, and impossible anywhere but on a speck of fertile soil anchored well off the coast. And no wonder that exile Islanders, in any part of Canada, speak of home as The Island and carry its memory as a talisman. No other soil is fit to bear that name.

Seeking more light on these matters, I strolled over to Prince of Wales College and sought out The Island's leading historian, Dr. Frank MacKinnon. This college principal is young for such a post, looks like a hard-driving executive of business, but is in fact a man of deep erudition who gladly threw up a promising career in Ontario to live in his simple boyhood home.

He does not find it as simple as it looks or as dull. The Island, he told me, has been extremely difficult to govern, and sometimes, in its riotous youth, was parlyzed by political chaos. A committee compiling a booklet to celebrate Charlottetown's centennial could think of nothing to record since the Confederation Conference, but plenty happened before that.

Ever since the Indian god Glooscap discovered "Abegweit," the "place resting on the waters," and, dipping his brush in the sunset, painted the soil a rusty red, all men have prized The Island. The first white men made it a French outpost of Louisbourg and called it Ile St. Jean. After the British conquest it became an annex of Nova Scotia and then a separate British colony.

All this time the Islanders cleared their forests, plowed their land, struggled for generations, often with bloodshed, against a brutal system of absentee landlordism, won responsible government at last, and took for their colony the Christian name of the Duke of Kent, who was too busy to inspect it.

The Islanders' trouble from the beginning was that neither Britain nor the prospective nation of Canada would take them seriously as they certainly took themselves. ("Don't be too boastful about your little island," cried Thomas D'Arcy McGee, the great orator of the Confederation debates, "or we'll send down a little tug and draw you up into one of our lakes.")

Local patriotism was so passionate, indeed, that The Island refused to join Confederation until 1873, six years after the original union, when political stalemate, graft in railway construction, and imminent ruin left no alternative. Some Islanders refused to recognize that alternative and had a habit of fastening black crepe to the doors of the Provincial Building on Dominion Day, the new nation's anniversary.

The facts of political life have long since been accepted, and so have the facts of economics. Its area and wealth strictly limited, The Island, like Nova Scotia and New Brunswick, has always exported its citizens to other provinces and could never afford immigration. But Dr. MacKinnon thinks that the varied racial origins of Scots, English, Irish, and French, in that numerical order, have prevented a monotony of character. A casual visitor can see at least that The Island is full of nonconforming and lively characters.

It is true, nevertheless, that an insular geography has produced an insular mind, as limited and tidy as the soil around it. The Island may not have a large view of Canadian affairs, but it sees the thing at hand with peculiar clarity. It may not view the nation through a telescope, but its local microscope is a fine instrument.

These people cannot give the nation leadership, and have provided no political ideas or any statesman of note. Instead, they offer an example of thrift and management lacking in richer provinces, of alliance between man and environment, of skilled concentration on indigenous resources, of specialized production and the elimination of waste; above all, an example of sane living which a prodigal, hurried, and increasingly neurotic nation badly needs.

If The Islanders lack glamour, so called, they also lack illusions. They have the old virtues that go with simple life and long residence in one place. They are realists and they are friendly. Still, there must be some latent poetry in them— their little kingdom is as neatly put together as a sonnet.

All these qualities, I was informed, could be found in the most eminent contemporary Islander. We tracked him with some difficulty to the outskirts of St. Peter's, a hamlet east of Charlottetown first settled by shipwrecked French sailors. He had lived there nearly one hundred years and practiced his profession for sixty-seven.

As we neared St. Peter's, we observed a tall man in overalls behind an old-fashioned house. Apparently he was sawing a branch off an apple tree of about his own age. At our approach he disappeared hurriedly into the house, but emerged a few moments later, dressed to receive us in the dark, well-worn serge, stiff collar, and enormous gold watch chain of the family physician.

Dr. Roderick J. M. Macdonald, the "Doctor Roddy" of Island legend, had a face which could bear only one adjective: it was beautiful, as a prophet's face on a church window is beautiful. The features were finely cut out of hard Scottish material and tinted red by the weather of the Gulf. Though he had been born here ninety-seven years before, Scotland was legibly written in every wrinkle and confirmed in his speech. The white mustache was cropped short with surgical precision. The eyes twinkled in perpetual merriment.

Dr. Roddy said he had been grafting one of his apple trees with a new variety. He could hardly expect to reap the fruit, but he thought it might please his daughter who keeps his house. This prospect set him chuckling as he led us through a surgery lined with shelves of medicine bottles and into his cosy nineteenth-century parlor.

There he stopped suddenly, looked me in the eye, and wagged his finger under my nose. "I'm old," he thundered, "but I'm not in my dotage! Young man, you're after something, by Gob!"

I admitted it, and my candor seemed to reassure him. Well, he had seen writing fellows before. He supposed they must write about something, but really he had little to tell them. Nothing much had happened in his life, though still and all it had been a good life, by Gob. (That curious word was the only semblance of an oath he would permit himself.)

No, nothing much had happened—only his boyhood here nearly ten years before Confederation; the days when his father built sailing ships in the bay yonder; education at Toronto University; and then, with horse and buggy in summer or saddle in winter, a lifetime of service to his people. By endless round of birth and death, of comedy and tragedy, he had held such a clinic on human nature as few Canadians will ever see.

Nothing, Dr. Roddy repeated, had happened to distinguish him in the least. As an afterthought, he recalled something rather unusual. The other day he had met a man whom he had ushered into the world, his first baby, just sixty-seven years ago that week. This memory made him heave with laughter.

Seventeen years before, as I learned later from one of the

participants, Dr. Roddy had invited his friends to a last birthday party, toasted them in Scotch whisky, and bade them farewell. They cried that night, but most of them were now dead while the doctor was still curing his neighbors, driving his car in summer, a horse in winter, and yet finding time to follow, with a young man's eagerness, the latest discoveries of medicine.

By Gob, he said, what medicine could do nowadays was a caution. Why, he had watched scores of men die of a simple disease like pneumonia. Things were certainly improving all the time, and he counted himself lucky to live in such an age —yes, and always "plenty to eat and drink and a very lovely companion," dead these many years.

Well, the long shift would soon be finished. He told me quite cheerfully that he was "waiting for the call, and that, you know, is the best thing of all." At the gate he invited me to repeat my visit. "By Gob," he added in an unfamiliar Island phrase, "don't make a bridge over my nose." Both of us understood well enough that we would never meet again.

I left him with a new respect for his Island and for the human race. Dr. Roddy returned to his garden with a saw to finish the graft on his apple tree.

What surprised me most, after I had turned the wheel over to my wife and examined the scenery at leisure, was not the beauty of The Island—I was used to that by now—but its deceptive size. More densely populated than any province or perhaps any American State, for all I know, with about fifty people to the square mile and eighty-five per cent of its surface under cultivation, it reminded me of the spacious western prairies. Its railway meandered in endless distance. Its inhabitants evidently had learned to expand space by sleight-of-hand.

All their possessions seemed to be made of the same material, built to a single architect's plan, and painted by one artist's hand. There really was no plan at all. Only instinct had made a collective farm of a million acres—collective because its farmers, all free to do as they pleased, had learned to tend, protect, and nourish their estate jointly.

There was more here than scenery and order. We came, for

example, upon bands of men, women, and children planting potatoes, apparently in a kind of week-end folk festival, and they told us that The Island grew over half of Canada's potato seed and sold this valuable product to a score of foreign countries. It has as many cattle as people, its bacon is recognized as probably the world's best, and it produces half the nation's canned chickens. The diatoms and food organisms carried down by the St. Lawrence feed swarms of fish and give The Island lobsters and Malpeque oysters their celebrated flavor. No speck of food is neglected. Even the edible seaweed called Irish moss was being harvested close to the beach by men and horses half submerged in the day's low tide.

Though nature is kind and recognizes the Islanders as friends, she demands infinite toil, patience, and experience in payment for returns that most Canadians would consider pitiably small. Such facts could be read at North Rustico, where we ate dinner in a dingy restaurant among lobster fishermen of French descent.

These men in oilskins and gum boots spoke English with no trace of foreign accent, but they had swarthy Norman faces. Their village by the shore, the squat houses, community pump, and towering wooden church had an unmistakable French air. The restaurant's superb meal of potato soup, fresh lobsters, and berry pie (at a price of sixty-five cents) could have been cooked by no other race. These people were poor and unaware of poverty.

That fact of itself was probably unique among North Americans, who usually are unaware of their wealth. But it occurred to me, in my talk with the fishermen, that I had overlooked another fact and The Island's largest achievement. Unlike some other provinces, it has achieved an understanding and goodwill between the British and French races so complete and unquestioned that nobody seems to think about it any more. The Islanders have taken both race and poverty in their stride and reduced them to irrelevancy.

Our purpose in North Rustico was to attend a political meeting and inspect real democracy in action at the grass roots. Finding that the election campaigners would not arrive before dark, we drove on to Cavendish beach. There twenty-

five unbroken miles of sand glistened beside the terra-cotta
cliffs, the green headlands were as lonely as any space in Canada, and the sun, abruptly turning the cliffs purple, slid down
into the metallic blue of the Mediterranean. Night was coming with a special blend of color, a private salute to the second
North American continent.

We increased our speed to find, before darkness overtook us,
a certain Canadian myth. Soon we were wandering through
such a labyrinth of deserted roads that we wondered how Father George Belcourt ever got around here, ninety years ago, in
that steam contraption, Canada's first automobile. At last we
stumbled by chance on our objective.

"Green Gables," the house of the immortal Anne, who was
once known to all North American children, stands on a grassy
knoll. It is a commonplace house of clapboard and rather ugly.
Nothing about it would attract a second look except the myth
of its departed owner. We felt a little disappointed until the
dusk fell, a robin sang from a gnarled apple tree, a brook
chattered in the darkness, and the air was suddenly filled with
the heavy incense of fruit blossom. Then we began to understand why Lucy Maud Montgomery could discern fairies in
her garden, could play with the cousins of Peter Pan, and in
this house produce her humble classic.

It was now time for the meeting. By nine o'clock about one
hundred electors of North Rustico had assembled in a new
community hall, the men fresh from their lobster boats or
milking stools and still wearing the gum boots and overalls of
the day's work, the women in their best mail-order dresses.
They sat diffidently at the back of the hall. The front seats
were left vacant, according to the local custom. We had
reached the ultimate grass roots of Canadian democracy.

After a whispered conference in the corridors, someone
nominated a chairman. A beefy young Hercules strode awk-
wardly to the platform, leaned over a chair, his eyes on the
floor, blushed scarlet, and invoked the mysteries of democracy
in these exact words: "As yez all know, I don't know much
about this here chairman business and I aim to conduct myself accordin'."

He called upon a nervous and stammering little person who

protested feebly that he had tried to do a good job in the provincial legislature, but was no speaker and would therefore call upon another candidate.

This man was a stranger in the district, a politician of talent and a smooth specimen of a breed recognizable anywhere in America. I knew that as soon as he opened his mouth to intimate his only ambition in public life. He had come here, he said, to meet and serve the fine people of North Rustico, and he added (the unfailing gambit of his kind) that he had been instantly impressed by the beauty of the district's ladies. This may have impressed the ladies, but they stared at the flatterer with dead-haddock eyes (the unfailing emblem of Canadian politics).

The third speaker, imported with his gift of oratory from Charlottetown, recalled his boyhood in North Rustico, told many tales of pioneer life, never mentioned the election, promised to be brief, and rambled on for nearly an hour.

If all this seemed a trifle obscure, a lean and handsome farmer, obviously uncomfortable in city clothes, got down to business, explained the farmers' problems, and talked a deal of sense that his audience understood.

At last the official representative of the government rose to flaunt the opposition's newspaper advertisements and announce that he would answer them point by point. His financial figures might amuse a mainland audience—fifty thousand dollars saved here, thirty thousand wisely spent there, all the seventy little bridges built on schedule, and no culverts as the opposition alleged—but anyone who felt amused must have been ignorant of democracy, of politics, the history of his country, and the dignity of man. The audience was not amused. It listened in respectful silence.

This meeting in North Rustico, though the nation would never hear of it, was repeating the political process that made Canada. The nation had been built by just such men as these, not with any great plan or abstract principles but solely by attention to common local problems and practical business as they turned up in the daily round. They happened to be small here, but they represented a large thing, nothing less than the nation's inner method and the whole democratic process reduced to essentials. We had found what we were looking for.

The grand finale was supplied by a wee creature who moved erratically like a jumping jack, walked back and forth across the platform, paused on each passage to lay his hand on the table as if it contained some magic current, and recited a formidable series of Irish jokes to conclude the meeting with laughter in the good old Canadian fashion. A piano-player was summoned; none appeared; the chairman began to sing "God Save the Queen" in a hoarse bellow, and the electorate of North Rustic went home to ponder its verdict.

We decided that democracy was safe on The Island, which understood it, and next morning we started westward from Charlottetown. As my wife was navigating with a map and a sure sense of indirection, we were soon hopelessly enmeshed in the Cotswolds of England, then in the red lanes of Devon, then in a dark German forest, and finally on a beach of golden sand. After pausing at a dozen villages to get our bearings we agreed that the national census figures were grossly distorted, that The Island held a million people at least. We remained lost for three hours, but it didn't matter. As nearly as any grown-up can be, we were happily lost in toyland.

At last we discovered and embarked on the big ferryboat at Borden and fell into talk with two of its passengers, a wise man and a fool.

One of them said he had come to live on The Island five years ago and loved it, though the clannish natives, whom he also loved, had not yet accepted him entirely. He was still a stranger from the other continent. Gazing back at the triple lines of blue, terra cotta, and green on the northern horizon, he pronounced his faith: "These folks are the best in Canada. I hope they never change." That was the voice of the wise man.

His companion said: "Don't worry. They'll never change. Everywhere else in the country you'll find nothing but progress. Here everything stands still. If they had any sense, they could do something with The Island. But they won't."

Thus spoke the fool.

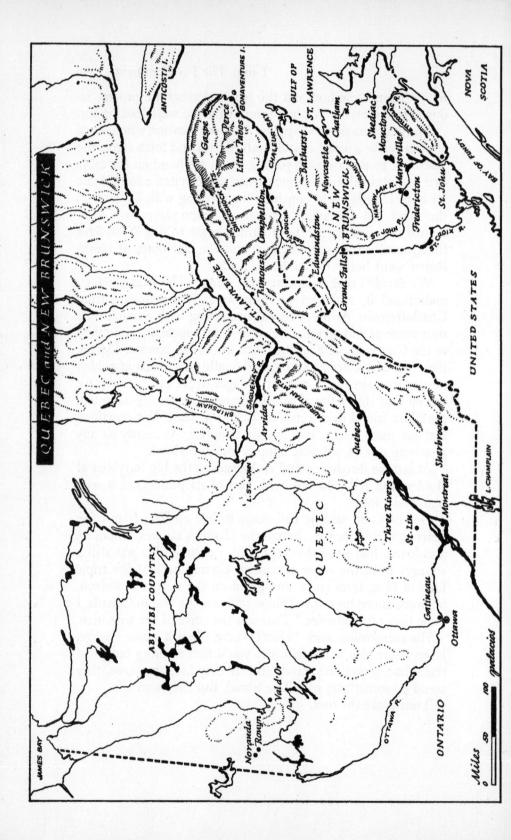

GREEN FLAMES

*T*he springtime of tradition and English poetry, the soft drift between winter and summer, is alien to Canada. A British constitution serves us well. The seasons of our ancestors cannot fit this land. Here spring comes overnight in explosive heaving, an agony of mammalian birth and then an ecstasy of growth.

One day, after weeks of trial, the arrows of the sun find their range upon the northern target, the shining arch of winter cracks, and half a continent begins to thaw. Overnight the mountain moss turns soft and releases its little store of moisture. Rocks drip. Icicles fall from the cliffs and shatter in the valleys. A heavy load slides from the spruce tree and the cabin roof. Snow turns to water.

Each drop finds its way into some small channel. Many channels, joining together, form a trickle. The trickles merge into a brook. The rivers are opaque with mud and the milk of glaciers. Another cargo of earth specks is putting out to sea.

As the winter rind is burst and riven, as ice splinters and dissolves at the river's edge or sinks, already half liquid, into the upland lake, the spring freshet scours new curves in the soft plains, new clefts in the rock of the Shield, new grooves in the canyons of the Rockies. Almost with intelligent motion and sure homing instinct, ice and water return to their parent ocean.

Now the soil of Canada awakens, not quietly and soberly like the soil of the poets' England, but in sudden start and convulsion. It heaves upward to eject the frost and then sinks to begin the work of bacteria, worm, root, and seed. They must work fast. Within six months cold will put them back to sleep.

In Canada we have no need for a Browning to tell us that April's here. It declares itself, as the French would say, in an unwritten language which all Canadians can read before they have learned English.

April declares itself first in the hoarse gutturals of geese flying northward in the night. The Canadian hears that message, as his fathers heard it long ago, and he feels again, even in his clangorous cities, the old longing for far-off places and the freedom of flight. Without road sign, map, or radar, the geese are flying north once more, certain of their exact destination and safe return, while man is lost under his own roof. But in that midnight whir and honking the Canadian knows for sure that April's here.

He has known spring long before April on the Pacific coast, where the snowdrop raised its white face in January, the crocus opened its gold chalice in February, and the daffodil nodded a solemn spinster head in March. He knows it, if he is a prairie man, when the first purple anemone appears on a southern slope; or if he is an eastern man, when the native orchids dance in lady-slippers, the swamp maples spill arterial blood, and the succulent fiddlehead excites the Maritime palate.

Today is spring. Tomorrow will be summer. Our country, reborn into new life out of winter's chilly womb, breathes deep and feels its strength. The fetters of its prison are shattered at one stroke. This is no time for leisurely bud and pastoral verse. Spring must end before even a sonnet can be written.

The winterbound human spirit melts with the ice. A nation flings the winter garments of repentance into the first spring fires and lights up in dangerous conflagration. The child divests himself of shoes and socks. Sensible city men are maddened by seed packages, hoes, shovels, and lawn-mowers in hardware stores. Middle-aged housewives attack the millinery stores in rebellion against their advancing years and the hard facts of life. Newspapers hastily rewrite last year's editorials, to welcome a guest already installed. Members of Parliament at Ottawa hear the old siren song, rush through the national budget, and, with a little luck and some backstage interparty arrangement, may be home by the first of June after spring has departed.

Throughout Canada spring explodes not only in the frozen earth but also in the human heart. Let it explode. It is the only safe explosion left, now that man has invented the ingredients of eternal atomic winter. The spring of Canada will explode anyway, even if no man is left to watch it. With all his nuclear knowledge, he can neither light nor extinguish the green flames of April.

———◆———

CHAPTER FOUR

The Land of Peter Emberley

OUR introduction to New Brunswick was admirably arranged by a lady historian at the town of Newcastle, a British tycoon then far away in London, and a dead wood-chopper from Prince Edward Island. These three had kindly conspired, without advance notice, to provide the setting for a strange little adventure and a continental discovery of some importance.

We reached Newcastle on a hot Sunday and inquired our way to a house which, we had been told, contained the inner essence of a people almost forgotten by most Canadians, of a land left far behind in their westward march.

The house did not strike us as distinguished or promising. Massive, square, and painted an ugly cream color, it stood on Newcastle's shady hill and cast a dismal frown on the Miramichi River below. We knew, however, that this unprepossessing structure held a notable story for all Canadians, for the English who have inherited its owner, and for Americans who admire his gaudy career. It was from a room in the third story, through a gable window about two feet square, that a boy named William Maxwell Aitken got his first view of the world, an oyster to be pried open with a golden lever bearing the heraldic arms of Lord Beaverbrook.

As we approached the house, I recalled a gay yet rather wistful little man enveloped in a sofa much too large for him —an elderly elf, a Wizard of Oz who was busily charming birds and governments from their perches, managing his newspaper empire, re-creating an imaginary British Empire, and occasionally writing books to explain how anyone can succeed by following his simple rules of thrift, sobriety, and attention to detail.

That was in London two years earlier. Now I wondered how the classic success story of our time could have started in this house and what it had to do with the quite opposite story of New Brunswick. I would soon find out.

Actually, like most things in Beaverbrook's crowded life, the beginning is commonly misrepresented. He was not born in Newcastle, as he would have wished and as the *Encyclopædia Britannica* asserts, but in Ontario, where at the age of ten months (so he likes to think) he informed his family: "Pack my diapers, I'm off for the Miramichi!" He remained in Newcastle for some fifteen years and departed suddenly on his adventures through western Canada and, later, in England.

But, like all New Brunswickers, he could never get this land out of his blood. He has repaid his debt to it with wild extravagance. The elf, for all his success, remains an exile. His farewell to the Miramichi may seem to be an accidental episode in a ravenous search for success of a sort. In fact, it explains of itself the life—some would say the tragedy—of New Brunswick. Most of this province's ablest sons in modern times— such as Beaverbrook, Prime Minister Bonar Law of Britain, and Prime Minister Richard Bedford Bennett of Canada—left home to enrich other lands and impoverish their own.

Remembering those melancholy facts, we entered the manse of Beaverbrook's father with a mixture of awe and great expectations. For a moment, only a moment, we were disappointed.

The whole building had been gutted and turned into a public library at the expense, naturally, of its owner. The parlor, once crammed with fashionable and hideous furniture as shown in old photographs, was empty except for the bookshelves. Young Max's bedroom upstairs was freshly painted but deserted, as if awaiting his return. Then, from the cavernous and vacant dining-room, we heard the native voice of New Brunswick, the sigh of this land's inconsolable nostalgia. It issued, oddly enough, out of a phonograph.

Some nameless minstrel from the wilderness had recorded his song and his heart on a celluloid tape, again at the Beaver's expense, as part of a worthy plan to preserve New Brunswick's pioneer culture. To tell the truth, the minstrel sang in a wailing falsetto, a rhythmic paroxysm of grief. To our unschooled ears his words and tune were preposterous.

Thus we heard the immemorial folk song of Peter Emberley. That ill-fated Prince Edward Islander was killed under a falling tree in the New Brunswick woods long ago. He had earned no distinction in life, but became a hero in death simply because a farmer named John Calhoun liked to write perhaps the worst doggerel in the language.

Miss Louise Manny, playmate of the younger Aitken children and now the librarian of the manse, has preserved the rustic balladry of her province, and just in the nick of time, for the race of New Brunswick's troubadours is dying out. Thanks to this strong-minded but charming historian, the old songs will never die.

She told us that they were much older than they seemed. Musicians had discovered in them the melodies of Elizabethan times and some snatches from the music of the Middle Ages brought here by the early settlers as unconscious racial memories and then used as the setting of some local rhyme.

Thus Peter Emberley is far more than an obscure logger; he is the reincarnation of a thousand forgotten medieval heroes; he speaks for New Brunswick, in Calhoun's strident ballad, more clearly than Beaverbrook with all the power of the press. Indeed, he is Beaverbrook's spokesman, and, like others of his kind, speaks for the whole New Brunswick race. He sings of violent death, of graves, moldering bones, of a lost hope and a great age now gone.

Another age has arrived here, unforeseen by Emberley, Calhoun, Beaverbrook, or any Canadian outside New Brunswick's narrow valleys, and with it one of the major experiments in North American life. But any study of this province must begin in the past because it dominates both present and future as in no other part of the nation, save Quebec.

The past not only endures in the old ballads, but also still expresses itself in new ones written to celebrate any event of local interest—a murder, an accident, an election, a joke. They are written in the backwoods by a people whose world barely reaches the next valley, whose ancestors are always beside them in the new age.

These people may claim, almost with an inverted pride, to inhabit the poorest province per capita in Canada, next to the new province of Newfoundland and the tiny garden of Prince Edward Island, but poverty and joint memories of the great age have knit them into a clan, almost a secret society and arcanum within the nation.

Anyway, as we listened to the song of Peter Emberley and observed the librarian's honorable emotion, which no westerner could share, we realized that the clan had maintained its secret communication intact. Only a clansman can translate it and then only to another clansman. Even Beaverbrook fails to translate it to anyone but a New Brunswicker. His multi-million-dollar homesickness, his gifts of public buildings, skating rinks, libraries, and monuments of all sorts to his people, as if in atonement for his desertion, tell us much, but not everything.

We found more significant exhibits, the first portents of the new age, on the outskirts of Newcastle.

Near the Miramichi's yawning mouth there stands a house somewhat like the ghostly Aitken manse but still the home of living people. It was built long ago by some wealthy sea captain and was inhabited, when we were invited to accept its hospitality, by a jolly soul as crimson and salty as his luncheon of broiled lobsters.

This man was worth some study not only as a person but also as a portent. And, talking to him over beer and lobsters on the cool porch, I remembered what I had read of another man more famous and less discerning.

On September 17, 1758, Colonel James Murray faithfully carried out in this place the orders of General James Wolfe by driving the last Acadians from the Miramichi Valley—or so he thought. "I am persuaded," Murray wrote to his commander, "that there is not now a French Man in the River Miramichi and it will be our fault if they are ever allowed to settle there again."

The future colony of New Brunswick was to be British forever, the most British colony of the newly won Empire.

What would Murray have learned if he could have lunched with us in the sea captain's old house? He would have learned from its present owner the total failure of his mission. He would have learned, among other things, that the Acadians, surviving every attempt to dislodge them, will soon turn New Brunswick into Canada's second predominantly French-speaking province.

I supposed that it would be dangerous to question my host, the descendant of a United Empire Loyalist family from New England, about such painful matters. But the question must be asked. Bracing myself for an explosion of Loyalist anger, I finally ventured to inquire how he would enjoy living as a member of an English-speaking minority. To my amazement, he was not angry at that prospect. He was not even alarmed.

The ethnic shift, the new age, and the most promising racial experiment in America were natural, he said, inevitable, and, to him, entirely agreeable. As a businessman he had found reliable associates among the French Canadians, and good friends with much to teach their neighbors of British stock. In another generation, he hoped, both races would be bilingual, as they should be, and still more friendly.

That reply was almost unbelievable to a Canadian from any province whose speech is predominantly English or French. Imagine what Ontario would say if it heard that it must soon face a French-Canadian majority, or how Quebec would regard the opposite prospect! My host's statement could hardly come from any English-speaking Canadian except a New Brunswicker. The clan might be secretive, it might regret the passage of the great age, but it was preparing itself for a greater.

How was it, I asked, that this community of two evenly balanced races had escaped the long and ugly racial tensions of Upper and Lower Canada that became Ontario and Quebec?

"We had something," my host explained, "that they didn't have. We had time. The thing has happened gradually, you see. We were never organized at the beginning in two separate blocs of race like Ontario and Quebec. We were always mixed up together, and race never became much of an issue with us. Each side had time to learn that the other was all right before any real trouble broke out. Time saved us."

Yes, time. New Brunswick has been learning the lessons of time, of success, failure, bitter disappointment, and recent recovery for three and a half centuries since the Acadians first settled along the Bay of Fundy. Nothing has turned out as Murray expected on the Miramichi, but the British soldier, who later fell hopelessly in love with the French of Quebec, would find little to disturb him in modern New Brunswick. Perhaps he would understand, if he were here today, that British civilization is not failing here because it is being outnumbered. It is achieving a success of a certain kind without parallel in Canada, with few parallels in this race-riven world.

From the porch of the sea captain's house we watched a Norwegian ship, successor to the myriad fleet of sail, loading mine props at the edge of the garden. The air was laden with the mixed scent of lilac and freshly peeled logs. The river glistened like brass, and from the opposite bank rose the ragged silhouette of Chatham. Newcastle and Chatham together seemed to provide a case history of the New Brunswick mind, a microcosm of its past and some explanation of its present.

Toward the end of the eighteenth century, the giant personage of Joseph Cunard appeared in Chatham. He soon crammed the basin with his shipyards and his lawns with peacocks. He drove to church in a shiny coach, his coachmen in livery, expected the town to welcome him from his incessant travels by a salute of gunfire, and, on the awful day when he faced bankruptcy, rode his horse through sullen mobs, a pistol in each bootleg.

Cunard, king of Chatham, faced across the river the king of Newcastle, Alexander Rankin. Their rival kingdoms long enjoyed an agreeable holiday of guerrilla warfare at every colonial election—broken heads, battles with stones, sods, and hunks of coal, barricaded streets, and finally, in 1843, cannon loaded with scrap iron but happily not fired.

It was hard to believe, in this quiet house and scented garden, that the almost empty basin once echoed to the clatter of shipwrights' hammers, the shouts of riot, and the sound of perpetual prosperity.

Why, the boom had barely paused for the Miramichi forest fire of 1825, though flames covered four hundred square miles, cremated nearly two hundred people, drove the rest into the river with the woodland animals, and, according to the local diarist, Robert Cooney, made the earth "reel from its ancient foundations" while "the harmony of creation appeared to have been deranged and about to revert into original chaos."

The people lived through the next winter in roofless cellars, went back to work in the spring, and, being New Brunswickers, immediately produced another ballad. But the great age already was doomed. Steam ruined the wooden ship and all the brave hopes of the North Shore. It seemed likely to ruin New Brunswick entire.

As the first tide of industry receded, leaving two sleepy towns on the Miramichi, another invisible tide had begun to rise. The Acadians were coming back. Slowly, and then with increasing momentum, the ironic wheel of history turned in full circle. Today the descendant of British folk could look forward without surprise or alarm to a new and more hopeful adventure.

The emergence of a second Canadian province containing a French majority—though by no means a reproduction or satellite of Quebec—deserved further inquiry at the center of politics. So we set off on a winding country road—I have no idea where it lies—across lonely hills, lush valleys, dark forests, and furious rivers. At last we came to Fredericton, capital of New Brunswick, incidentally, but for national purposes the genuine original and apotheosis of the Canadian home town.

In the dozen years since we had seen it last, Fredericton had changed distressingly on the surface. How deep did the change go?

Sharp spires still pierced a cloud of spring foliage and floated upside-down in the river. The current of the St. John moved in majestic strides as Villebon watched it from the first French fort, as the Loyalists saw it from their boats, as Main John Glasier, in stovepipe hat and bushy brown wig, mastered it from the deck of his celebrated ship, *Morning Dew*, and even drove logs over its Grand Falls without removing hat or wig.

The river, alas, was deserted. Captain Peabody's floating store from Boston; the snorting fleet of side-wheelers that once paddled up from Saint John with sleek white flanks and piercing toot of whistle; the captains, the pilots, the merchant princes of lumber; that humble genius Benjamin Franklin Tibbits, the clockmaker who invented the first compound engine here, revolutionized the use of steam, and died broke; the drunken engineer who blew up the good ship *Ben Beveridge* in a moment of spite—all had departed, leaving no mark on the river but Fredericton.

It is mark enough, the loveliest town in Canada, so perfect in every line, its ingredients so subtly mixed and matured to such ripeness, that no stone, brick, or board in all its singular anatomy should ever be changed and no vandal finger should be allowed to rub a speck from its mellow patina. A town, in short, or rather the imagined image and daydream of a town where a shady veranda, a girl, a guitar, and a moon on the river might rescue a man from this rude age and return him to the innocency of his youth when all the world was young.

Or was it conceivable that Fredericton might become just another normal town and lose its character in a nation that has no characters to spare? We set out on an early morning walk and found everything apparently in order.

The velvet turf of the Loyalists' graveyard lay undisturbed in the middle of the business district. The Parliament Buildings, their absurd dome shaped like King George III's nightcap, remained as homely and yet as beautiful as ever. The original Audubon prints—one of the last two complete sets in existence, as we were told, and Fredericton's most valuable possession—reposed securely in the fireproof vault of the archives. The brown clapboard house of Bliss Carman, Canada's greatest poet and leader of New Brunswick's humble Renaissance, was in good repair.

Down the street that monstrous golden hand on a church steeple still pointed its gilt forefinger to heaven in a gesture of eternity. The English cathedral presided with Gothic grin and silent elegy over Gray's imitation English churchyard. The university meditated, unruffled, on the hill. The painted iron dolphins gamboled in their fountain. A solid roof of green, on the soaring pillars of the Loyalists' trees, covered the whole town, leakproof.

But superficially Fredericton was changing faster than any other community in the Maritimes. It had become a little city of twenty thousand people. It was swelling up and down the riverbank; it had built a luxurious hotel (named for Beaverbrook, of course) out of its own capital; replaced the rabbit warren of *The Gleaner's* editorial office and its Dickensian inmates with a newspaper of three daily editions; and, as the final proof of its new opulence, had produced a formidable parking problem. A parking problem in Fredericton! We began to fear the worst, and now we found it.

Fredericton no longer could find space for that majestic stuffed frog of a hundred pounds weight, a beloved fake but a national figure, who used to stare coldly from the door of the Barker House and seemed to defy time as he defied nature. We searched for out lost friend in vain. Some Philistine had consigned the punctured remains of Fredericton's most famous resident to an unknown garret. Had the inner stuffing of Fredericton also oozed out? Was Canada losing its home town?

That question assailed me as I approached the inner sanctum of the university. There I found an answer, but not at once. (The answers of the clan are always slow, grudging, and oblique.)

When Beaverbrook built the Bonar Law library extension in honor of his old political chieftain, he spared no money or imagination. The splendid common room would not be out of place in Oxford or Cambridge. It is dominated by portraits of Bonar Law, David Lloyd George, and the Canadian, Lord Bennett. The adjoining archives contain the three statesmen's papers, for which any university would give its eye teeth. No one but the Beaver could have brought them to this unlikely place.

The professors who received me here in the good old English ceremony of afternoon tea and sticky tarts are the final expression and delicate bloom of a very special civilization. Though their civilization is small and poor, it is the locus and darling of their scholarship. Everything that has ever happened in New Brunswick since Villebon built his fort near by, almost every human being ever born along the St. John River must be known to these men. The three leading poets of Fredericton—Bliss Carman, Charles G. D. Roberts, and Francis Joseph Sherman—are revered, analyzed, documented, and endlessly debated as if they had ushered in a new age of poetry. Perhaps, in Canadian terms, they did. Whatever their merits, they have been elevated to the stature of Keats, Shelley, and Byron in a miniature Romantic Revival. All true New Brunswickers, I suspect, are incurable romantics. May they never be cured.

An educated cynic might say that this worship of provincial deities is only a defense mechanism against the disappointing facts of New Brunswick's economic experience in modern times, but on a hill of weathered buildings, in the quiet of the scholars' workshop, an ignorant man like me might properly feel that he had stumbled upon a modest Acropolis, a remote suburb of Athens.

In any case, if the scholars were analyzing a small civilization as they might analyze a first-rate national power, they have preserved an important chunk of Canada while most of the same treasure is lost in other provinces. Here nostalgia has been elevated into a science, or an art. The past with all its little glories emerges in a long sigh, the authentic folk sound of a province which has felt, like no other area in Canada, the sudden change from wealth to poverty.

Yes, but there is a very different future ahead. The economic revolution has marched in frontal attack upon most of the other provinces. It has crept slowly, almost silently into the narrow valleys of New Brunswick, and it is coming to stay. The professors and some of the province's leading politicians told me of the huge hydro-power scheme on the upper St.

John, which of itself will largely transform the provincial economy, of new mineral discoveries in the north, and of other sure omens of the revolution.

In another fashion New Brunswick is passing through an experience unknown elsewhere in Canada. The university's statistics confirmed what the old Loyalist had told me at Newcastle: a high French birthrate must soon assure an English-speaking minority in the Loyalists' sacred preserve, where they had established, as they thought, "the most gentlemanlike government on earth."

The professors took the prospect of a French-speaking majority quite calmly, as a mathematical fact, but warned me not to confuse New Brunswick with Quebec, since the histories, cultures, and attitudes of the French stock in the two provinces were entirely different.

The Acadian culture was separated from the culture of Quebec from the beginning by a trackless jungle. It was banished and almost extinguished by the Dispersal of 1755. It has returned, survived, grown on its own roots, and never felt itself to be a part of a single French bloc. It belongs solely to New Brunswick and an Acadian fringe in Nova Scotia. It is a unique element in the nation's life, as its peaceful relations with the British stock are also unique.

This phenomenon, overlooked by most of the nation, was explained to me in an Acadian home not far from the university. The distinguished figure who welcomed me there was unmistakably French in look, manner, and mind, but just as unmistakably Canadian, and he spoke better English than I can ever hope to speak. He would be insulted, no doubt, if he were called a Frenchman after his people's residence in this land since DeMonts's settlement at Port Royal. He would be a little hurt if he were confused with the French of Quebec.

The first thing to understand, he told me, was that Acadian culture had not based itself on "nationalism" as that word is used in Quebec to denote a belligerent racial isolation. It was not belligerent because its rights of language, religion, and education were not challenged here. The Acadians felt no need to isolate themselves because they were entirely secure. They would never form a racial or even a political bloc with Quebec. True enough, many people from Quebec had moved into the forest, farm, and fishing industries of New Brunswick and formed almost solid communities of their own language, like the upriver town of Edmundston, but they were being absorbed rapidly in the Acadian culture and found no cause here to resent the dwindling English-speaking majority.

The Acadian gentleman still retained some inherited French instincts. Though he was pressed for time and due at an important official meeting, his Gallic manners compelled him to escort me on foot to the hotel. There he raised his hat in farewell and gave me a little message for all Canadians.

"Tell Canada," he said, "that New Brunswick is the crucible of a great national experiment. Tell it that the experiment is working out better here than any other place in the world. People ask what New Brunswick contributes to Canadian life. That is our real contribution. Someday the nation, and perhaps the world, will appreciate its value."

This sounded much too good to be true, so I questioned some of the English-speaking politicians in the Parliament Buildings who, I felt sure, would have different views. I was wrong. These men endorsed in every detail what the Acadian had told me. The French-speaking New Brunswickers, they said, had attracted no attention until recent years. In their labors of mere survival, they had found little time for politics, were generally poor and often ill-educated. Now they were learning fast, were insisting that their sons study English to prosper in a dual society, and were training a generation of youngsters who would soon make their names in government. Future politics, however, would not be split on racial lines, as had often happened in other provinces, simply because any durable government must seek support among both races and could not rely on either alone.

Such a hopeful and friendly racial evolution, though it directly affects only some five hundred and fifty thousand people in New Brunswick, must interest any observer of the current race-mad world. Nevertheless, with all the history books, bluebooks, and assorted information supplied by the professors and the politicians, I was still wondering what kind of people the New Brunswickers really were when I encountered, by chance, a striking piece of evidence.

Across the St. John, on the foaming Nashwaak River, a few miles from Fredericton, stands the deserted cotton factory of Alexander Gibson. This blond, bearded giant of six-feet-six arrived here by wagon in 1862. He wore a beaver hat and swallowtail coat, and he had only ten thousand dollars in his pocket. Yet this odd genius of industry managed to build lumber mills, railways, a mansion for himself, and the town of Marysville for his workmen, whose debts he once canceled by tossing all his ledgers into the office stove.

"Boss" Gibson was a strict Methodist and a gambler. He gambled everything he owned and won a fortune. His life, like Beaverbrook's, thus represented, as a historian of Fredericton observed, one aspect of the ambivalent New Brunswick nature. The other is represented by the cotton factory, a gigantic, vacant cavern of brick.

The death of its largest industry failed to halt Fredericton's growth, for the new revolution already begins to dwarf the work of the early giants, but New Brunswick as a whole lost the gamble of Gibson's heroic day once the original pine forests were cut out and steam replaced sail. The resulting wounds of the spirit have never quite healed.

"The gamblers," said the local historian, "died or moved out west, or maybe to England, like the Beaver. Most of the gambling spirit went with them. The rest of us, who stayed home, were different from most Canadians. They had so much wealth that they could afford to keep on gambling. We couldn't. We knew that if we lost any gamble, we'd lose our shirts. That's why we're cautious or, you might say, timid. We had to be."

At the sight of Gibson's cavern he heaved a wrenching sigh, the authentic folk sound, always faintly audible throughout New Brunswick. It is no more authentic, however, than the quiet chuckle of a folk accustomed to the ups and downs of life.

This country was designed by nature as a cradle of contentment. Its gently rolling landscape, fair to the eye, soothing to the soul, is different from any other in Canada—not rugged enough to be called grand and appalling like the western mountains, not wild enough to be called spectacular, yet too wild and solitary to be tamed or spoiled. It is friendly to man and wholly feminine, the true motherland of the clan.

When we drove out of Fredericton, the swelling bosom of the river was printed with the sun's red gules, and its shoulders were modestly decked in a lace of green. Spring had come at one stride, lighted the maples with the flame of scarlet bud, spangled the hills with white stars of blossom, set the birch moving in ghostly dance, and thawed out the crooked old limbs of the pines that once possessed the entire valley.

There are larger rivers in Canada than the St. John, none lovelier, and no other inhabited river so free of man's disfiguring spoor. Having lately seen the Rhine, we thought that it must have been very like this, long ago, before man populated and scarred it.

There were scars here, too, after man had cut the old pine forest, but new growth has covered them, except on the plateau around Gagetown. There the atomic age has inflicted a new scar.

As we passed by an old farming community, army workmen were removing the last of the farmers' houses and barns to prepare a vast training ground for Canadian troops. A few lingering residents loaded their furniture into trucks, taking with them doors and window frames for some new home where their fathers' long struggle against the wilderness would begin again. Sure, one of these men said, he had been well paid for his land, but it didn't seem right somehow that he must leave a valley farmed by his folks for so long. His wife beside him in the truck clutched a few poor possessions and wept silently. Another struggle, the struggle for the world, had moved all the way from the Rhine of Europe to the remote Rhine of Canada.

We crossed the eccentric falls of the St. John that casually reverse themselves at every change of Fundy's tide and, toward evening, reached the city at the river's mouth to make our only unpleasant discovery in the Maritimes.

A daring impostor, it appeared, had written a book about

Canada under my name some dozen years ago and described Saint John as homely, grimy, and forlorn. Of course I indignantly disclaimed all responsibility for this slander. With a little effort, I almost believed my denial. For any man who cannot see the beauty of this place must have no sense of line, contour, or composition. He must be blind to form and color, deaf to the music of the sea. Let no such man be trusted.

Saint John, the mate of female Fredericton, is male, muscular, and hard. Best of all, it has managed to retain in man's work the natural scheme of a granite coast. Native stone bursts through the floor of the streets to remind the inhabitants of their origins. All the buildings and disjointed towers seem to be merely the jagged upthrusts and careless top stories of the continental shelf. The town is anchored deep and immovable in the enduring stuff of the planet.

Where the builders could not afford stone, even their wooden houses, leaning together for support like aged men around a fire, possess a kind of tragic symmetry which always fascinates painters and is best captured in the water-colors of a native artist, Mr. Jack Humphrey.

The Atlantic gales have boomed ceaselessly up this harbor, but they could never dislodge the first French fort of Charles de la Tour, the British settlement of Parrtown, and the city built by the timber boom. They have washed Saint John's face in salt spray, gouged its cheeks, and given it a seaman's shrewd, narrow gleam. It squints at the sea with the stone wrinkles of time. What goes on behind those steady eyes?

A stranger cannot hope to analyze a civic character so old, wise, and reticent, but I began to suspect, after talking to its citizens in ancient parlors and modern offices, that Saint John, like Halifax, is split between the nostalgia of the old and the impatient energies of the young.

A city which was once the fourth shipping port of the world and has seen other ports on both Canadian coasts far outstrip it in business must feel a bitter disappointment not easily disguised. The wistfulness of genteel poverty lies heavy here like the sea fog and makes the old cling for compensation to a lavish past of wealth, boundless hope, political fury, and sometimes riot.

What other bustling Canadian city of fifty thousand people would keep the Loyalists' graveyard, a valuable piece of real estate, green and pampered among its business buildings? Who but a Saint John Loyalist would pray for quick death so that he might be buried in the last available grave and opportunely die one night in 1853, before the graveyard was officially closed next morning?

The Loyalist legend, born when the refugee ships dumped their human cargoes on the beach of Parrtown, is fading out, but its mark will never be erased so long as the buildings sprawl in Victorian corpulence, the streets still climb and curve across the naked hills of granite, and men can smell the ocean and see the ships at their doors.

Though wistfulness is a discernible flavor in Saint John, so is the smoky smell of labor. The sigh of the old is almost drowned by the impatient shout of the young. This town is commonly accounted one of the dullest in the nation, especially by Canadians who have never seen it, but its intellectual life is suddenly quickening. It has produced some excellent writers, painters, sculptors, and craftsmen, and they find their inspiration right here at home. None is more interesting than Kjeld Deichmann and his wife, Erica.

In search of this pair we drove along a crooked road, crossed a lake on a dilapidated ferry, and finally found a splendid Mad Hatter's house.

This astounding structure had swelled and multiplied, room by room, into passages, alcoves, and stairways so complicated that you almost needed a guide to travel from the front door to the kitchen. Kjeld had built it of lumber and hand-hewn beams from abandoned farmhouses. Erica had filled it with secondhand furniture, acquired for a dollar or two at some country auction, had scraped the vandals' paint from good English oak or New Brunswick maple and uncovered the craft of long-dead workmen. And to anchor this queer ark securely in the soil of New Brunswick, Kjeld had modeled a contour map of the province in colored concrete on the living-room floor.

We followed him to his workshop and watched this former Danish wood-carver and painter, now an ardent Canadian pot-

ter, spin his wheel while an exquisite jar rose under his hand
as Adam must have risen from clay in Eden. Erica, a woman
of fragile grace like her handiwork, was painting other jars in
her own fanciful designs taken straight out of the forest.

The ruddy, cheerful man with his aura of white hair, the
woman of delicate features and deft hands, had both come
here as foreigners and brought their skills with them. But it
was not their skills, it was the discovery of New Brunswick,
the beauty of hills, woods, and rivers around them, that
changed the craftsmen into artists.

Late at night we dragged ourselves from the Mad Hatter's
hospitable house and drove north into the darkness. A spring
moon guided us through the forest, gilded a broad valley of
farmland in lumps and chasms of silver, danced on a hundred
chattering streams, and brought us safe to Moncton.

They used to call this second city of New Brunswick simply
The Bend. It had nothing to distinguish it except the bore
of the Petitcodiac River, which rushes inland like a minor
tidal wave, exactly on the minute, so that you can set your
watch by its arrival. Then Moncton became the main railway
junction of the Maritimes, then a thriving business city, and
then the unofficial capital of the Acadian race.

A community unlike any other in the nation, because it is
evenly divided between two races and virtually bilingual,
Moncton may be called the inner crucible of the New Brunswick experiment. The contents of the crucible are significant
mainly because they are outwardly invisible. An English-speaking Canadian will not find Moncton a French city, like the
cities of Quebec. A French-speaking Canadian from Quebec
will not find it English. It is purely Canadian, the pivot and
symbol of the nation's dual culture. So well is the experiment
succeeding that the stranger is unaware of it.

The world's largest lobster crop was coming in and hurrying by iced trucks to the American market as we drove along
the Shediac shore, a district lamentably unlike most of New
Brunswick. It looked unpainted and run-down. The Acadians
about here, small farmers and fishermen, are not given to decoration and seem to lack the gardeners' instinct of the British
stock, but they are friendly and communicative.

A hitch-hiking youth turned out to be a cutter of pulpwood from the interior and, though he evidently didn't know it, the heir to a great tradition. He had heard only vague rumors of the old timber drives in the days of Peter Emberley. What I wanted to learn, however, was his feeling toward his English-speaking neighbors. My question surprised him. He guessed he'd never thought of that. "I work with anybody," he said. "Some English, some French. It's all the same to me."

A well-dressed and well-spoken Acadian youth thumbed a ride near the towering paper mills of Bathurst. He was going home to Campbellton after being graduated from St. Joseph's University, outside Moncton, but he would not remain at home. He was going on to Montreal, Toronto, or Vancouver. The Maritime export of young men has never ceased. Even a few of the original Acadian New Brunswickers are moving out. But not many.

We reached the narrow western corner of Cartier's Bay of Chaleur at sunset to watch a shattering spectacle of hill, river, and sea. As in his time, the westering sun hung like an orange over the blur of a mysterious continent. His first landfall of Gaspé loomed dimly to the northward through a purple haze. The pulp logs of the Restigouche swirled down in a wild current and piled up at its mouth in booms ten acres wide.

Inland a piece we found a hotel on the grassy riverbank and millionaire anglers assembled there with rod, fly, whisky, and other essential tools for the first day of the salmon season. They were not concerned with abstractions like the New Brunswick experiment but only with a rich men's sport. They may have noted, however, in the dining-room, which could have been moved intact from any inn of rural France, a pretty Acadian waitress who spoke no word of English.

She told us in French that she had not been as far as Saint John or even Moncton. Fredericton lay in the valley of a distant river, in another world beyond her imagination. That girl and her kind will remain and flourish in New Brunswick.

Through the window we could see, across an invisible line, the land called French Canada. Though we had visited it many times before, Quebec was as strange to us, as inwardly unknown, as it must have been to Cartier.

WHEN SAP IS FLOWING

❧

*I*f one were asked to name the most typically Canadian festival of the year, the answer would be easy: the festival of spring syrup.

It is not typical of the whole nation, to be sure. Hard maple and its magic contents are concentrated in the Laurentian valley, with offshoots into the Maritimes and New England. But for mysterious, psychic reasons imbedded deep in our folklore, all Canadians regard maple syrup as their own exclusive property.

A mass nostalgia pours through the press and the Canadian mind once juice starts to pour from the eastern forests, bubbles in huge caldrons, and issues at last in a brown liquor or, better still, in golden sugar more precious and much scarcer than metallic gold.

The spigot in the maple trunk simultaneously releases a tide of sap and the imagination of Homo sapiens (canadensis) even though most of us nowadays have never seen a sugar bush in spring freshet. This is not a flow of liquid. It is a gush of pure myth.

The Americans also tap the maple, but Canadians were the first white men to taste its elixir. Frenchmen by the St. Lawrence learned the secret from the Indians. Who taught it to the Indians no one can tell us. What inspired and originative mind, what genius of wild speculation, first collected maple sap in some birch-bark bucket, boiled it with hot stones, swallowed the result, and perfected one of man's truly great inventions? Or was this revelation accidental—a drip of sap somehow falling into an Indian fireplace, to be licked by an enterprising dog and then by its lucky owner? We shall never know. Enough that we have syrup and sugar.

The crude chemistry of the first mineral smelter has been improved to produce remarkable results, among them the hydrogen bomb. The chemistry of the Canadian woods has changed little, and its annual discharge is no danger to anyone, except the danger of commercial substitutes and synthetic imitations. They will not fool any boy who was brought up near a sugar bush.

He could borrow an augur from his uncle's toolshed, quickly bore a hole into the maple's soft cambium layer, and contrive a spigot from one of those hollow wooden handles customarily used by virtuous Ontario housewives when they smuggled parcels across the river from the American side.

Then, in niggard drops, so slowly that a boy grew mad with impatience, the colorless, tasteless nectar oozed into a rusty pail or the family washtub, giving no hint of its inner virtue, until at last the moment of alchemy arrived.

A fire of pungent hardwood burned in the clearing. The sap boiled and shrank hour by hour. The pail was replenished again and again. At dusk, for all the day's labors, there were only a few cupfuls of the sticky stuff.

It was drunk red hot—one could hardly wait for it to reach the ultimate refinement of sugar—or spread on the snow to make a viscid confection whose memory, in the mind of any Ontario boy, is too deep for tears. He in his old age, and nobody else, will understand why the news of dripping sap every spring is the news of childhood recovered for a moment, of a Canada young, sweet, and lost.

CHAPTER FIVE

The Lost Peasant

THE MAN facing me across a rail fence looked exactly like one of those whittled wooden figures which tourists buy in Quebec and take home as the image of a backward race. That image is true of individual peasants. As the image of the French Canadian race it is false; just as the man behind the fence represented one old, authentic aspect of Canadian life, but denied, and knew quite well that he denied, the modern nature of his people.

His face was angular, bony, and rough. It could have been hacked out by a hurried whittler and daubed crudely with red paint. His hard blue eyes held a look of shrewdness, perhaps of suspicion. His body was permanently bent and worn out with labor. But his mind—a cell of the most durable and daring racial mind in Canada—was neither bent nor worn out. The face and body might be shaped like a tourist's clumsy curio. Their owner was thinking furiously.

Like all his people, he was trying to adjust himself not merely to the physical changes of a new era but also to a deeper spiritual change. One of the strangest and least understood facts of contemporary America could be discerned in this aged figure, though no foreigner was likely to discern it.

Here, one might think, was only a peasant plowing an acre or two of niggard earth outside the dreary hamlet of Little

Pabos, on the shore of the Gaspé peninsula. His single horse, as bony and tired as its master, seemed glad to pause in the furrow. A black dog lay down, panting, beside him. The plowman acknowledged my awkward attempt to greet him in French and gave me a knowing smile.

Why, yes, it was a cold spring, he said in pretty fair English. Crops would be late. The land? Well, it wasn't like the rich land of the St. Lawrence Valley. Still, a man could live on it. No, he had never seen the great river. He had never crossed the peninsula which is thrust eastward like the blunt nose of the continent to sniff the Atlantic's flavor. His world stretched hardly a dozen miles from this barren shore, but the legend of the St. Lawrence was part of his hereditary estate. He pointed northward with his thumb—they had fine farms and many cattle over there.

"Where from?" he asked, and when I told him I was from the Pacific coast he dropped the reins, strode across the furrows, and peered at me closely as if I could tell him something of importance.

"Vancouver!" He pronounced the name with wonderment. It was a kind of magic bond between us. "My boy," he added, "goes to Vancouver. Dat's long way, yes? He sends de photos. Ah, de big trees! She must be good country out dere, eh?"

I said it was a reasonably good country and hoped his boy would like it. Oh, yes, the boy liked it, all right. He was making big wages in the woods and sending back money every month. A second boy had gone to Toronto and worked in a factory. The other nine children were scattered among the St. Lawrence towns.

They would never live again in Gaspé, where their family had lived so long. They were gone for good, their father said. And why should they come back?

He stared at his narrow rectangle of soil, the ramshackle cottage, the three cows, and his wife, who, bucket in hand, was dropping potatoes along the furrows.

Down the treeless road a few houses leaned against the Atlantic gales and clustered around a shiny new store and a garage. The bitter wind off Cartier's Bay of Heat rattled the houses, almost lifted a passing cartload of manure from the road, and sent the petticoats of a stout lady flying as she attacked her garden with a mattock.

The youngsters of Little Pabos, like youngsters all over the nation, celebrated, by purchases of Coke and candy at the store, the birthday of an English woman, the Queen of Canada. Queenship, the link between a French race and a British constitution, the central paradox and compromise of Canadian life—the known facts—were improbable enough in this remote spot. The mind of the peasant was more improbable, and, to most North Americans, entirely unknown.

"De land," he went on, "is too small. She's not big enough for my boys. So dey go away."

His farm had been cut up again and again and divided between the sons of some twelve generations until it could be divided no more. That division and scarcity of land, repeated on countless French Canadian farms, was the beginning of Quebec's economic upheaval and, more important, of its spiritual transformation.

"Too small," the peasant repeated. "So de boys can't stay 'ome."

The village boys have been going away for a long time. In the days of this man's father, less than one century ago, the landless sons of Quebec poured into New England, half a million of them, between 1860 and 1890, and bred there a French Canadian stock of some two millions. Now the industrial revolution offers plenty of jobs in Canada, and the young are moving to the city, are pushing beyond Quebec into Ontario, the prairies, and British Columbia, and in that movement are being themselves changed as they have already changed French Canada beyond recognition.

"Big pay up dere in de city," the peasant said. "Nice house. Big car. Frigerator. Television, too. Dat's fine t'ing for young man, eh?"

I agreed it was a fine thing, but I was thinking of something else. I was trying to imagine the ceaseless wanderlust, the restless energy and thirst for adventure, the roving instincts inherited from ancestral Norsemen in Normandy, that had first carried these people across the ocean, had sent them paddling to the edge of the Rockies and down the Mississippi to the Gulf of Mexico while men of British stock were fenced east of the Alleghenies by a thin line of French power.

These Norman people, as Hilaire Belloc once said of their mother race in France, had marched forth perpetually to be sucked homeward, having accomplished nothing but an epic. The epic of the French Canadians seemed to end with the British Conquest of 1759. Their conquerors expected at first that this handful of ruined rustics would soon lose their native qualities and accept a superior British civilization. Actually the real epic was only beginning.

In less than two hundred years the French Canadians not only have fastened their own civilization—more French in some ways than France itself—upon their Laurentian homeland, but also, growing from sixty thousand to some five millions, a third of the nation, have burst the bounds of Quebec, resumed the old westward march on the moccasin trails of their fathers, and colored the whole life of Canada. In this process they have ceased to be French in anything but tongue; they have become nothing but Canadians. If they are thus nothing but North Americans, they remain a stubborn enclave, or series of enclaves, within the life of the continent.

The peasant behind the fence doubtless knew little of this epic factually. Yet he knew it better than I, who had studied it in books. He knew it racially. The long racial memory, going back to Cartier's landfall a few miles from Little Pabos, was unbroken in this man.

"De land," he said for the third time, "is too small for de boys."

I asked him if he sometimes felt lonely for his children. He didn't answer, but his eyes searched mine for communication. He hungered, I could see, for some knowledge of the far-off, mysterious land where his sons and daughters had gone, never to return. There were yearning, hurt, and bewilderment in those old eyes. He wanted to know what was happening to his family, to the life it had once lived here, to the larger life beyond the hills, the life he would never see.

I could give him no answer. We were both citizens of the same nation and aliens to each other, both Canadians and forever strangers. At that moment of contact across a fence as formidable as any iron curtain, I felt, like a physical blow, the awful fact of Canada's duality.

No words can convey it. A library of travel books written by breathless spinsters, another library on the Quebec Problem by tortured pedants, nearly two hundred years under a common monarchy, nearly one hundred years of political partnership in a common state, all the debates of Parliament, and all the professors in our universities tell us nothing understandable about the sovereign fact of Canada. It is too deep for words. It is never translated. Neither English nor French, as spoken by the lips, can be rendered into the language of two separate minds.

This peasant on the other side of an impervious rail fence, this man of strong natural intelligence, of unequaled experience on his land, of a willpower racially indestructible, has been called a member of a conquered race, and that memory, I suppose, was never long absent from his thoughts, or from the thoughts of any man in Quebec.

"*Je me souviens*," is the watchword of these people. They all remember the same thing, the wrong thing, and turn it upside down, exactly as we do outside Quebec. A conquered race? Maybe an inferior race? At least a weakness and tragic schism in our national character—so think many English-speaking Canadians.

When I looked into the peasant's eyes, guessed their wordless contents, and knew he was a better man than I could ever hope to be, I almost laughed aloud at the irony and falsehood that so often masquerade as the truth about French Canada.

Conquered? Inferior? Weak? Why, this man and his people, the handful besieged by the whole force of the British Empire and apparently destroyed, have achieved a conquest with no recorded parallel, have given us our second heritage, the treasures of French civilization, and, for all the confusing eddies on the surface of politics, have made possible the transcontinental state. Strangers to us, yes. But they are the oldest, most deeply grained and fundamental Canadians in this land.

Our roots in the British Isles have never been cut. The roots of French Canada in France were twice cut beyond repair—by the so-called Conquest and by France's Revolution. In the rest of Canada we are still torn between history and geography. In Quebec and its suburbs geography won the struggle long ago.

That is part of the Canadian duality, but even the sovereign fact is overtopped by the Canadian land, only by the land. For the common love of this land, the dream of a separate Canadian society shared by Canadians of every race, is the national solvent, the ultimate fact. It has always united Canadians through all their quarrels, through one rebellion and many terrifying collisions. As I was soon to find in Quebec, it is now uniting them much more rapidly than most of us realize.

The historic record is printed in every schoolbook. Most Canadians have begun to learn, for example, that less than half their population is of British ancestry, that, like this peasant of Gaspé, all of us belong to some racial minority. Nevertheless, the direct discovery of the French Canadian, even if one has been in Quebec many times before, is always a shattering surprise—the discovery, I mean, that the French Canadian is a human being, not a label; a man, not a tourist poster; a person, not a problem; that his society is not a solid lump of race, religion, politics, and prejudice, but is as varied, complex, troubled, and fractured by these times as humanity is everywhere.

It may be, indeed, more troubled than most of Canadian society because here the revolution of the machine is so rapid, after its long delay, so sudden and unexpected, and cuts so deep across a settled way of life and thought.

The same revolution is under way, of course, from Newfoundland to British Columbia. In Quebec it is comparatively larger in size and almost different in kind. As nowhere else it threatens the age-old habits of a race, it touches even the religion of that race, and, since modern industry cannot be isolated, it dooms the isolation of an ancient peasant society.

This abrupt change, by far the largest since the so-called Conquest, is proclaimed by every industrial smokestack beside the St. Lawrence. It issues from every machine in the factories. It clamors over every labor dispute, dominates every maneuver of politics, and is uttered by farmers over their fences.

Quebec has ceased to be a simple farm community, an island of anachronism in the sea of modern America. Its livelihood is earned mainly by the engines of an industry which must soon be one of the most productive on the continent. Two thirds of its people are urban. The quaint French Canada of yesterday lives only in a few shrinking pockets, in the tourist advertisements and the holiday diaries of schoolmarms from Boston.

Statistics reveal the economic process. Behind it the human process can be seen only in the little, nameless people in the little, nameless places.

As the peasant chatted with me at the roadside, a shiny new Cadillac went by in a billow of dust. It contained only the driver, a priest in black clerical garb.

"Nice maysheen," the peasant said and chuckled to himself. That machine and that quiet laugh seemed to tell me more about the changing life of Gaspé than any statistic. Not long ago the priest of every village on this coast used to light a bonfire and ring the churchbell to guide the fishermen out of the Atlantic fog. Now the priest traveled in an expensive car and the peasant watched him with an ironic smile.

The peasant smiled, but he could hardly know that his Church, supposedly the most conservative force in the modern world, has supplied some of Quebec's most radical thinking, or that the Church, more than any other institution, is feeling the impact of the revolution.

I asked the peasant whether his sons still went to church in Vancouver and Toronto. But yes, they were faithful Catholics, of course. Then he remarked dryly that his married sons had only two children each. He gave me a quizzical look. For all his ignorance and isolation, he knew that something more important than industry was changing his people.

We shook hands in farewell. His hand felt hard and rough. His eye still held the unanswered question: what was the future of his people in a new kind of world? I soon saw part of the answer for myself in the big garage of Little Pabos.

The owner of this prosperous establishment, a tall, pale man, strikingly handsome in his well-tailored city clothes, explained in good English that my car, though only a month out of the factory, was suffering from grave mechanical disorders. He tried to summon the right English word and added: "It is organic."

A young mechanic with a dark, narrow face and quick, nervous grin, had plunged like a surgeon into the bowels of the engine and spread most of its organs across the floor. I took him at first to be a clumsy village roustabout. Now I realized that he was a mechanic of genius. He had discovered that some minute but vital part was missing from the engine; he had fashioned a new part on his lathe and was installing it.

When he reassembled all the organs and listened to the heartbeat with his stethoscope, he scowled in disgust and took the whole engine apart again, refusing to pause even for lunch.

The mechanic, as his employer informed me, had been raised on one of the postage-stamp farms at the edge of the sea, had spent five winters studying mechanics in Montreal, and had returned in the spring to Little Pabos, but in all his journeys had learned no English. He was the product of the new age. The local *seigneur* of Little Pabos had turned into a wealthy garage-owner. The farm hand had become an expert of machinery. A market place or a fish wharf had once been the forum of the village. Now its forum was a machine shop.

While the mechanic reassembled the engine for the second time, after five hours' work, two young men in greasy overalls brought their truck to the garage and waited patiently, smoking noxious black pipes. They spoke English with an Irish accent—descendants, I suppose, of immigrants from the great Irish famine more than one hundred years ago. Like the mechanic, they had been raised on the farm and now worked in the new Gaspé mines to the northward. The rich ore there, they said, had been known to prospectors for half a century, but until recently no one had bothered to develop it. Today a large mining industry was going ahead full-blast.

Yes, these youths guessed they were Irish, but were not clear about it. Did they get along well with the French Canadians? They eyed me rather coldly at that question. Nobody around here, they replied, ever thought about such things. Everybody was the same and got along fine.

A frail, bespectacled youth in an over-padded suit had been eavesdropping on our conversation. He told me privately that he had been born in Gaspé and taken by his parents to live in St. Boniface, the French Canadian suburb of Winnipeg. Lately he had come here to tend bar in some mining town. He liked his native province, but could speak hardly a word of his native tongue. That was a serious handicap. The miners who frequented the bar expected a French boy to speak French. So he was learning his own language from scratch.

"These guys," he whispered, "look dumb when you first see them. But they're not. They're just as smart as us when you know them. I'm getting to kind of like them." An exile was rediscovering his race.

Two slick-looking fellows stopped their car at the garage to demonstrate some newfangled metal polish. A farmer offered his battered jalopy for this demonstration, and in a flash the salesmen applied a dazzling sheen to one side of the bonnet. The loitering crowd watched this performance solemnly, as their fathers used to watch some traveling peddler or conjurer. Then they laughed as the salesmen refused to complete the polishing job and left the car alternately streaked in shine and mud.

No one would buy a can of the polish. The salesmen drove off in disgust. The crowd laughed again at their failure, and the owner regarded his piebald jalopy with a sheepish grin. Maupassant, I reflected, would have understood this scene. Little Pabos reproduced exactly, save for the modern clothes and machinery, the old Norman village and its thrifty, skeptical inhabitants.

The operation on my car was now complete, the patient fully recovered, the surgeon satisfied. My wife at the wheel (I always placed her there if the scenery promised to be interesting), we swung around the wriggling shore of Gaspé. It is almost as beautiful as the tourist folders say in their routine of professional hyperbole, and it is far more interesting.

Black headlands are stretched into the ocean like the fingers of a Negroid hand, palm downward. White foam explodes on rusty cliffs. Hamlets innumerable are fastened in ragged garments to the clothesline of the road. Around every turn a metallic church steeple glistens against the green of the forest and the blue of the sea, some marble Virgin watches the traveler from a hillside, or a solitary wooden cross, successor to the first Canadian cross planted here by Cartier, lists under the weight of the weather.

Then the road swings inland, through tightly folded valleys, gulches of dark timber, and multitudes of lost villages. And always, everywhere, children by the roadside, and behind every house diapers hanging out to dry, the humble banners of fertility, the legible headlines of another great national fact.

Toward evening we rounded a hairpin turn and almost collided with the harsh fantasy of the Pierced Rock. We stopped the car and gasped.

A ship of bronze, five times larger than any man-made ship, glowed hot in the sunset a few yards from shore, her hull bored clean as by a torpedo, her rudder broken from the stern—a dead, deserted, specter ship of hallucination and delirium, ravaged and scuttled in her last harbor. The seagulls wheeled and screamed around her in a cloud of white. The waves beat wildly against her sides. Grain by grain, century by century, her stone substance was dissolving into the sea.

As the blood-red sun slid down behind the western hills and its reflection set the Atlantic on fire, we thought that the ship suddenly quivered and lurched inland to crush the helpless village beneath her bow. We were not the only spectators to observe this illusion of movement. Out beyond the bay a black island called Bonaventure watched the wreck like a surfacing whale, one bright eye winking in the sunset with astonishment.

Though Percé's famous rock has been beached here for quite a long time, its life will be short in geological time. Exactly thirteen thousand years hence, the geologists calculate, it must finally erode and disappear. The villagers have noted little change in it lately, but on June 7, 1845, Phillip Le Boutillier looked from his store to see the ship's stern fall into the sea with deafening detonation of sound, dust, and frightened waterfowl. Someone will see that sight again.

Percé has built a substantial tourist trade around one of nature's more whimsical freaks, has primped itself up, rouged its cheeks, and dressed in Sunday best for visitors. Happily, the tourists had not yet arrived. We found on the beach only two fishermen painting their little schooner. In their black berets and rough sweaters they might have been working by any beach in France. The Gaspé boats have changed, but the fishermen must be unchangeable.

Where, I asked, did they fish? The younger man pointed his paint brush vaguely to the open sea, that graveyard of many brave ships since Cartier first breached the continental mystery here. The older partner, who spoke English, said the fishing had been bad lately and the weather ruinous. A year ago the village had gone to bed on a calm night, the fleet bobbing peacefully at anchor, and next morning every craft in Percé lay smashed on the rocks. The fishermen shrugged. They knew the Atlantic hurricanes.

Darkness fell, the phantom ship of bronze slipped her mooring and faded into the nothingness whence she had come, and a rotund figure walked down to the beach.

At first glance he might have been the village *avocat*, in black coat and stiff collar, but a second glance penetrated that disguise. We saw at once, from his swelling vest, his vinous cheeks and crafty eye that Shakespeare's Justice, with fair round belly and good capon lined, full of wise saws and modern instances, had stepped briefly out of the forest of Arden to play his little part in Gaspé.

He greeted us ceremoniously in perfect English, noting that my car bore a British Columbia license. That was remarkable, very. He had always wanted to visit the west and see what the people there were like.

"Don't we surprise you here, my friend?" he inquired. "Of course. It is everywhere the same—the human comedy."

He stopped smiling and added: "Perhaps it is the tragedy we should say. The tragedy of Canada. We are all in it together, the same boat, but the French, the English, what do they know about each other? Nothing."

He glanced at me to make sure I caught his meaning and demanded sharply: "Shall we fight? No, there are too many of us to kill, so we must get along. It is formidable. We would get along very well except for a few old people, too set in their ways. But the young will be different. It is the education. It is changing everything in Quebec. When you go home, think about that. Think about it very much. And remember we are all the same"—he thrust a plump finger into the left side of his vest—"in here."

Having delivered this extraordinary speech, which seemed rehearsed, pat, and probably delivered many times before, the Justice saluted me with his cane and rolled away.

While dining on exquisitely creamed lobsters, we thought about the utterance of that curious figure on the beach. We thought about it very much and wished every Canadian had heard it.

A pretty girl, evidently the owner's daughter, showed us to a comfortable room in a summer boardinghouse and disappeared down the road. Left alone in the house, we examined at leisure the invariable French Canadian gallery of family photographs, the portraits of the Queen and Winston Churchill torn from some magazine and framed in massive gilt, the little glass domes of artificial flowers usually placed on graves but now hanging on the walls with labels to commemorate some dead relative, the usual combination of fine hooked rugs and cheap, flashy furniture. These were the family's heirlooms, and they were trusted without question to strangers.

At midnight, remembering Gaspé's best-known legend, I got out of bed to stare at the sea. Surely a man with any luck should get at least a glimpse of that other phantom ship which burns and sinks here at regular intervals. I watched and listened in vain for the well-known flames, the groaning sailors and clanking chains. No ship appeared that night. The phantoms refused to perform for visitors.

Next morning we followed a winding route around the sheer cliffs and tidal flats of the peninsula, whose nose was chilled by wind, spray, and mist. But the coast was warmer than the country inland, where the road lurched and dipped like a roller coaster through the recesses of the Shickshocks.

Winter still possessed the mountains. Snowdrifts two feet deep were sweating in the May sun. Here and there farmers plowed some crooked valley. Men with little axes and hand saws cut pulp logs and marked their names on the butts. Even the mechanical saw had not reached a people who spoke no English, hardly looked up as we passed, and might have been a thousand miles from civilization.

As suddenly as it had risen, the road rolled down the southern shoulder of the St. Lawrence Gulf, that long gash of geography, that yawning mouth of the nation which, with its river, carries the nation's cargoes halfway across the continent. The Gulf was piled deep in fog today. We could not see across it, but along this southern shore we began to see, in its latest version, the nation's oldest process.

Since Cartier explored it and Champlain seized it, man has always clung to the St. Lawrence system, fought his wars for its possession, divided it between two states, and built the continental economy around it. Here in Quebec he clings to the riverbank with special tenacity.

A double line of farms and industry marks French Canada's chief heritage, its heartland. The stark smokestacks, the towns clustered around these grimy altars of commerce, the logs in booms or mountainous pyramids, the paper streaming off the rollers, the people no longer following the plow but punching the time clock, all inform the traveler of Quebec's new age.

In economic and human terms this change is wide and deep; in geographical terms narrow and thin. The double shelf of the river was colored green by agriculture long ago. Now it is dappled by the black smudges of industry. Yet only a few miles away the land has been little altered, except for a few towns and camps, since Cartier first glimpsed it from his ship.

We drove westward against the steady eastward march of the revolution. The villages began to look more prosperous, better painted, and (I have to admit it) quaint and toylike as in the travel booklets. Their houses wore those familiar gimcrack porches of the Christmas cards, the gaudy false shutters, hipped roofs, and dormers, all designed like shelves of confectionery from the kitchen of some fanciful chef. The revolution had not touched them yet, and, one hopes, will never alter them, but it was moving this way.

At a hotel in one of these river towns the agents of the revolution could be seen reconnoitering the next advance.

The same figure who presides over every country hotel in France, the massive female of generous bosom and calculating eye, carved half a beef in the kitchen, her powerful bare arms spattered with blood. Her daughters waited on table and giggled shyly. The chicken was cooked as only a French woman can cook it, and the decorations had a true Gallic tinge. Lace antimacassars protected the mail-order easy chairs. The immaculate silver spittoon was intended for ornament only. Exotic birds fluttered, in strident prints, about the walls. A high-button boot in pink glass held three artificial carnations.

Two men drove from the west in a big car, entered the dining-room, crossed themselves hurriedly, and began an assault on the pea soup. They were travelers from Montreal, sleek men, expensively dressed, obviously contemptuous of this village, and they sold machinery which they discussed with the enthusiasm of their kind. They were bringing the machine to Gaspé. They were pushing back the frontier. And in this village they were strangers, like us. Even as they talked the life now being changed by such men suddenly revealed itself just outside the window.

A tiny stick of wood, dropped by a cart, lay in a puddle near the travelers' car. Out of a doorway hobbled an ancient woman, who clutched the stick in her hands and carried it triumphantly to her stove. Maupassant's "Piece of String" told no more than that stick about the nature of Quebec's Norman folk. They had not changed much in this village far from Normandy, but the machine would soon change them.

Rimouski, where we spent the night, is a thoroughly modern city, rebuilt after a fire to embrace the most costly and ugliest improvements of modern architecture. Its hotel is luxurious enough for Montreal or New York. Even in these new surroundings, however, the Norman has not lost his instinct of thrift, his strong grasp on essentials.

There being no vacant rooms in the hotel, we were conducted to the splendid stone annex at the rear and a suite of surprising grandeur. When my wife opened the bathroom door, a blushing gentleman of at least three hundred pounds staggered to his feet, collected himself with Latin aplomb, bowed gallantly from the waist, and said: "Welcome, Madam! I am de owner. We share de bath."

His bulk, I thought, would make it difficult to share the largest bath, but I saw then (as my wife retreated with a scream) what had happened. The owner of the hotel was renting us his daughter's private room, while she had been banished to a chesterfield in the parlor for the night. These people are reckless in hospitality, and they never miss a dollar.

After the wrestling match that evening (an affair enlivened by a certain Gallic fury and the shrill squeals of a fleshy woman who wore a fortune in diamonds) we fell into talk with an engineer from some neighboring factory.

This well-spoken young man was a portent of the times. In his sort Quebec had begun to educate its own technicians and supply the native managers of the revolution. The old educational system, which consigned all scholars to the humanities and thus gave the best jobs in the new industries to English-speaking Canadians, was being overhauled at last. And high time, too, the engineer said. Actually, he assured us, the myth of his people as instinctively rural and agricultural had never been more than a myth anyway.

"We always liked the town," he explained. "Why, it took twenty years after Champlain got settled in Quebec before they cleared an acre of land. If a boy couldn't get a job in town, he took to the woods. We were town people, or *coureurs-de-bois*, or soldiers by preference. Out west you see big farms, far apart. Here the towns are close together because we're social animals and always have been. This idea that we weren't made for industry is ridiculous. We take to it like a duck to water. We're far more urban by nature than you English."

Perhaps he exaggerated, but urban civilization is packed tight along the river. So many cities and towns that no traveler can remember their names, so many villages that a car must slow down at every mile, so many children by the roadside that a driver moves through an almost uninterrupted school zone, are producing, wholesale, that modern species, the industrial man, and quietly spreading the uniformity of the industrial age in a French version. How, I wondered, was the process affecting the largest and oldest force in this society?

Soon I found myself in a certain village, far from the main road, pacing the sunny, walled garden of a monastery with a monk of serene look, powerful mind, and quiet speech. Yes, he said, it was true, all too true—the country boy who moved to the city often lost touch with the Church. The village curé knew every family down to the last infant. How could the overworked priest possibly keep such close touch with his flock in the new cities?

The former peasant, now a factory worker, met men of strange ideas and, as the monk put it, was "exposed for the first time to the big world." Often the old faith was weakened and maintained only in form. There, the monk believed, was easily the greatest fact in French Canada today.

As he spoke, the roar of three huge trucks, each carrying five new automobiles from the factory, interrupted our talk. They were part of that larger avalanche which the Faith must meet and guide.

"Of course," this saintly little man admitted, "the impact of the new things is very great when a society is in such sudden change. The Church may lose in numbers. But numbers are not everything, you know. Quebec is being educated. We are gaining in quality."

He volunteered a piece of information which, from such a source, astounded me: "You Protestants imagine that the Church is a monolith, a single thing, inflexible. How absurd! It is single only in a few basic doctrines. Once or twice in a century, perhaps, the Pope pronounces certain fundamentals. Apart from the articles of faith, we think as we please. Do you realize that some of the most radical social thinking in Quebec today is in the Church, in Laval University especially?

"Oh, no, my friend, the Church is not monolithic. It is full of conflicting thoughts, what some people might even call social heresies. Why, there's more difference between me and a Jesuit, for instance, in all things but the Faith, than there is between a Methodist and a Christian Scientist. And never forget this or you'll never understand Quebec—the Church, too, is changing. Not in the Faith, of course, but in everything else. It has always grown with society. That's why it remains so strong."

Driving westward, we gave a lift to a university student of mechanical engineering. He apologized for his indifferent English, but hoped to master the language and practice his profession somewhere out west. The English, he said, had proved far abler than his people in industry, up to now anyway, and more venturesome in enterprise. He must acquire English to get on.

I asked him what he knew of Papineau, Lafontaine, and Riel, French Canadian heroes whose legends, I supposed, must be taught to every Quebec boy at his mother's knee. He said he had heard those names at school, but couldn't remember much about them. Had been too busy studying mechanics, he guessed.

This answer dumfounded me. It seemed to shatter another legend, the legend of a French race brooding day and night on ancient wrongs and triumphs. When will English-speaking Canadians discard the notion that these people of Quebec, because they speak a different language, are one and all obsessed only with racial memories?

The river was narrowing now, the sun shining, and the north bank emerging from the mist. Presently we saw the channel split by the Isle of Orleans and behind it the tangled towers of Quebec City on the black cliff where Canada began.

SUMMER'S MADMEN

*A*fter a winter of reasonable unity Canada is split, by June, into factions forever irreconcilable. Two distinct kinds of men, almost two different species, go their separate ways.

The orthodox and civilized live on as usual in town. The heretics, most Canadian of Canadians, begin the tribe's oldest summer ritual. With the overpowering impulse of the wild goose, the death wish of the lemming, they swarm to the wilderness.

Now, throughout the land, a mass migration is heading toward the summer shack. The student of our folkways will find on every road out of town a steady stream of cars overloaded with food, bedding, lumber, tools, paint, cement, and no one knows what else—more than enough, you would think, to sustain an army's campaign. All the passengers are bound for some quiet waterfront by the outer gate of paradise, for a dilapidated house of no conceivable value and thus valuable beyond price.

Some people say that Canada has contributed no great thing to the world's culture. They have overlooked the Canadian summer shack. No doubt other peoples have country resorts, perhaps better and certainly more elaborate than ours, but it can be proved, I think, that our shack is indigenous, peculiar, Canadian, and mad.

Though aliens may misunderstand it and foreign architects despise it, though it may violate every rule of construction and defy the laws of gravity, the shack remains the truest symbol of Canadian civilization because, of course, it is a revolt against civilization at large. Moreover, it is a miracle.

The shack is usually made of cardboard, fastened to a rock

by a few rusty nails, built like an incompetent swallow's nest
or a gopher's hole, and supported by some obscure principle
unknown to science. Like all durable things, it rests on the
foundation of a dream. It is held together by nothing more
than invisible hoops of pure affection and human faith—sufficient to resist not only the fierce Canadian winter but also
the deranged climate of mankind.

A summer shackman sets out on a trail that may appear
new, but is as old as the white man's life in Canada, a branch
of Champlain's trail leading straight from Quebec. Every year
since 1608 the first odyssey has been repeated.

The latest version differs superficially from the original, is
commonly carried by an automobile rather than a birchbark
canoe, but inwardly it is unchanged and unchangeable. A
shackman seeks summer, as his fathers have always sought it,
in the only place where the summer of Canada can be found.

As he emerges from the woods, he sees in his shack one of
the few certainties left on earth. Empires may reel, stock markets fall, and bombs explode, but the shack will be there. It
has been waiting patiently for its owner. Its windows light up
at his approach with a glitter of welcome. Its monstrous shape
is charged with memories of laughter, tears, and vanished children.

When, at the sacramental moment, the shackman finds a
rusty key (secreted, last autumn, where anyone could find it),
turns a broken lock, and shoulders open a warped door, he
enters a dank, musty cell, like a mountain cavern or the lair of
woodland beasts. But when the fire is lighted, the bedding
dried out, and the first meal of summer cooked, the cell instantly becomes a cloister in the New Jerusalem.

Then begins the heretic's summer of freedom, which the
orthodox would call a sentence of hard labor, a cruel, unnatural punishment; freedom to mend the ever leaking roof,
to paint the decaying boat, to fix the unworkable pump, to cut
firewood and perform that infinite toil of preparation which the
summer guest will take as his due while complaining bitterly
about the service. The freedom, in short, of voluntary servi-
tude, the summer slave system of a free country.

Opening camp is not really a labor. It is a transfiguration. The shackman is so transfigured that the orthodox will hardly recognize him in a fortnight. For only here in the open, away from human beings, can a man rediscover his humanity and be himself, do what he likes, build what he pleases, and return to the wisdom of a child building sand castles and perceiving the ultimate.

The nation is safe in the hands of the species that made it in the first place of native materials. No doubts about the future alarm the shackman. He mends his roof as if it would last forever. He adds a clumsy porch as if he were building for the ages. He paints his water-logged boat as if it would carry him across the river of immortality. If the final bomb should drop and civilization perish, somewhere, somehow a shackman and his wife will survive—the first Canadians and the last.

CHAPTER SIX

The Fortress

THE ROCK of Quebec, slanting black across the St. Lawrence, was the primary fortress of America for nearly two hundred years, the focal point and strategic hinge of the continent. Many men have stood there watching the river and its freight of human events. From the rock, Champlain and his garrison watched the descent of that first hungry winter and then the sails of the first English fleet. Here Frontenac defied the second fleet from New England, Montcalm heard the last fleet announce the doom of New France, Carleton saved Canada from the American Revolution, and, in our time, Churchill and Roosevelt planned the world's largest war.

The rock has always been held by giants. Though it is no longer a military center, it remains a fortress. It is the spiritual fortress of a great people. Any man standing on the rock sees with his eyes the noblest sight in Canada and, with his imagination, the tragedy and triumph of the French Canadian race. It has lived from the beginning, and still lives, under siege.

A May moon was anchored in the river as I climbed the rock. The spires of Quebec City shone like an intricate crucifix against the rounded breasts of the Laurentians. Man's tiny lights, a myriad dance of fireflies, glowed and winked all the way down to Cartier's Isle of Bacchus. Above me the obese English citadel grinned in the moonlight. The heavy scent of lilac gushed out of some secret garden.

I walked down the silent streets of midnight and came upon a vague figure kneeling in a churchyard. Apparently he had dug a hole in a flower bed—why, I could not guess. Now, under the rays of an electric torch, he was sifting the damp soil through his fingers. I paused in alarm. Was this a grave-robber or a madman?

He was neither. The flashlight revealed the shovel hat, black vestments, and aged face of a priest. A gentle voice bade me good-night in French. I replied in English, and the priest said: "Don't be alarmed, sir. I was only digging worms. To-morrow morning, you see, I go fishing."

We talked at some length about fishing in various places. The priest sighed. He would like to fish in the great lakes and rivers of my western country, but he didn't expect to see them. They were so far away.

That man lived in the fortress under siege. He could escape down the St. Lawrence for a day's fishing, but no farther. I wished him an angler's good luck, and he began to dig again in the soil dug by Louis Hébert, the first Canadian farmer, long ago.

Next morning Quebec no longer looked like a fortress, but it always deceives the visitor from English-speaking Canada unless he is a very clever or a very dull man. The clever man sees through the façade of America's most spectacular city and suspects the turmoil behind it. The dull man sees nothing beyond the spectacle contrived for tourists. An average Anglo-Saxon (always as naïve and romantic at heart as the Latin is cold and logical) finds his judgment melting before nature's lavish work and man's reckless architecture upon the riverbank.

No Canadian is worthy of the name if he can sail up the river and, as he catches his first glimpse of the rock and its towers athwart the western sky, feel no constriction of the throat and sudden dampness of the eye. Such a man is not fit to be called a Canadian. If he is not embraced at once, as in the arms of a dark enchantress, and dazzled by a pair of ageless eyes, he is not fit, whatever his nationality, to be called a man.

Not long before, from the deck of an Atlantic liner, I had seen the face of the fortress flushed by a rosy dawn. The returning Canadians beside me were silent within the ancestral gateway of their home. The foreigners chattered and exclaimed at a sight more European and antique than most of Europe's cities. But few of us grasped the modern contents of Quebec.

In the depth of many a Canadian winter I had looked out from the tower of the Chateau Frontenac upon a river of solid ice, a town smoothed and muffled by snow.

In the first days of spring I had seen the ice chunks float downward on the current and upward again on the ocean tide, the Laurentians turn from white to green overnight, as the page of a book is turned, the first ships grope their way up the channel, the farmers assemble in the old market place with the first syrup and sugar of the maple, the ancient cabbies, horses, and carriages emerge from their barns, and Quebec blink in the sun after its long imprisonment.

Then, in autumn, I had seen the cold come shouting down from the north, the Laurentians turn a page of mottled gold and scarlet, the ice creep out from the riverbank, the first snow fleck the rock, and Quebec batten down its houses and stoke its fires for yet another winter.

Now spring was here again, and, as always when I walk these sloping streets in a blur of historic memories and certain private ones, all purpose oozed out of me. I had come this time to learn something about current French Canadian affairs, but they seemed trivial, temporary, and hardly worth pursuit in the long history of this place.

Though I have said it before, and have been ridiculed as a driveling romantic, it is quite true that the ghosts of Quebec overtop all living men. Practical persons may see only the buildings of modern business and the crush of traffic. I confess that at every corner I almost expect to meet Champlain or Frontenac or Bishop Laval on his way to church. Wolfe and Montcalm cannot be far from Maître Abraham's grassy field beside the river, even if the new subdivisions of alien ranch-style bungalows crowd it from the northward. Carleton fought in this dark alley. Montgomery, the American, died beneath that cliff in a New Year's blizzard. Kent and his mistress, Julie, surely revisit now and then the square white house built to their Georgian design. The unhappy Angélique des Meloises must sometimes flit, cloaked and masked, from some hidden door on Grande Allée in search of her faithless Bigot. Or, if the ghosts are too remote, there must be somewhere in this town a few living men who, as children, saw John A. Macdonald and the bearded Fathers of Confederation gather here, less than one hundred years ago, to build a nation on nothing more than paper and faith.

Scorn not the giant phantoms of Quebec. Few of the figures, large and small, who stride these streets in plain view today will be remembered a few years hence when the dead will remain alive.

Buried deep and forever lost in the rubble are the bones of the town's founder. Deep also, and well hidden from the stranger, is the enigma of his race. A reporter must conduct his clumsy excavations as best he may, scratching only the surface.

As it happened, I was jerked violently back into the twentieth century by a wild ride, with a mad taxi-driver, through the teeming labyrinth of Lower Town, where laundry hung and women gossiped between the noisome tenements, children played football in the gutters, and tourists gaped at what they took to be the charming quaintness of a foreign civilization.

Thus by successive stages of bewilderment—a pilgrimage to the candlelit shrine of Notre Dame des Victoires, which survived the cannon balls of Phips's blundering armada, a tour of the finest parliament buildings in Canada, an hour in the quiet home of Catholic priests, a visit to the Citadel and its stiff scarlet sentries, finally an evening on the town to hear a songstress from France and see native society on parade—I remembered at last that I was not here to see the sights but to communicate, if I could, with French Canadians. I had come to study the fortress under siege.

This is not only the capital of a great province, the manager of vast natural resources, and the stronghold of a race, but also the core of its struggle with another race. The outcome of that struggle has always been the paramount question in Canadian life, and the answers—hopeful or discouraging, friendly or hostile—have always come mainly out of Quebec City.

The twin forces of the French Canadian nature have erupted repeatedly here through the medium of furious politics: on the one hand, the centrifugal force of separatism and racial mystique which tries to isolate French Canada from the nation, to keep the race pure, the culture undiluted, the Faith invulnerable, Champlain's old dream intact; on the other hand, the centripetal force which would preserve French Canada's ideals but in full co-operation, friendship, and understanding with the other race.

So the inner contest of Quebec has raged ever since Wolfe's soldiers hauled down the lilies of France, has moved through countless outward variations, has sometimes produced crises almost fatal to the national state, and has thus swelled and subsided in tidal rhythm.

The personalities, the political maneuvers, the banners and slogans have often changed. The inner contest has never changed. It is now, as it always has been, a contest between the French Canadians who see, know, and love only Quebec, and those who have seen the nation whole, have perceived Quebec's great future in a dual Canadian society and welcomed it.

The English-speaking Canadian usually forgets, underestimates, or misunderstands the separatist movements called Nationalism that threatened, in the nineteenth century, to disrupt the frail Confederation laboriously built here in Quebec City; the mystical and impossible project of an independent French Canadian state; the bitter, wrenching clash between the liberal leaders of Quebec politics and the conservative leaders of the Church.

Three such crises mark the record in our century: in 1911 the destruction of Wilfrid Laurier, a French Canadian prime minister at Ottawa, by his own people because he was not French Canadian enough; in 1917 an outright schism between the two races, with riot and bloodshed, because the French Canadians would not agree to conscript their sons for what they considered England's war; in 1944 the same conscription issue again, but this time settled without violence and with little bitterness by the centripetal forces of co-operation; and then the arrival of a second French Canadian prime minister, Louis St. Laurent, whose whole life in politics was aimed at racial reconciliation.

In the United States the forces of separatism produced a long civil war. In Canada they produced Papineau's rebellion of the Patriotes in 1837, a comic tragedy of a few weeks, followed by more than a century of that legal warfare known as politics.

Even a generation ago no man could be sure of its outcome. As late as 1921, Henri Bourassa, most gifted of the Nationalist leaders, was announcing that Confederation might last twenty or thirty years but "it is fatally wounded," while Canon Lionel Groulx, prophet of the separate Laurentian state, declared that Canada was "headed inevitably towards a breakup . . . only the date remains still unknown." An English-speaking prime minister, Lord Bennett, told me, some twenty years ago, that I might live to see the nation split on the line of the Ottawa River.

All these men were wrong. They had been watching the side eddies, not the main current of Quebec life. The main current, in alliance with English-speaking Canadians, gave us responsible government, Confederation, and the nation we know today. Always, on that main current, the greatest figures of French Canada have been moderates working with the moderates of other provinces. Not once in all the collisions of the races has a French Canadian Nationalist ever controlled the federal politics of Quebec.

The main current may slow down, twist, or sometimes seem to reverse itself. It may be disguised by contrary movements on the surface. The anxious watcher on the shore will often be distracted by the shouts of local demagogues, by the deceptive ebullience of the French race, by racialists of English tongue, and by overlearned treatises from the pens of foreign experts. Nevertheless, the current carrying two races in a joint voyage which neither can escape still moves inexorably like the St. Lawrence.

"*Mon cher Henri,*" Laurier once said to Bourassa, "Quebec does not have opinions but only sentiments." The Nationalists have always tried to manipulate those oldest sentiments of Quebec's life and one half of its nature—the xenophobia, the sense of isolation and grievance, the resentments, the nostalgia, and the folk memory of the Conquest. In local politics, though seldom in the politics of Ottawa, this manipulation has often been successful, and has succeeded abundantly in our time. But in our time the main current has suddenly accelerated.

Is Quebec moving closer to the rest of Canada or further away? I put that question to many men, high and low, and invariably got the same reply, thus phrased by an eminent Catholic churchman: "Don't be deceived by the clamor on the surface. Anyone who has read our history knows that the relations between Quebec and English Canada are incomparably better today than they've ever been. Why, in my lifetime, and I'm not an old man, the situation has changed almost beyond belief. And remember another thing—we're French by heredity, yes. But we're molded by British institutions. Politically we're British. We use the British institutions of politics to fight for our rights. Next time there's trouble, as of course there will be, remember that if your own province were the only English-speaking Protestant community in America you'd fight for your rights, just as we do. And I dare say you'd be just as prickly about it as we are."

Later that day I called on one of the wisest men in Quebec. He smiled at my questions. How did I expect, he asked, to understand French Canada when it could hardly understand itself?

We looked down from his office in a new business block upon the garden of some religious order. Inside the high stone walls, a few yards from a crowded street, two nuns in black robes and white veils were planting geraniums. That garden was a fortress within the fortress, and it remained inviolable.

"Quite a contrast, isn't it?" my friend said. "But, then, Quebec is just one huge contrast. You remember Groulx's phrase—'*Notre maître, le passé.*' He was wrong, though. The past isn't our master any more. Nothing can stop the future. That's all you need to know."

What was the future? The industrial age, of course. It must be an age of uniformity since business recognized no separate race or language, not within America anyway. So the Canadian struggle of the future would not be between races but between classes and economic interests.

"Both sides," he predicted, "will be organized right across the country, horizontally, not in little racial knots, vertically. Nobody talks about the most obvious fact staring us in the face. It is that Quebec has become an industrial province and most of its people are industrial workers. Ah, that will mean many things. Already we have produced an urban proletariat. The proletariat will produce a movement of the left, and neither government nor Church can stop it. Our future belongs to the party that can control the workers' vote.

"The movement of the left here," he added reassuringly, "will look pretty conservative in the other provinces because we're probably the most conservative people in America, but it'll look pretty radical beside our present governments."

And the end of all this? "Why, the amalgamation of race and language, of course. Not now. Not soon. But in time."

Then this French Canadian aristocrat of some twelve generations, and a strict Catholic, hazarded a prophecy which I had never heard in Quebec before: "The Faith will live. Our language will die, simply because we are outnumbered on a continent of English, and English is the language of North American business. But let me tell you this, and write it down for *les anglais*—if our culture were to die, Canada would lose something very precious, the thing that distinguishes Canadians, above everything else, from the Americans. Without it we would probably have joined the Americans long ago. If it dies, I think we will join them one of these days."

That culture, he said, was not dying. it was only changing and accommodating itself to the industrial age.

"We survived the Conquest," he chuckled. "I guess we can survive the machine."

My friend is a conservative, a rich man, and the heir of many *grands seigneurs*. Yet his opinions, as distinct from his wishes and disposition, are too radical even for the French Canadian politicians of the extreme left. Uttered publicly, they would defeat any candidate in Quebec. But those long thoughts about the future, uttered privately by a few men, bring the English-speaking Canadian up with a round turn, make him realize how absurdly little he knows about the French Canadian mind, that mind which has been compelled, if race, culture, and Faith shall survive, to think harder than any other mind in America. The result of such thinking, for nearly two hundred years, is perhaps the hardest mind in America.

"You English," said one of Quebec's oldest politicians, a veteran scarred by many battles, "imagine that because we are Latin and excitable and make a lot of noise at elections, we must be light-minded and frivolous. You forget we're French and the French are the most logical people in the world. We're almost too logical for democratic politics, but we're learning your English art of compromise because we have to.

"Quebec itself, a race and culture of its own within North American society, has to be a compromise. Yes, but don't misunderstand the French Canadian voter just because he enjoys making a noise. Once he gets into the polling booth he's the coldest and toughest voter in the country. He votes for his own interests, for the party that seems most likely to protect them. And if he votes for one party in the province and an opposite party in Ottawa, as he's been voting steadily for the last twenty years, the purpose is the same—to protect Quebec. That's no paradox, as you English seem to think. It's French logic."

Though all these candid talks and many others had told me little about Quebec, they had told me enough to demolish the usual caricature of a pleasant but rather retarded race in an unchanging, stolid, picturesque homeland.

Yet North Americans read the usual travel books and conclude that Quebec remains a stubborn anachronism and precious museum piece sheltered from the brawling civilization of the continent. If you sample the growing torrent of serious books on the French Canadian Problem (may God forgive the inventor of that label), you may imagine Quebec as a community of downtrodden, desperate workers, obscurantist clergy, and political lunatics scheming to destroy the Canadian state.

Or if the reader ignores the statistics, he may still think that the French Canadian people, pursuing their *ravanche des berceaux*, their Revenge of the Cradles, must soon form a Canadian majority when in fact the French Canadian minority is slightly smaller than it was a generation ago and, as a percentage of the nation, seems unlikely to grow in the visible future, though it is itself growing fast and spreading steadily from Quebec to other provinces.

Leaving these larger speculations to the experts, who only confuse the reader (and probably themselves), we set out for the countryside to see the reality of Quebec at first hand. We had not traveled many days before we began to understand that the French Canadians were not only a people of peculiar greatness, with many qualities that most of Canada lacks, a people of profound inner strength, but also a people who, even while relatively poor and writhing in the grip of new problems, were somehow happier than the rest of us.

To be sure, our first specimen of this breed did not look happy. This aged hitchhiker was distinguished by a face of wrinkled leather, a battered black homburg hat, a red shirt, and a belt six inches wide encrusted with glass jewels and a silver crucifix. He told us he had wandered all over Canada in his time, working at many jobs, and had fought as a volunteer in the First World War.

The memory of that adventure set him talking in the voice of his kind. "My brother," he said, "was in the war, too, but he didn't come back. I got hit at Vimy, but I came back with a game leg. What did the government do for me? Nothing. What's the use of fighting? The big shots tell us to fight, but they don't fight, not them. They fly around in the big plane, eat good, and smoke cigars. They make conscription so we can fight for them. I tell you, it's crazy. Next time we'll all be killed. A good thing, too. No more trouble when you're dead. But some will be left. They'll start over—a new system."

I asked him why his people didn't start the new system now. "Hell," he retorted, "they're too dumb. They don't go anywheres. They never see Canada. But a few hear about the big wages out in Ontario and B.C. and they go there and then they smarten up. Say, I'd be right out in Vancouver now —there's a town for you—if I wasn't an old crock. I was dumb, too, or I wouldn't of come home."

But he had come home, and I could see that, for all his English veneer, he was glad to be among his own people again. Armed with a suitable letter from some politician, he was going to an easy job in a paper mill. "It'll be a cinch," he said, "after what I've been through out west." We dropped him off at a smoky industrial town, and he walked down the street, limping from the wounds of Vimy Ridge but whistling merrily.

Darkness overtook us on a side road far from the river. We were lucky to find a village and a cozy little hotel folded between the Laurentians. The proprietor, a solemn little man in a bowler hat and black serge suit, eyed me suspiciously through thick horn-rimmed glasses. After accepting a second drink in the kitchen, he evidently decided that I could be trusted.

For many years, he said, he had been the local organizer of the ruling political party. His district, I gathered, was well and tightly organized, the government's patronage distributed where it would do the most good. When I remarked that the speeches of the Quebec Nationalists sometimes alarmed English-speaking Canada, a grin of flashing dentures appeared beneath my host's mustache.

"You don't understand," he said. "That talk is for politics. Listen to it with one ear. Listen with the other ear to the people and watch what really happens. Not like the speeches, eh? No, no, that is the horse of a new color."

He winked, pressed his finger against my chest, and added: "The people are not children any more. They know what time it is of the day. Quebec is changing."

It is changing mainly because man has mastered an alchemy which transmutes the sterile Pre-Cambrian Shield into gold.

The upland reservoir, hurling its waters to the Atlantic and Hudson Bay, holds perhaps half of Canada's potential hydro power, and of itself will nourish a major workshop of the continental economy. In Quebec the Shield also holds the iron ore of Ungava, other minerals and timber in the perfect combination of industry—a treasury beyond measurement, only a portion of it yet tapped.

Yet, when you see it, man's work has made only an occasional scratch upon the surface. Saguenay's dark gorges look as empty as when Cartier reported them gleaming with "diamants and leaves of fine gold as thicke as a man's nayle." They lead not to Cartier's Kingdom of Saguenay, but to the soaring dams of Shipsaw and the factories of Arvida that turn bauxite from Guiana into aluminum. The same spill and lash of water carries the upland logs down to the river and powers the mills to turn them into paper. Then, if you move a little way from the riverbank, the land rolls on to the north as the first Frenchmen must have seen it.

The northern farm country of Maria Chapdelaine around Lake St. John, the newly rich mining towns like Rouyn-Noranda and Val d'Or, the whole industrial complex of the Abitibi country with its spreading network of roads and railways, give Quebec a new dimension. But its life, as from the beginning, is attached to the central river, at once the stomach and the lung of its economy. The St. Lawrence digests the food of the hinterland, inhales the traffic of the Atlantic, and exhales the traffic of the Canadian interior all the way to the Great Lakes.

One thousand miles of roads, rivers, towns, villages, and mountain forest, a long detour through the ski country and the Gatineau, where log cabins, black rail fences, and covered bridges remain unchanged on the edge of Canada's capital, and then a drive through the fat St. Lawrence farmlands, all split and checkered by family division and jungles of fence posts, brought us at last to the meeting-place of two great rivers. One hot evening, we saw the final autograph of the revolution scrawled across the sky by the smoke and lights of Montreal.

How fertile was that "grain of mustard seed" planted here by Maisonneuve when he founded, at the base of Mount Royal, his Ville Marie and dedicated it to the Virgin! And how quickly Montreal lost her own virginity!

An immortal trollop with a heart of gold, this city has been called—always a mistress, never a wife—or a metropolitan wen and parasitic growth forever swelling across its island and ravening through the farmlands on the river's banks. Nouns and adjectives all wither in this colossal presence. It is simply Montreal, a civilization, a state of mind, and the only true city in Canada, beside which all others, however large, are only grown-up towns or camps of steel and concrete.

Yes, a city not by the mere measurement of size, not by its proud title of the second French-speaking community in the world, but by the measurement of time, wealth, diversity, and urban instinct, its violent clash of slum and mansion, its men of secret power in mahogany boardrooms, its middle class in endless vistas of ugly houses, its proletariat swarming through the unspeakable rabbit warrens of the east end. All this amorphous jumble somehow has been welded together in a single organism. That is Montreal, and its very name sounds like the thunder of its streets, the gurgle of its two rivers.

Here is an island joined to the mainland by many bridges and yet forever an island in the life of Canada, spiritually separate and alone. The nation's life flows past and washes the island, but cannot erode it. So it has flowed through the nation's jugular since 1642, and from the flood Montreal takes what it wants at pleasure. As it once exchanged fur for French coin, it now transforms the toil of unknown men throughout the hinterland all the way to the Pacific into the products of its factories, into the profits of its counting houses, into its own wealth or poverty.

Montreal, the sleek entrepreneur and greedy broker of our economy, is crapulous, they say, with vice and crime. It is continually reforming and always unreformed. Maybe so, but most of its inhabitants, far more than one million people, have never entered a night club, met *les filles*, or made a dishonest dollar.

In short, for all its virtues and vices, all its shocking contrast of money and destitution, all its legendry, fable and fact, this is the heart of Quebec's revolution, the Canadian metropolis of a metropolitan age.

Though I have seen it many times, Montreal always fills me anew with the horror, the admiration, and the envy of a country boy seeing his first city in all its wickedness. A walk of half an hour will take you from some hideous night spot, awriggle with nudes on a Sunday night, to the splendid avenue of trees on Sherbrooke Street, the quiet campus of McGill University, and then past the stone houses of the rich to the top of Mount Royal, whence, like Cartier, you can see the island moated by its rivers and laced loosely to the shore by its bridges.

Or, if you are pursuing a certain quarry, as I was, you will find yourself in some queer places—a French Canadian home of wealth heaped up and bursting with bric-a-brac, bronze busts, and furniture of monstrous, distended girth; Bourassa's dingy office of *Le Devoir*, where soft-spoken journalists, perhaps the ablest in the nation, write their corrosive editorials in his still potent acid; an English club of smooth, disarming, dark-clothed men whose word sets other men blasting mountains, clearing forests, boring oil wells, and building dams in the wilderness; dark holes and corners inhabited by scribblers, poets, artists, agitators, and passionate reformers, all breaking their heads and hearts against the unbreakable walls and canyons of the city; a business block of glass and stone beside an old church and immaculate green churchyard; a rectangle of skyscrapers glaring impotently upon a grassy square and the serene granite figure of Laurier; the Chateau de Ramezay, untroubled by all the surge of traffic around it as when Ben Franklin printed in its cellar his futile propaganda of the American Revolution; and, in the suburbs, a farmhouse, here and there, surrounded by a rising sea of identical new bungalows as the voracious parasite spreads across its island, leaps its moat, and penetrates deeper into the mainland.

The quarry having eluded us for the moment, we breasted the week-end tide of traffic in search of the house where Laurier and Quebec's greatest myth were born. It stands only an hour's drive from Montreal, if you know the way. Few Canadians know the way. In all that automotive torrent we saw no car turn off the main northern highway and follow the gravel road to St. Lin.

Half a mile off the highway, we lost our bearings in a country of lush fields long fattened on manure, of stone churches, villages innumerable, and stolid peasantry—an authentic scene from France at the margin of our greatest city. Where was St. Lin?

A barefoot boy, fishing with a willow pole in a muddy brook, gestured wildly, but spoke no English. A farmer in suit of Sunday black pointed eastward from the seat of his buggy. His gigantic wife pointed westward with her green parasol and lectured us at length, to no avail. A man behind a plow, whom I ventured to address in my ghastly French, heard me gravely and replied: "Maybe we better speak English." I should have expected that rebuke. The plowman was obviously a Scot (the descendant of a soldier in Murray's army, as it turned out), and wore a beard like a flaming heather.

After following his careful directions for some ten miles, we were still lost. Five wedding processions passed us in beribboned cars, honking for all they were worth, and in a roadside garden we saw an embarrassed groom being photographed beside his bashful bride while the lads of the village hoisted appropriate refreshments on the porch. One could hardly interrupt a wedding, so we drove on at random until at last we saw a man on a leisurely farm horse.

The rider seemed to be asleep, his head sunk on his chest. This time I used neither French nor English and, ignoring St. Lin, uttered the single magic word "Laurier."

Instantly the man awoke, threw himself from his horse, pushed a swarthy face through the window of our car, and spoke for some minutes in extreme agitation. I caught only Laurier's name, repeated many times, and the notion that St. Lin lay straight ahead.

My guess was right for once. Five hours out of Montreal, we stumbled upon a village which, without its myth, would be indistinguishable from scores of others around it. St. Lin consists of a leafy main street, a chuffling little sawmill, a pond full of logs, a quiet stream, and, on a side street, the home of Laurier's grandfather.

Originally the cottage was made of logs, but it is now covered by a veneer of red brick and surrounded by a lawn and flower beds, thanks to Laurier's friend and successor, Prime Minister Mackenzie King. This squat, unornamented building cannot be more than thirty feet square. It is humble even by the standards of St. Lin. The meager rooms are cluttered with the family's stiff-backed rocking chairs, a clock propelled by wooden works, a loom, a massive stove, a butter churn, and the hand-made cradle of the myth.

A plump old man of jovial countenance, whose likeness can be seen in any village of France, led us up the twisted stairs and proudly opened a door in the eaves to reveal a narrow bed and a mattress of straw. This, he said, was Sir Wilfrid's bed.

We looked about the bare cubicle, little larger than a clothes closet, and tried to imagine the boy who slept there, dreaming a boy's dreams of a world beyond the single pane of glass.

What kind of boy was the greatest son of French Canada?

From his photographs on the walls, a handsome boy, rather gangling and frail, the face not yet matured into the lines of almost feminine beauty, the hair still dark and thick before it turned into the famous plume of white curls. A lonely boy, too, by all accounts, given to books and moods of silence, but probably much like the boys who played beside the millpond today in imitation ten-gallon hats and brandished the toy western six-shooters of another Canadian myth.

Why should these cramped walls have been the shell of a greatness unique in Canada? Why should St. Lin, of all places, produce the ultimate idol and folk father of his race, a figure more powerful than any other French Canadian alive or dead, a colossus still astride the nation's history? No one, I suppose, can explain such things as a career beginning in this obscure village and ending, like the story of his race, in tragedy and triumph.

The guide shrugged his shoulders and smiled shrewdly at my questions. He seemed to hold an incommunicable secret.

"Laurier," he said, "was big man, very big. So nobody can stop 'im. I don't know 'ow to say it. We say *gentil, très gentil*. Dat's Laurier."

Had he ever seen the great man himself? But of course. It was long ago, in 1911, the year of Laurier's defeat. Just before that fateful election, which destroyed his government and turned him forever into the wilderness of opposition, Laurier had come home to St. Lin on a sentimental journey. Ah, that was big day for sure.

"My fadder," the guide explained, "is Laurier's friend, very old friend, you understand, and makes politics in St. Lin. So he gets up de parade. We meet Laurier wit' t'ree cars and seventy boys on 'orses. I am on a 'orse very wild, and I am scare. We all ride wit' Laurier beside 'is car. But Laurier don't like it. No, 'e wants to see 'is 'ouse. So we all turn round, the parade bust up, 'orses running away—oh, she's a big mess, all right. But dere's Laurier standing by de gate in top 'at, tail coat, very fine. A man is taking de photo, everybody is yelling, my 'orse is rearing up and I am falling down. Just den de camera goes off. I 'ave dat photo at 'ome now. Dere's Laurier, and right be'ind 'im is me on my 'orse, all reared up and falling off. I never forget dat day. Laurier, 'e don't forget it, too, I bet."

We walked down the street to the huge and rather ugly church of St. Lin. Beside it stood a carved figure of the Christ. It was dated 1917. This no doubt was a coincidence, but the date told Laurier's tragedy and triumph. In 1917, opposing wartime conscription, he quarreled with English-speaking Canada, entered his private Gethsemane, smashed his career forever, returned to the heart of his own people, and there became immortal.

Many dark, unfathomable currents flowed from the conscription crisis of 1917. But when we returned to Montreal and ran our quarry to earth in a night club, he declared that all those currents were generally misunderstood outside Quebec.

Roger Lemelin, a writer of genius and the clearest modern interpreter of his race, was giving a farewell party to the television actors of his popular *Les Plouffes* family. Half a dozen men and women ate snails and drank wine with evident melancholy at the end of their winter season. Lemelin himself was not melancholy. He said he was not melancholy enough for his own good.

This remarkable person of towering body, rough-hewn face, and burning eyes lifted his voice above the din of the night club and, speaking in the flawless English which he learned by six months of study in a hospital bed, hurled at me a morsel of his credo.

"I am," he bawled, "a great beast! You understand—a beast! I am an adolescent! Life is suffering, and when I have suffered, then I will be a man!"

Yes, but what of his people, the real people of Quebec, who, on Lemelin's pages, shed their peasant mask and emerge in urban reality?

"The people?" he cried. "Oh, yes, the people! I will tell you what is wrong with your concept of the Quebec people. You hear of the people in terms of politics only—false terms, always. What you need, what you don't get, is Quebec in human terms. I try to paint it in those terms, but the traffic is all one way. No one paints the rest of Canada for us in human terms. Why is that?"

Possibly, I thought, because English-speaking Canada had

no Lemelin, but I did not venture to answer his question and interrupt his verdict.

Engorging a snail, he went on: "The politicians only divide us. The people unite—always. Nothing can stop that union in the end. Quebec, you see, is the life of the parish, expanded to the parish of the province but no farther—yet. But it will expand. Ah, yes, and there is no real hate for English Canada, as you imagine, only synthetic hate invented and exploited by the politicians in both places. That will pass."

Another snail, and then: "Make no mistake, the great movement is toward the center, not the other way. The streams all flow together, and all the politicians are only chips on the surface. Nothing can stop the main current. Why?" He glared at me and answered himself: "Because all of us are only people, that's why."

I walked away through the hushed streets as the first light glinted on the river, the electric cross grew dim on Cartier's royal mountain, and the broken skyline of Montreal turned black against the dawn.

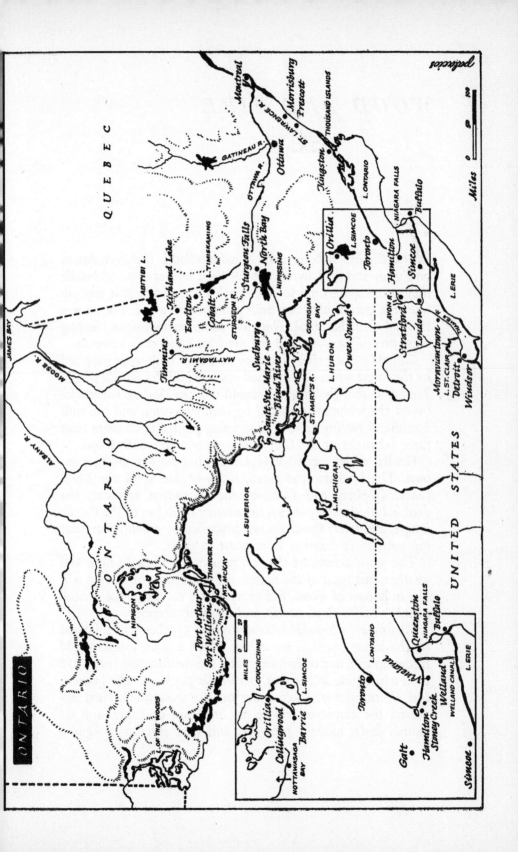

WOOD AND FIRE

*T*he English fishermen of Newfoundland, the Frenchmen on Fundy and St. Lawrence, built their houses of wood before they could spare time to build with stone. From that day onward the nation has been built primarily of wood. The ax was the first Canadian tool. The plow came second, since clearing must precede sowing, and the machine came only yesterday.

Canada's first export industry and cash crop were supplied by the forest when no plow had yet touched the central plains. Timber is still the great Canadian crop in modern times. Between the whipsaw, powered by man's muscles, and the mill machinery cutting lumber or grinding pulp, stretch more than three centuries of the Canadian's experiments with wood.

He has often wasted it recklessly, but he has made it his own. The bucksaw and small, single-bladed ax of the Maritimes, Quebec, and Ontario, the seven-foot crosscut, the double-bitted swamping ax, the narrow falling ax of the Pacific jungle, and lately the chain saw propelled by gasoline have cut the path of civilization from coast to coast.

The stone houses of the east remain, immune to time and weather, but most of the nation lives and probably always will live in houses of wood. For everywhere, except in the central plains, wood is close, handy, and relatively cheap.

Champlain's lop-sided Habitation at Quebec was followed by the more practical log cabin, which a good axman could throw up in a day or two from any tree within easy reach. He used white pine in the east, perishable poplar on the prairies, and almost imperishable cedar on the west coast. Next appeared the clapboard house, in imitation of stone, and its clumsy lines, hideous fretwork, and dark interior disfigured

most of the nation for a century. At last Canada has learned
to make beautiful wooden houses of native design and many
other things, from paper to cloth.

With the use of wood, the Canadian inevitably learned the
use of fire. Perhaps nowhere else has fire been such a friend
and enemy to man. As an essential tool against the wilderness,
fire has consumed, in the debris of man's clearings, more
sound wood and natural wealth than he can ever reckon. He
burned his way across the continent, and bonfires celebrated
his conquest. He warmed himself twice with wood, by Tho-
reau's method, once in the cutting and again in the burning,
before coal mine, oil well, and gas pipeline brought easier fuels
from the depths of the earth.

But fire was always his worst enemy. A stone chimney standing among the embers of a cabin is everywhere the monument
to the Canadian's toil upon the land. The skeletons of trees
over thousands of miles of blackened soil are the memorials of
his folly.

Fire never fails to fascinate him. He has learned not only its
dangers and uses but also its beauty. No painter ever conceived
a color or shaped a design lovelier than flame rising high into
the air, lapping in forked tongues, breaking off in crimson
splinters, falling and rising again in the hot woodland dance
of passion. No sound is sweeter than the voice of the flame, as
if, on its funeral pyre, the forest were uttering for the last time
all the remembered songs of its life.

The hiss of spring sap comes from the clearing fire, the
crackle of summer, the moan of winter, the chirp of birds, and,
above all, a giant's laughter mocking man's attempt to destroy an older life than his beneath the ashes. The tree burns,
but its spirits escape their flesh in a sigh of resurrection.

These sounds the Canadian has heard through generations
of woodcraft. He has long smelled the incense of wood smoke.
He has felt the handle of ax and saw, has seen the chips fly and
the sawdust pour out of the kerf. He has known the satisfaction of building with his own hands. The grain of wood has
entered, you might almost say, the inward grain of the nation.

CHAPTER SEVEN

—◆◆—

The Homeland

THOUGH we had both been born in Ontario, we crossed the Ottawa not as natives coming home but as strangers entering a second foreign country. At first glance the river which divides the two Canadas, Gallic and Anglo-Saxon, seems to be almost an international boundary, as clear to the traveler's eye as any in Europe. It is almost a surprise to find no customs house or immigration officials.

On the Ottawa's eastern bank the faces of Quebec, the speech, the gay architecture, and the little farms worked mainly by men and horses are all French. On the western, Ontario bank you find British faces, or the faces of new immigrant peoples, the English tongue, stern Protestant church towers, old stone or brick houses apparently transported intact from the British Isles, and big farms worked by machinery.

Ontario is as strange a country as Quebec to its exiled natives, but the roots of half the nation west of the Lakes are sunk and moored forever in the old family soil. Otherwise, why should a stranger from the west, finding himself beside the St. Lawrence just west of Montreal, learn with personal hurt that a strip of this land will soon lie deep under the waters of the new Seaway? What is it to him?

The approaching flood hurts because this is his fathers' homeland, long cleared, farmed, and dumbly loved; because, perhaps, he has played here as a boy, fished in summer, skated in winter, and—if he was a regular Ontario boy, well trained at Sunday school and taught at home to respect the law—he smuggled his first skates, his baseball bat or rifle across the ice from the American side.

That boy is dead, though still walking about, but he does not forget. He remembers Ontario, but he cannot hope to understand it. For if Ontario is the richest, the best-known, and the most powerful region of Canada, it is also the most mysterious. Every other region has been typed, at least in caricature. Ontario has no recognizable image, accurate or inaccurate. In the national gallery its portrait is a blur.

Great machines were graving new lines in that vague, composite face as we drove up the St. Lawrence. The Seaway's monstrous ditches scarred the green meadows. Square mountains of concrete had erupted in the placid current like volcanoes. Once again, as he has been doing over and over again for more than one hundred years, man was reshaping America's central channel for his purposes.

Some three miles east of Morrisburg we came upon a Church called St. John's, the oldest Protestant church built by the United Empire Loyalists when they reached Upper Canada from the American colonies and brought with them the second ingredient of the Canadian state.

The Seaway's waters were about to close over a tiny steeple, three graveyards, and the bones of the original German settlers from New York State. No doubt the inundation is complete by this time. Another patch of Ontario is sicklied o'er with the pale cast of progress. Mere sentiment and ancestral memories cannot halt these enterprises of great international pith and moment.

The minister of St. John's, the Reverend Ferdinand Louis Howald, is a descendant of Swiss folk and grandson of a Loyalist. He received me in the study of his big brick house, wearing a look of tranquillity under his shock of white hair. Like Noah, he awaited the flood with confidence, and meanwhile, inspired by a powerful pipe, wrote next Sunday's sermon in his shirtsleeves.

The minister was proud of his church. When the Seaway had drowned it, he would miss it like an old friend. But no doubt these navigation and power works were all for the best. Anyway, the memorial windows of St. John's would be saved and installed in a new building. Perhaps a few descendants of the Loyalists would dig up and re-bury the bones of their ancestors before the graveyards were flooded.

Mr. Howald sighed with resignation. It would take more than the Seaway, the diversion of the river, the concrete dams, the sudden upheaval in North America's transportation system, to shake this Christian gentleman.

Ontario must be getting used to violent change, for it is the true vortex of the Canadian revolution. Not many places in the world have changed so rapidly, but the changes have been uneven, chaotic, and diverse in Ontario, have only served, in fact, to prove that there is no actual entity of that name. Instead, there is a loose congeries of separate civilizations lumped together for administrative purposes. Hence the blurred portrait and the mystery.

That night we found our way to a fine old stone house on the riverbank and were welcomed by one of Canada's most famous scholars. "Never talk," said he, "about Ontario. There's no such place. There's no such thing as an Ontario person. The name is only a political, not even a geographical expression. Why, I can show you at least half a dozen typical Ontarios and as many typical Ontario breeds. They're identified, for convenience, on the map. They have one provincial governmet. But they're as different as Nova Scotia is from British Columbia. Ontario is just a fiction."

Nevertheless, that fiction must be explored. We started up-river on a highway swarming with freight trucks, those new rivals of the St. Lawrence ships, but the river didn't seem to be doing too badly, even without the unbuilt Seaway canals. Its fleet ambled along through lush fields, hedges of hawthorn in white blossom, elms spouting like green fountains, and herds of overstuffed cattle knee-deep in grass. We were now in the heartland of English-speaking Canada beside its original main street of water. Apart from the traffic, nothing seemed to have changed since my boyhood.

Thus we came, full of illusions, to Prescott, where, as I have been reliably informed, I was born about a century ago. Certainly it seemed that long when I beheld what progress had done to a certain house at the corner of Dibble and Edward streets.

Fifteen years earlier I had found the elms of the garden reduced to stumps, the stables gone, the shady porch torn off, and everything wonderfully improved by progress. Still, some fragments of the old days had remained even then. A genial old man who had known me as a baby inhabited the house and showed me over it. Remembering a relic left long ago in the attic, he climbed up the narrow stairs and descended with a little plaster-of-Paris bust of Sir John A. Macdonald, my grandfather's friend. It stands on my mantelpiece as I write this on the other side of the continent. The native never quite escapes Ontario.

That kindly householder had disappeared when I stopped at Prescott again. The house which had seen so many generations of birth in one bedroom was entertaining another visitor. It had become an undertaking parlor. I turned away without seeking entry. Most Canadian boys must make the same discovery in their Ontario birthplace—they can't come home again.

What had happened to Prescott and to every other town along the river? The obese windmill, fortress of the American invaders in 1838, was turned into a lighthouse, and snored comfortably in the sun. Fort Wellington looked natural enough within its walls of sod. But everything else had changed.

Where was the old grocery store, that dark nest of spicy pungence, and its owner, Mr. Mayberry, who gave a boy some striped candy sticks on every errand? Where was the tobacco store with its tank of live fish in the window, the rumor of card games and other shocking vices in the back room? Where was the jewelry store and another back room in which a boy saw his first motion picture of flickering cowboys and Indians? And where all the clamorous family of grandparents, cousins, uncles, and those saintly aunts who supported the church and high tariffs and smuggled systemically from Ogdensburg, upholstered with contraband under their ample skirts?

As I was ruminating on a futile question, an aged citizen of Prescott shuffled up Dibble Street. "I'll tell you what it is," he said. "The town has growed." Yes, he remembered my people, but that was long ago. "Things," he added, "ain't what they was by a damn sight."

In those few words he had uttered the obituary of an age, of an Ontario beyond resurrection, of a native folk scattered from here to the Pacific coast but still holding a secret morsel of this place in their hearts.

It was comforting to find that Kingston still stood at the eastern end of Lake Ontario, changeless and serene as the capital of that lost age and the home town of Macdonald. Town and man shared a hereditary look. Both were fashioned here of hard gray limestone, were carved with the same wrinkles, and wore the same tired smile.

Professor Arthur Lower, Canada's leading historian, who lives not far from the dreaming towers and bulbous domes of Kingston, told us how it had achieved its perfect symmetry, as if designed by a single architect.

It was founded by Frontenac as the westernmost fortress of New France, beside the Indian village of Cataraqui and not far upstream from the Thousand Islands. A scrubby little town of wood was built here about one century later by the Loyalists. Then the Scottish masons who had completed Colonel By's worthless military canal between Lake Ontario and the Ottawa River turned up, unemployed, in Kingston. Possessing only one idea, these men reproduced on every street the stone house of lean, square lines that they had learned to build in Scotland.

Later on, this sound sedimentary layer of local limestone was overlaid in places by some hideous Victorian gingerbread, but these blemishes on Kingston's sober face are well covered by endless avenues of trees. More important, its mind has been little marred by Ontario's recent progress, and is, indeed, no part of the modern Ontario mind. Since its university can afford long, quiet thoughts, the scholars of Queen's have always been influential in the nation's affairs and sometimes dominant in Ottawa's inner brain trust. Probably Macdonald would still be at home in his home town.

We saluted his bronze statue among the chestnut trees of the park, lunched at the hotel where he had enjoyed so many nights of bibulous revelry, and drove westward along the lake shore. A dozen busy towns and innumerable villages, all suburbs of a great metropolis, told us that we were now approaching the hub of modern Ontario. Toward evening a smudge of smoke appeared against the sunset. There could be no more doubt about it. We confronted the awful presence of Toronto.

Every Canadian traveler and visiting fireman thinks he knows Toronto, and usually dismisses it with a sigh or a sneer. In fact, no one really knows it, not even its own inhabitants. For Toronto has grown past all knowledge and boasts that it is growing faster than any other city in the world. It has become, like the province around it, a series of diverse elements loosely knitted together by stitches of steel and concrete, articulated by the first Canadian subway, glued by the adhesive of business, but not yet fused like its only rival, Montreal.

There are as many Torontos, I suppose, as the numerous Ontarios that feed its divided body—a Toronto of old-timers saddened by the jungle of skyscrapers around their tranquil homes, of newcomers dazzled by their first glimpse of Babylon; a staid provincial capital of Toronto at Queen's Park; a financial capital of brassy tycoons in Bay Street; a capital of learning at Canada's largest university; a Toronto of churchgoers, organized crime, and commercialized vice; a Toronto of writers, artists, musicians, and scholars nurturing that tender little plant called Canadian Culture; a Toronto of old Loyalist stock, who founded muddy York long ago and retained its muddy prejudices; a dozen Torontos of foreign stocks speaking their own languages, eating their own diets, and thinking their own thoughts in Canada's central melting-pot.

York was a village in a swamp beside Lake Ontario. Toronto, York's successor, was a town of fixed customs and cohesive mind. The several Torontos of our time compose neither a village nor a town, and have yet to become a city. They are a series of communities in shifting combination, continual flux, and perpetual expansion.

Yet great things have happened here. When William Lyon Mackenzie, a furious little creature in flaming red wig and three overcoats, led his mob of country bumpkins to the barricades of Gallows Hill in the Rebellion of 1837 and fled to sanctuary in the United States, he had unconsciously altered the history of the world. But Toronto is too busy nowadays to remember that its comic-opera revolution doomed the existing British Empire governed from London and, by a century of experiment, finally issued in the Commonwealth of independent nations. If that curious structure can be said to have any birthplace, it is this sprawling, ill-jointed civic colossus by the lake.

We tried to find Gallows Hill, but it was swamped by an ocean of concrete. A friendly policeman said he had never heard that name. Had he heard of Montgomery's Tavern? Well, he seemed to recall that there was a business building of some sort hereabouts marked by a bronze plaque. That might be the place, but its location escaped him.

We abandoned the search for the headquarters of Mackenzie's revolution. What was the use of a bronze plaque under the concrete ocean?

In all the endless suburban checkerboards, where a man can hardly find his own house among ten thousand others of identical design, how many Torontonians know the story of the ruined Rebel, whose treason was expunged and family honor restored by his grandson, Mackenzie King?

How many can remember even yesterday's familiar caricature of Toronto—the spinster lady in Victorian lace who abhorred drink, Sunday sports, and the morals of her French neighbor down the St. Lawrence? She is gone, or retired into some obscure mansion with blinds tightly drawn. Her voice may grumble sometimes in the morning's *Globe and Mail*, but it is lost in the afternoon screams of *The Star* and *The Telegram*, the new voices of a Toronto in birth but not yet born, and all the more shrill and positive because they are so uncertain.

Still, if Toronto sucks into its insatiable maw, through the gullet of the Lakes, half the nation's farmstuffs, minerals, timber, oil, and water power, and uses them to nourish a distended and dropsical body, its mind is nourished by new people with new ideas from every corner of Canada and from many foreign lands. It is slowly building a second Canadian city. The shiny smugness, the well-fed, aldermanic look, and the self-infatuation that so repel strangers will disappear in time. A folk who could invent the Commonwealth in the swamp of York can surely invent something better than this overgrown country town and second-class New York.

With mixed feelings of dread and hope, we set off for the Niagara country, that sharp southward arrowhead which penetrates the forty-ninth parallel and which the repeated American invasions failed to blunt.

A cloud of factory fumes at the western point of Lake Ontario marked a second metropolis. Hamilton, as we entered its crowded streets, seemed to be the largest small town of the nation, and, strangely enough, is our third shipping port, a long way from sea.

Burlington Heights, the Loyalist village of fierce old Allan MacNab, became this formidable center of industry through a queer accident. When they were building railways hereabouts, about one hundred years ago, the steel rails from England buckled in the Canadian frost and were re-rolled in Hamilton. Thus began Canada's greatest steel industry, a laboring population two fifths of foreign extraction, and a local aristocracy so proud of its big small town that one of its leading members, moved to the head office of his firm in Toronto, talked to me about his promotion almost with tears, like a man sentenced to a Siberian concentration camp.

He and others guaranteed, if we remained for a few days, to

prove that Hamilton was the best and least-appreciated city in the nation, but we took their word for it and headed south, only to find that we were going west.

Our flight through the battlefields of the War of 1812 was as badly organized as the American invasions. Like the invaders, we lost our bearings in the maze of the escarpment that rings the lake shore, then in canyons of spring greenery, and finally in an orchard of red cherries where the Americans were routed at Stoney Creek.

A farmer allowed that some kind of fight had occurred in this vicinity, he wasn't sure how or when, and kindly directed us back to Hamilton. For the second time we ran the gauntlet of the town traffic before we rediscovered the broad and brutal Queen Elizabeth Highway. To keep abreast of the natives, we moved toward Niagara at a moderate speed of seventy-five miles an hour.

Now we were in another Ontario, another climatic belt, and the Ruhr of Canada. A year earlier we had driven exactly the same sort of road, built by Adolf Hitler, through exactly the same combination of factories and smokestacks in the middle of green fields, the same orchards and vineyards, the same process which is turning a peasantry into a proletariat—a common world-wide process, but focused and perfected here as nowhere else in Canada.

I say it is perfected because most of the swelling satellite towns of Toronto are being admirably planned, though of course the old, planless villages were much better. The new factories are as modern, comfortable, and sightly as factories can be. The influx of urban workers, many of them recent immigrants, seems to get along well with the farmers who have tilled this land since Loyalist times.

To the old-timer of the Niagara Peninsula it is tragic, just the same, to see the hungry jaws of industry biting deeper every day into the orchards, the apple trees cut down to make way for a factory, the vineyards overrun by bungaloid subdivisions in mathematical squares.

This local revolution, electrically propelled by the falling water of Niagara, interested us so much that we returned in the autumn for a second look. The springtime foam of blossom had disappeared, but the Peninsula was lovelier than ever. Its orchards bent under the heaviest apple crop of modern times. The vineyards were stained with purple fruit. The upland woods of the escarpment had turned to brief red and yellow. In every village street the air was flavored with the smell of burning leaves. And on a quiet road we met the spirit of Niagara.

The man behind his wayside stand of apples had acquired, by long association, the color, shape, and tang of his product. He was a rosy apple on two legs.

His great-grandfather from upper New York, he told us, had brought the adjoining orchard with him in his pocket, toward the end of the eighteenth century. In his pocket?

"Why sure," the apple man said. "They dried out the seeds down there in the States, they brought 'em up here and then planted 'em yonder."

He pointed to the neat rows of trees around his neat stone house. Well, these weren't exactly the trees planted from seed by his great-grandfather, but they came from the same stock. One of them, gnarled like its owner, was at least one hundred years old. It had been grafted with scions of Ben Davis just before the last war, and it had yielded more apples than ever this autumn.

"It's the soil," said the apple man, fixing on us a fanatic eye. "There's something in the soil you won't find anywheres else. The soil and the moisture and a little frost and the wind off the lake. Especially the wind. Don't ask me why. Ask God. But it makes apples."

He thrust a Northern Spy into my hand and compelled me to eat it, free of charge. I had to sample several other varieties. They were fine apples, all right, but I had tasted better.

Being a peaceful man and a cowardly traitor to my own province, I did not dare to admit that I came from British Columbia, home of the world's best apples, and was really a Western Spy. Our endless national debate between the eastern and western apples is not a thing to be taken lightly. The apple of discord, if introduced into politics (where issues of such gravity are wisely avoided), would doubtless split Confederation.

So I ventured to remark only that the Okanagan Valley, on the western slope of the Rockies, seemed to produce quite decent fruit. At that the spirit of Niagara exploded.

The apple man's face took on a deeper crimson. He grasped me by the arm, looked straight into my eyes, and pronounced a solemn warning: "Don't let yourself be fooled, son! There's no apples in the Okanagan. Not real apples. Oh, yes, they're colored, all right, they win prizes, but it's just color. Might as well be paint—lipstick, I call it. No flavor. Why? Because they're irrigated, that's why! It's agin nature. Look at that"— he pointed to his row of glistening teeth—"I haven't lost a tooth in seventy-eight years. That's apples. Niagara apples."

I attempted to divert his fury by asking the apple man if he intended to sell his orchard. The question only incensed him the more.

"Sell it?" he cried. "Why, my great-granddaddy planted it! No, sir, it'll stand as long as I do. Oh, they've offered me a mint of money for a subdivision. A subdivision when we can grow the only apples in the country! Sure, they're gobblin' up all the best land under the sun. But they won't get mine, not while I'm around. Look, you can only sell land once. Apples go on forever if you look after 'em. And there's only one Niagara."

When we got out of his grip at last, our stomachs and car were full of apples much inferior to the product of our own little Pacific-coast orchard. But of course we did not utter that fact aloud in Niagara. A people who could defend this land against overwhelming American armies would defend its reputation against Canadians, if necessary, by a civil war.

We were looking for the house of John Decew, to which Laura Secord, Canada's legendary heroine, brought the news of an impending American attack at Beaver Dams on June 24, 1813. As my wife was Decew's great-great-granddaughter, we intended to bring home a snapshot for his great-great-great-grandchildren. Alas, when we finally found it, hidden in the secret valleys of the escarpment, there was little left of the house to photograph—only a square of stone walls two feet thick, a waterfall splashing into a mossy cavern, and an abandoned millhouse.

Meditating on life's accidents that have spread the offspring of Niagara's first miller across a continent, we sought our way out of a solitary upland only a few miles from the Queen Elizabeth autobahn. Fortunately we were still lost or we might not have met Joseph Edward Culp.

Mr. Culp (or Joe Ed, as everyone seemed to call him) was a brown nut of a man eighty-four years old, though he would pass for sixty at most. He was driving his car alone as we hailed him and, by a lucky chance, was carrying in massive scrapbooks and diaries the genealogy of his people.

Great-grandfather Culp, a German by descent and a Mennonite by religion, had come from the States in 1803, the usual apple seeds in his pocket, and his descendants had been farming around Vineland ever since. Joe Ed had conducted a meticulous study of his ancestors all the way back to Germany, recording every birth, marriage, and death for six generations. Now he was compiling an exhaustive chronicle of the town council, library board, and United Church of Vineland.

It was not an easy job, and he had grown lazy in his old age, so he said, like everybody else. If a man wanted to be healthy and happy, he must work hard all his life, Joe Ed affirmed. He was a living proof of his theory and of something else—the deep folk memory of the Loyalists and their undying love for this Niagara earth.

We found our way at last and descended from the escarpment to the garden shelf of Lake Ontario. Its almost tropical growth, dense population, clotted traffic, and ever expanding factories amaze and rather terrify the westerner. But in this most southern of the many Ontarios something more fundamental than economic change is under way. Here, indeed, the central dilemma of all humankind is being solved, or not solved. Man is trying to learn how to live with the machine and yet remain a man.

The factory workers in automobiles crowding the town

streets once crowded by farmers in wagons; the emancipated working girls in their invariable uniform of gay bandanna, tight sweater, and blue jeans; the dark, potent faces of the immigrants from Europe—these are the shifting atoms in a chemistry more complex and far less calculable than atomic fission. What is coming out of Ontario's gigantic test tube? What kind of city, what kind of society, what kind of human being?

From a hill near Welland one can see both the current symptoms of this process and a glimpse of its beginnings.

Farms, towns, factories, and smoke roll out to the northern horizon. The towers of the Niagara electrical grid dance in well-ordered ballet, with outflung arms and pirouette of steel legs. Directly below the hill lies Canada's most revealing monument, the three Welland Canals, triple autograph of the nation in stone.

Today's revolution began right here when Canadians undertook their first big construction job and bypassed the continental barricade of Niagara Falls. First they made a narrow, winding ditch and queer little locks, rising in places by seven separate steps to the mile. Then they made a wider, straighter ditch, larger locks, and higher steps. Finally they made the beeline of the present Welland Canal, a broad man-made river carrying an unbroken procession of ships, day and night.

Most of the stone walls are still in place as the masons left them in the old canals, and should last as long as Egypt's pyramids. Aeons hence, if visitors from distant planets ask what manner of folk once lived in Canada, let them look at these three ditches. They tell our story better than any written word. They could have been built only by a folk of imagination, courage, and faith hidden under a deceptive look of mere competence and thrift.

A visitor in any European town is shown the ruins of some cathedral, castle, or royal tomb. In a Canadian town the proud citizenry always showed us the new factory, the marble-faced bank, or the improved sewage system. These are our castles, cathedrals, and tombs. As a national monument I prefer the three canals. They say just about everything that needs to be said, and their message is indelible.

A barefoot boy was fishing that afternoon from the wall of the oldest ditch. The water ran cleanly through the deserted lock and provided good sport (though the current in other places is polluted by the discharge of the paper mills). That boy was not thinking of history, but he might have been posed by a photographer to provide a symbolic picture of Canada's lost youth.

Behind him, in silhouette, a cigar-shaped ship, heavy with grain, wallowed into the locks of the new canal. The upper gates swung shut as smoothly as your front door. The water gushed out, the ship sank like a toy in a bathtub. The lower gates opened, and she glided downstream with a toot of thanks from her whistle. The barefoot boy, the narrow ditch, the broad ditch, and the big ship—there was our history in capsule.

When the St. Lawrence channel is finally gouged out by the Seaway, when all the hydro power is harnessed, when the revolution of Niagara is complete, what then? We can be sure of only one thing: some small boy will still fish in the old ditch dug by the Loyalists. Everything else will change. The boy is changeless. He is Canada—no, he is youth everywhere —and immortal.

A few miles from Welland (I revert to our earlier, springtime journey to make the reader's confusion equal to my own in this topsy-turvy peninsula) we found the rebuilt wooden fort of General Isaac Brock and the river road where he galloped to his death on Queenston Heights.

As that ride won the first critical skirmish of the American invasion, and probably saved the chance of an independent Canadian state, Queenston should be a place for meditation. No one seemed to be meditating on the pleasant hill or beside Brock's gun pits. A steady stream of cars raced along the river cliff. How many drivers remembered the doomed man on horseback, galloping alone into the rainy dawn?

A towering granite shaft and Brock's ill-carved figure remind the thoughtful traveler of a decisive moment in the nation's life. And just below that rather ugly monument stands the house of another decisive Canadian, William Lyon Mackenzie, who published his first radical newspaper here. This building is also a national shrine.

The memorials to the loyal soldier and the rebellious scribbler tell a strange tale. Brock's column was being raised just as Mackenzie launched his rebellion. Since copies of the Rebel's *Colonial Advocate* had been buried in the base of the monument with other current documents, the outraged government of Upper Canada necessarily tore the stones apart, burned the offending journals, and started work all over again.

Those passions have burned out. Brock looks benignly down on Mackenzie's little house, which workmen were repairing at government expense as we passed by. Beside Niagara Falls, Mackenzie King made sure that his grandfather's lifework should be understood by erecting there a splendid marble arch and vault in honor of the Rebel and his unfortunate followers, Peter Matthews and Sam Lount, who were hanged for their principles at York. History has moved in its own calm rhythm, disregarding the brief prejudices of men.

The Falls were moving in the same fashion. As there is nothing new to say or think about them, we did not pause long to watch the waters of four Great Lakes leap down the stepladder of the continent. The mechanics of the cataract, as Winston Churchill found, have not changed for quite a while. It still revolves like a mangle wringing out a ragged white sheet, and it soon bores the observer by its monotonous motion, even when nature's virgin white is turned to trollop hues by incongruous floodlights—one of man's more notable insults to God.

Man is spoiling the falls, but not far off he has built and stubbornly preserves the ideal Ontario town. Simcoe, a relic untouched by the furious change around it, lives spaciously in big brick houses, shady streets, and the perfume of blossom.

Such surroundings and a long experience of life create a definite type of man, one clear portrait in the blurred gallery of the many Ontarios. We found that man in a mellow mansion and listened all evening to his recollections. They seemed to us a social document of some importance, but will perish with him like so much of the nation's story.

Three generations of his family had spanned the entire British civilization of Ontario from its beginnings. In him this adventure had produced an athlete's body, an eagle's face, and the broad, powerful hands that are shaped only by the plow handle, the ax, and the saw. But he was no ordinary farmer. He was a historian of this old countryside, a student of the people, vegetation, animals, and insects.

His Loyalist grandfather had come to Canada from New Jersey in 1796. His mother had once ridden back there alone on a sidesaddle of doeskin which he still kept as a souvenir. She must have been a brave and thrifty woman. Her son remembered her homemade gloves, her candles of tallow, and, in bad times, her flour ground out of beechnuts. That was only a generation ago in a land now throbbing with the machines of mass production. An impatient young nation might pause now and then to observe the speed of its journey.

Outside Simcoe our friend had traced the rutted tracks on which the Loyalists, with eight yoke of oxen, had hauled white pine—some of it forty feet long and six feet in diameter—to some local water mill. The descendant of those men had spent all his spare hours in the new forest cataloguing every native plant and had distinguished a few unknown to botany. Meanwhile he had watched the forest's retreat, the advance of the plow, the arrival of industry. All this progress appeared to him a questionable success.

"On a farm now," he said, "we've got water, plumbing, electricity, natural gas, and God knows what all, even television. But I doubt we're half as happy as our fathers. So I've kept my old privy as a kind of reminder. I can see the whole farm from there every morning. Helps a man to think. And remember."

There was the Loyalist folk memory again, the oldest in English-speaking Canada. It grows dimmer in every generation, but in rural Ontario it is still a powerful force, and it colors both private life and public policy. It remains a little core of sanity in a mad world.

Only a few miles west of Simcoe we found another folk and another memory. Here a worthless land of fine brown dust, abandoned by the Loyalist settlers long ago, has been turned into Canada's opulent tobacco industry, mostly by the labor of immigrants. New towns of shiny bungalows, farms polka-dotted with greenhouses and red-roofed drying kilns, curious machines to tend the tobacco seedlings, above all, the unmistakable foreign faces, announce a new Ontario barely three decades old, a little enclave of separate methods, customs, and people who make a fortune out of smoke.

We stopped to watch a tractor hauling two girls of remarkable beam—obviously recent immigrants—on a kind of wheeled rack. Their trained hands planted tobacco seedlings in the steady motion of a machine. A youth walked slowly across the field and, wherever a plant had died, replaced it with another which he dropped from a cone of metal and squirted with a dash of water and fertilizer. This operation had been almost completely mechanized, and required perhaps three seconds. Mass production had moved out of the cities to the tobacco fields.

"We've done all right," the youth said, pausing at the end of the row to replenish his basket of plants. "This land was worth five dollars an acre a few years back. We were going broke tryin' to farm it. Now it's worth a thousand, anyway. See that old guy over there?" He pointed to a swarthy and bearded man who drove the tractor, two stout daughters behind him. "He's got a hundred acres. Worth a hundred thousand, I guess, and he's only been out from Europe fifteen years. Can't hardly speak a word of English. They're mostly foreigners around here. But we're Canadians," he added quickly.

The old racial melting-pot, once centered in Winnipeg, and now in Toronto, was bubbling merrily in the rich little Ontario of nicotine.

Farther along that road an old dairyman leaned across his gate, watched his new neighbors, and smoked his pipe. He told us he didn't hold with tobacco. Not as a crop, anyway.

"Hell," he said, "these foreigners aren't farmers at all.

They're mechanics and chemists. They were so starved for land in Europe they just go crazy over here, plowin' and growin' more all the time, and more damned chemicals and sprays than you can shake a stick at. And they're takin' the country right over from us Canadians. But wait. They'll overload the market with tobacco, and then bang she goes. I'll stick to cows."

We left him cursing tobacco, smoking his pipe, and happily contemplating his herd of sleek Holsteins. Two hours later we ate our lunch on a beach of sand as lonely as it must have been in Loyalist times, our eyes dazzled by the blue-green glitter of Lake Erie. And by the middle of the afternoon we beheld the jagged skyline of Detroit, a miniature Manhattan, across the flat gardenlands of the Windsor country. Here was another Ontario, much closer, physically and spiritually, to the American metropolis than to Niagara or Toronto.

Having watched with amazement the unbroken stream of ships in the narrow trench between two nations, and having listened to the mingled grunts of their whistles, we asked a distinguished Windsor journalist how the boundary had been maintained when the people of his town crossed over to Detroit as easily as they crossed their own streets, and when the automobile factories on the American side paid substantially higher wages than the similar Canadian factories could afford. The journalist, like all his countrymen, just didn't know the answer to the sovereign question of Canadian life.

"Somehow," he said, "our people like it on this side. Twenty years ago I think a referendum in this town would have given a majority for union with the States. Not now. This is a labor town, a radical town, and a quarter of it is of French Canadian blood. But it's no suburb of Detroit. It's strictly Canadian."

The towers of Detroit rose up before us like a mirage on the site first settled by French Canadians under De la Mothe Cadillac long ago. That same mirage had beckoned Canada for nearly two centuries, but always faded under our Canadian sun.

From Windsor we wandered idly up the little Thames, on the line of the Canadians' retreat to the battlefield of

Moraviantown. No one about here seemed able to trace the disastrous strategy of Chief Tecumseh's last stand until we fell into talk with an American tourist. He held us for an hour describing the campaign of 1813 as if it had occurred yesterday. (Why is it that Canadians know so little and Americans so much about their national history?)

The Thames naturally brought us to London, the old farm town which is now ringed with industries, and then to Stratford on its imitation Avon, complete with swans.

Stratford has lately become one of the most interesting spots in America, and at that moment was suffering the final throes of preparation for its Shakespearean Festival. Sculptors, painters, and costumers worked against time to make a colossal bust of Pompey for *Julius Caesar*, a gross of Roman helmets, armor of plastic, and enough women's gowns to stock a department store.

Caesar, Brutus, and Cassius rehearsed under a big circus tent. Though clad in sweat shirts, slacks, and sneakers, they brought the Roman Forum suddenly to life. Nowhere, not even in the Old Vic itself, had we felt so keenly the magic of the master's lines as they fell trippingly from the lips of these Canadian youngsters.

Robins chattered outside the tent, and a heavy whiff of lilac blew through the canvas walls. Shakespeare would have been at home here. He would have approved the performance of his play, repaired to the coffee bar for a snack with the players, or lolled on the grass beside an Avon very like the original.

The inhabitants of Stratford are a little bewildered to find their sleepy town transformed overnight into the shrine and local habitation of airy nothings from another Stratford far away. One corner at least of Ontario has escaped the economic revolution and felt instead a revolution of culture. Stratford has become an independent city-state of poetry, drama, and imagination.

"Shakespeare," said the proprietor of a delicatessen shop where we purchased a picnic lunch, "isn't my dish. Still and all, they tell me he's quite good if you like that stuff. Why,

you can't get a room for miles around when they open the
Festival. I'll say this much for Shakespeare—he's sure good
for business."

It was hard to tear ourselves away from Elizabethan England and drive into the drab Ontario fronting on Lake Huron
and removed by several centuries from Shakespeare. We were
now in the historic Huron Tract, that far western wilderness
to which the first settlers came by lake to clear the forest,
build roads, and push their farms to the rocks of Georgian
Bay. This is harsh country after the garden soil of Niagara and
the Lake Erie shore, but the farmers cherish the broad fields,
the fences of boulders, the painted Pre-Cambrian rocks, and
the metallic vistas of the lake.

An editor in the solid brick town of Owen Sound assured
us he wouldn't take five times his present salary to work in
Toronto, and apparently Toronto sees his point. A large part
of the city population surges out here in summertime to litter
the beaches of Georgian Bay with holiday cottages, to foul
the air with the smell of speed boats, and to create several
pretty fair imitations of Coney Island. A westerner, used to
ample space, finds himself jostled by these holiday crowds.
When we came to the fishermen near Collingwood who stood
in solid rank to cast their spoons at Nottawasaga Bay, and
then a pathetic Toronto millionaire fishing with expensive
tackle in a culvert by the roadside, we fled from this repulsive
urban annex into the quiet of Huronia, the land of the
Jesuits' martyrdom.

Orillia, on Lake Couchiching, a town famous in Ontario's
legendry, was filled that Saturday afternoon by hordes of
Toronto refugees bound for the healthful follies of their summer camps. But the mansions and spacious estates of the rich
along the lake shore were well sealed by massive gates against
these brief birds of passage, and Bill Deacon, literary editor
of the Toronto *Globe and Mail*—a romantic, historian, and
confirmed camping man—assured us that the old small-
town virtues of Orillia would break through the thin crust of
the week-end on Monday morning.

Mr. Deacon and many like him regard Orillia as sacred

ground. A splendid statue in bronze marks Champlain's passage here. Moreover, Orillia produced a genuine literary masterpiece and one of the greatest modern Canadians. This is Stephen Leacock's town, the Mariposa of his immortal *Sunshine Sketches*. Barrie, down the lake, long claimed that distinction for itself, but written proofs, as Mr. Deacon demonstrated, have extinguished such pretensions.

In the public library of Orillia the bust by Elizabeth Wyn Wood—a leonine head that capture's Leacock's inner wistfulness and melancholy beneath his brave banter and wonderful nonsense—presides over a collection of his manuscripts in a glass case. And among these records is a letter in Leacock's penmanship stating definitely that Orillia is Mariposa slightly distorted.

We were glad to have that vital question settled after years of doubt, but we knew by now that Leacock's land, like all the many rural Ontarios, was terra incognita to us, its people strangers though they were our people by ancestry. It was time to visit yet another Ontario, which, by political definition only, is called the capital of Canada.

MEN WITHOUT NAMES

W hen we have studied all the written records and the un-written legends, we still have overlooked and can never find some of the most decisive Canadians in our history.

At the head of the list any historian would surely place, if he could find it, the name of the man who first stripped the bark from a birch tree and made it into a canoe; for it was this flimsy, buoyant craft of Canada, unlike any other, that carried men, both Indian and white, from the eastern to the western coast and revealed the makings of the nation. The canoe was the first Canadian invention of genius, but the inventor will remain forever nameless.

So will that other seminal mind which shaped a pipe of stone, was soothed by the smoke of tobacco or some wild weed, thereby creating a medical problem, a vice, and the solace of mankind. He may have been an American Indian or a Canadian, but, whoever he was, most of our adult population is in his debt, or his clutches.

Again, what history book records the name of that decisive Canadian (probably a woman) who sat down one day and, in a prodigious act of imagination, combined buffalo meat with blueberries, added grease, and produced pemmican on the Canadian prairie? Nobody knows that woman, though she had discovered the complement of the canoe, had perfected the essential diet of the explorers, filled with all essential vitamins and energy enough to nourish the long western voyage.

One would also place pretty high on the roll of honor that master chemist who first changed maple sap to syrup. While Banting, a Canadian, is rightly remembered for insulin, the maker of syrup, a still more improbable discovery, lies in some unmarked grave beside the St. Lawrence. History is seldom just.

We remember Louis Hébert, the original French Canadian

farmer, plowing his field behind the first Canadian ox, close to the walls of Quebec, and there clearing a convenient battlefield for Wolfe and Montcalm. We forget that there were other Canadian farmers long before Hébert's time. Indians planted corn, beans, and pumpkins to found our farm economy. We cultivate the first farmer's plants today and sow his seeds. We have lost his name.

In the art of architecture we have no recorded names worthy to stand with Michelangelo and Christopher Wren. Yet neither of them, nor any white man, ever hit on a principle of construction more remarkable than the igloo of the Canadian Eskimo. Some inspired architect had built domes of snow centuries before Michelangelo drew his plans for St. Peter's and Tamerlane stole the onion-shaped domes of Asia Minor, dragged them by camel train to Samarkand, whence they traveled to Russia, and finally arrived, with the Ukrainian immigrants, in the Canadian west. The igloo melts in spring, but outlasts the ages. What pre-Canadian first used the winter's snow to build a house against winter?

Even in the unlikely field of political thought this country had its decisive thinkers before the white man introduced his form of government. The Iroquois confederacy, stretching across an unmarked line which would someday be an international boundary, was a system of collective security when no one had thought of the United Nations. It presented the ideal of world citizenship and international law, it proposed permanent disarmament under the Tree of Peace, and it enforced a democratic franchise. True enough, those policies worked indifferently, the Iroquois being otherwise engaged in massacring the first white Canadians, but the idea was there, and the early statesmen were less destructive than their successors in the age of enlightenment.

A small part of the Canadian story is written down and remembered. By far the longest and largest part is lost. We shall never even know for sure what white man from Europe first saw this land and called it good. We don't know who gave it the name of Canada, where the word came from, or what it meant then. We only know, or think we know, what it means to us, and that dimly.

CHAPTER EIGHT

The Cliff

OTTAWA should be approached from the north side of its river, preferably by a detour through the winding, mossy ways of the Gatineau Valley. They led us to the old, familiar tangle of gray towers afloat in a green mist. But every road in Canada, every trail through forest, prairie, and tundra, leads at last to Ottawa. Every traveler who hopes to understand the nation must come here.

For Ottawa, with all its faults and disguises, its smiling face and incessant hidden war, its endless adventure and blind groping that men call politics, is the nation's brain—not its heart, mind you, but its brain, radiating impulses, wise or foolish, to every nerve and muscle of the half-continent.

Inevitably we came back, as so many times before, to the falls of Chaudière, where Champlain propitiated the Indian gods with an offering of tobacco, to the sheer cliff on which his successors built a capital before they built a nation, to the abiding enigma of that nation's life.

Six months earlier the Hill of Parliament had stood solid and white above the river like a wedding cake from the oven of a mad baker. The towers were rimed with hoarfrost and dripped massive icicles. New snow lightly dusted the bronze shoulders of many a statesman's statue. The Royal Canadian Mounted Police, dismounted and bundled in buffalo skins, shivered and stamped their feet on the slippery driveway.

Looming above its rivals, the thin finger of the Victory Tower pointed sternly to a sky of blue steel.

Now the Hill was melting in the spring. A green cataract tumbled down the cliff, and a caldron of foliage bubbled around the buildings of government. The Tower of Victory seemed likely to slide at any moment into the Ottawa. Spring was almost finished, and the explosion of the Laurentian summer could be expected hourly.

We crossed the river on its death-trap bridge, entered perhaps the worst-managed traffic in Canada, and drove up to the Hill. There we stopped and gazed at the insane and splendid stone jumble, a semicircular Stonehenge of wild disorder, that Canadians reared up, without clear purpose or sufficient money, to declare their faith. The buildings were crazy, all right, they defied all the laws of symmetry, they sprouted and proliferated in ridiculous stalks and careless blossoms of granite, but in their spring dance they were all laughing together at the absurdity of man, at a joke which somehow became a nation.

In any season since I first saw it as a scared cub reporter nearly forty years ago, the central tower makes me pause a moment in humility; not because it is an original masterpiece of architecture—it is, in fact, a Gothic imitation from Europe, a remote offspring of Big Ben's tower by the Thames—but because its sinewy lines have caught by chance the harsh beauty, the distance, the loneliness, and the human struggle of our land. And as I stood before this sharp arrow aimed at the sun, the carillon bells chimed out suddenly in triumphant peal. A silent nation had found its voice.

I paused also to read again those proud words graven over the front door of Parliament: "The wholesome sea is at her gates, her gates both east and west." As a youth they had meant little to me. An old man must read them with new wonder, perhaps new comprehension, and with memories of ships and men on two seacoasts.

Then, as I stepped into the circular anteroom, whose single tree of stone spreads its carved branches in voluptuous groining, I encountered a woman, evidently an American tourist.

She and her two small sons were gazing upward at the roof of a petrified forest, and it seemed to puzzle them.

"It's grand," she informed me. "Not as big as the Capitol in Washington, you know, but prettier. Tell me, what does it stand for? We know what Washington means to us. What does this mean to you?"

I couldn't tell her. No one has yet articulated the meaning of Canada or of its mighty symbol in Ottawa. That question, it seemed to me, had become increasingly difficult to answer of late. The capital around the monument is supposed to be the mirror of Canada, but it is often a very clouded glass. Small wonder when Ottawa reflects a nation in whirling change beyond the control of government, when any nation is only one atom in a world-wide chemistry beyond human control.

In Ottawa's combined hothouse, whispering gallery, and Delphic oracle, some honest, competent, and average Canadians, the common denominator of the nation, were governing sixteen millions of their fellow citizens. I could not believe, after seeing the Canadian folk for myself, that Ottawa had sensed the true motion of the nation's mind. The thing we were building between the oceans was not the thing specified in the blueprints of Ottawa, proclaimed in the debates of Parliament, or shouted in the slogans of politics.

Nevertheless, it is in Ottawa that the total process must be examined because here it is centralized and, so far as men manage it at all, is managed. Here all the conflicting forces of our life come into naked collision; and here they are tamed, reconciled, and compromised before they can split the nation and end it.

There are, of course, two Ottawas—the cosy, rather provincial Ontario town built by Colonel By on the river cliff and the separate kingdom of the Hill.

When Queen Victoria selected Ottawa for the capital of an unborn nation, hardly yet a gleam in Macdonald's eye, she had not seen this site and never would see it.

When Goldwin Smith, that prophet of ineluctable Canadian-American amalgamation, announced that Ottawa was a "sub-Arctic lumber village converted by royal mandate into a political cockpit," he (and most Englishmen) did not foresee either the present nation or its capital.

When George Brown, the reluctant ally of Macdonald in the Confederation scheme, looked at the half-finished Parliament buildings, he concluded that all the revenue of the new state would not keep them heated or clean.

Later on, when Laurier remarked that "it is hard to say anything good" of Ottawa and that "it is not a handsome city and does not appear destined to become one," he could not imagine the Ontario town now spread miles beyond his Sandy Hill, the majestic Chateau named for him, the mansions of Rockcliffe, the spacious driveways, the prime minister's stately residence, the still finer city planned for the future.

To be sure, the dingy defile of Sparks Street and the other streets of business remain much as Laurier knew them. His own ugly house is preserved intact, with all its litter of Victorian horrors, as a monument to his heir, Mackenzie King. The industrial skyline and smoke of Hull, across the river, mar the whole civic design. Some surviving slums still crawl to the edge of Parliament Hill.

But if the architects and town-planners are allowed to complete their work; if the projected green belt is preserved on the city's rim; if new avenues are driven from the Hill through the business section (one fancies the encrusted old gentlemen of the Rideau Club gently lifted, chairs and all, by steamshovel, the American ambassador respectfully removed from Wellington Street and deposited elsewhere); if Ottawa has the time, money, and imagination, it will become a worthy capital, unlike any other in the world.

Meanwhile Ottawa the Ontario town lives its own life outside the stone walls of the Hill, is no more interested than any other Canadian town in the adventures of politics, is more concerned with the growth pains of a community already bursting at the seams and with its lovely playground in the Gatineau Hills.

Ottawa the capital is a town within a town, a structure purely political, an uninterrupted public debate and private conversation piece, sometimes an unpleasant intrigue, and always, like any capital, a ferocious struggle for power.

This struggle flows in two parallel streams that seldom merge.

A social struggle (its banner the stuffed shirt, its diet the cocktail and canapé) neatly laminates Ottawa in concentric rings of power, ranging from foreign ambassadors, cabinet ministers, deputy ministers, and high officials down to the humblest clerk.

A struggle for real power in a tight hierarchy, almost a priestcraft, radiates out of the cabinet chamber into Parliament and thence into every electoral constituency and hamlet of Canada.

A stranger may read a few books and quickly learn the public anatomy of Canadian government: the monarchial system brought from Britain and maintained by the symbol of a Governor-General who represents the Queen of Canada, a resident of London, England; the American federal system of ten sovereign provinces; the government sitting in and responsible to the elected House of Commons; the Senate appointed for life as a reward for party service, theoretically sharing equal power with the Commons but practically almost powerless; and, behind all this constitutional machinery, the regnant party system, which is not mentioned in the written constitution, which enforces its own laws, supports its own dynasties, rewards its retainers, punishes its rebels, and makes a national party actually a state within the state.

A spectator in the public galleries sees only the formal postures, the ritual dance and stylized counterpoint of parliamentary speeches, tiresome quibbles, party maneuvers, family jokes among the family of the Hill, and little triumphs rarely noticed beyond its walls.

The real game behind the scenes is played by accepted rules, for the most part fairly, always fiercely and for keeps. It is played on the Hill all day and at night in many an unknown house of politician, civil servant, or journalist, where a casual gathering at a buffet supper may change the whole course of national events.

The players are nearly all honest and usually poor; more honest, I believe, than the average man of business and invariably poorer. This intimate society abhors Ottawa's public social life, calls its eminent members by their first names, and knows from hour to hour what is happening in the cabinet and in the back concessions of the nation. Of all capitals Ottawa, in the vital regions of power, must be the most democratic, folksy, and unpretentious of our times.

Whatever its public posture may be at the moment, whatever principles it may mouth, whatever policies it may announce, the primary purpose of government in Ottawa, under any party, is to reconcile the conflicting interests of a far-flung nation and a diverse people; especially to reconcile the two major Canadian races.

Government pretends to be logical, consistent, and principled. In fact it is completely pragmatic, as it must be in such a contradictory state.

The successful Canadian party issues sublime pronunciamentos. It claims to be unified and dedicated in its sacred belief. Everyone in Ottawa knows that the party, if it is to succeed, can be only a loose assortment of pressure groups constantly at war.

A cabinet must maintain the fiction of unbroken solidarity before the public as if all its members thought alike. Behind the double doors of the East Block it is only a coalition of rival forces in constant disagreement, tension, and compromise.

The outsider cannot see through this flux or identify the real center of power. It shifts almost daily because the issues and the personalities are constantly shifting.

At the top a prime minister in the Canadian system possesses power which the written and even the unwritten constitution never mention. He holds almost a unilateral veto over his cabinet and party, provided he has mastered the nation, as only five prime ministers since Confederation have mastered it. But often decisive power may rest with some anonymous official since he alone knows the answer to some cabinet problem. He may invent the cabinet's policy, and, if he does, will invariably deny any knowledge of it. The principle of anonymity, plus the fact of personal ability, have given Canada a magnificent and, of course, unappreciated civil service.

Despite this apparent confusion, Ottawa has usually provided competent, though rarely brilliant or spectacular, government. Canada will not long tolerate brilliant or spectacular government, and only in Laurier's case would it tolerate a brilliant and spectacular prime minister.

The colors of our politics cannot be primary colors since the compromise of a divided state is always gray. So, of necessity, are the men who manage the process. Nevertheless, the resulting national policies usually meet the essential test: they work.

Anyway, the electorate, though never satisfied with its government, seldom changes it. One party has been in office, at this writing, for thirty-six years except for a five-year interruption. The nation continues to thrive, as it sometimes thinks, in the face of Ottawa's continual blunders.

Perhaps more than in any other nation the politicians of Ottawa have learned perforce the art of compromise. At best it is the highest art of statesmenship; at worst, a disguise for mere cowardice.

Once a workable compromise among the racial, geographic, economic, and class pressures of a multiform society has been devised by the politicians and their experts in secret, it is announced as the lifelong ideal and hallowed doctrine of the government. It may have been invented last night, and may contradict all previous announcements.

Consistency is not the hobgoblin of Ottawa's mind. If the policy meets the primary test and works, at least temporarily, no one asks who originated it or attempts to explain its inconsistencies. If it fails to work, it is quietly changed without notice or, if necessary, reversed, while any government in retreat pretends always to be advancing on an unalterable course toward a known goal.

The goal in Ottawa, as in any democratic capital, is unknown. Such logic must be left to philosophers and communists. The Canadian politician is not looking ahead to Utopia. He will be satisfied to survive the next election. In times of crisis he cannot see further than next week-end.

Though both goal and future route are unknown, it is possible to identify the basic pressures that are reshaping Canadian society more rapidly than most Canadians realize. And these pressures are now organized as they were never organized until recent times.

Before the present generation there were only three concentrated and organized powers in Canadian society: government, business, and agriculture. They were not very concentrated or, by modern standards, powerful because they reflected a diffused and relatively primitive economy.

Today the Canadian situation is different, not only in size but also in kind. Four colossi have been fully organized, concentrated, and equipped to exert power: government, business, labor unions, and farmers.

Power used to be geographical, or horizontal, in a contest between regions and zones of economic interest. Now it is growing more and more vertical, in disregard of geography. Business, labor unions, and farmers in all parts of the nation generally stand behind the same objectives, and their leadership is centered in their national headquarters. Society thus organized is largely a battle of the new colossi. The individual is becoming almost socially powerless except as a member of his group.

The paramount social event of our times, as reflected in Ottawa, is not the new distribution of power, striking as it may be, but the emergence of the planned welfare state.

In the usual tradition of Canadian affairs, that concept was born with no public announcement, the offspring of reluctant parents, out of wedlock.

Some twenty-five years ago Mackenzie King, the skilled midwife of this accouchement, damned the new theory of social "planning" as if it were a dirty word and the antithesis of historic Canadian Liberalism. He denounced the whole Keynesian theory of state spending for prosperity, extolled the balanced budget, ridiculed the economics of the American

New Deal, and privately chortled at the economic ignorance of his good friend Franklin Roosevelt. By 1935 he was in bed with the planners.

The state had underwritten the expanding economy, guaranteed full employment, and undertaken to plan the major business of society while neither state nor society knew what this would involve. Once the state seized the central banking mechanism—that is to say, the management of the whole credit system usually called money—a social revolution had been launched without a drop of bloodshed or even a bloody nose. There was no turning back.

The society evolving from the fundamental decisions of the thirties had become a commonplace by the fifties, but it was not the society that its occupants generally supposed.

It was no longer capitalistic by any known definition of the past. It was not socialistic either, though the Canadian state is managing the money system, the wheat market, the largest national railway, the main airlines, radio, and television.

Like everything else of importance in Canada, the new society was a compromise and a blur without name. The system of free enterprise as we knew it a generation ago had become only a historic relic, however it might be lauded on ceremonial occasions, and deserved to be embalmed in a glass tomb as Lenin is embalmed to commemorate a lost Marxism.

Whatever the present society may be called, the most obvious political fact in Canada today, as in other democratic countries, is the irresistible flow of power into the hands of the state. Ottawa now wields power that its predecessors would have considered unthinkable, undesirable, and dangerous.

The most obvious question in the Canadian society today is whether the state knows how to wield this power wisely. Recent years have been too rich, smooth, and easy to answer that question. It will be answered only in harder times. The total Canadian answer will involve the entire continent.

As the continent was originally bisected, after nearly two centuries of war, the richest half went to the newborn American Republic, the poorer to the northern British colonies not yet a nation.

The United States had the best of the Atlantic shelf, the South of cotton and tobacco, most of the great central plains, underlaid with oil, and the most productive Pacific littoral.

Canada, though larger than its neighbor, had only a narrow agricultural belt on the St. Lawrence, a stone waste along the Great Lakes, a prairie grain belt only about three hundred miles from south to north, the forest of British Columbia, and, across more than two thirds of its area, the sterile Pre-Cambrian Shield.

But the old assessment of the two nations' wealth has lately been revised.

On the one hand, the United States has dug up, cut down, burned, eroded, used, or wasted a substantial part of its natural wealth, and now requires vast imports of raw materials from Canada, without which it could hardly operate its peacetime economy and certainly could not begin to fight a war.

On the other hand, Canada has struck oil on its prairies, has discovered unsuspected minerals of all sorts in the Shield, has learned that the Shield's innumerable lakes and slowly melting snow provide one of the earth's greatest reservoirs of electrical power, and has rapidly built one of the world's major industrial complexes.

Out of these deep changes on both sides of the border there now emerges again, in new form, the oldest problem of Canadian life—the problem of the North American boundary, for which Americans and Canadians were fighting as late as 1866 in the last Fenian raids, and were negotiating, in the case of the Alaska Panhandle, as late as 1903. Since this is not a book of history or economics, it will be sufficient to say that the biggest decisions of Canadian life (apart from foreign affairs) in the present generation will revolve around the proper division of the wealth available on both sides of the boundary.

Canada was content until modern times to be mainly a producer of raw materials that were mainly processed in the United States and shipped back across the boundary to the Canadian consumer.

The United States was content to buy these things without owning their sources in the Canadian earth. By loading its tariff in favor of raw-material imports and against Canadian manufactures, the United States always managed to maintain what it considered a huge "favorable" balance of trade. Canada managed somehow to support its resulting deficit by earnings of hard money in the world market, mainly in Britain.

This was the North Atlantic Triangle of the economic textbooks. It was smashed by the Second World War and Britain's dollar shortage. The old assumptions and arrangements on which the joint North American economy lived for so long have been repealed.

Canada is not content to be mainly a producer of raw materials for American factories. It has become an industrial nation in its own right. But it continues to be one of the world's four largest international traders, vitally dependent on exports and imports; and, having built an east-west economic system in defiance of geography, it now finds the great currents of business flowing north and south. The United States buys most of Canada's exports and supplies most of its imports. More and more the Canadian eggs are concentrated in the single American basket.

Moreover, the United States has conducted a far-reaching invasion of the Canadian economy, has built or bought many great industries and such primary resources as mines, oil, gas, and timber. This movement of investment capital north across the border has covered, so far, a huge and growing Canadian deficit in the American market.

Thus economic progress—so far as it is financed by American money—collides anew, and on a massive scale, with the growing nationalism of Canada.

The question worrying Ottawa today, therefore, is whether in this process Canada will sometime become, as many Canadians fear, a mere economic appendage, satellite, and milch cow of the American economy as it is already an outpost of the American defense system.

That question has been posed over and over again in Canadian politics since Macdonald invented his National Policy of tariff protection and built the Canadian Pacific Railway to support a poor, unnatural Canadian economy for purely political and patriotic reasons. Canada has always found a satisfactory answer and, I believe, will find it again.

Today Canada is no longer a poor relation in the North American family. It is rich, and its economy, however unnatural, is working better than Macdonald ever hoped. The natural wealth of Canada is no longer a luxury to the United States; it is a necessity, while the Canadian market is by far the largest foreign cash market for American goods.

The two ideal neighbors, whose neighborliness is the admiration of the world and the theme of every visiting banquet orator, have entered the second half of the twentieth century in an entirely new economic context.

These fundamental North American changes will not be digested easily on either side of the border. It is not too much to say that the main impetus of Canadian politics in economic affairs is a determination to make a better business deal with the United States. A complex and awkward agenda faces the neighbors.

If government at Ottawa were confined to the internal business of Canada, it would be difficult enough. Those difficulties are doubled by the necessity of dealing daily and hourly with the American giant, which defends Canada from foreign attack and, in terms of real power, bestrides the whole continent.

The problems of government are tripled by a third factor, the oldest in Canadian life and the most formidable because it is not only political but also spiritual and therefore incalculable.

The American people instantly cut their roots in Europe by their Revolution, or thought they did. They are finding now that they cannot escape and must always rescue the old world in times of danger, but they began their adventure as an independent nation without a backward look at their ancestors. Their life was committed totally to North America. Spiritually they were undivided, untroubled in their conscience, and whole.

Canada has never cut its roots in the old world. Constitutionally it is a member of a world-wide Commonwealth centered in London. Spiritually it is attached to Britain by ties much stronger than constitution and infinitely deeper than politics. The forces of geography draw it ever more deeply into America. The forces of history draw it toward the old world.

This split personality may be ignored for years at a time, but any quarrel involving Canada's two great friends, Britain and the United States, immediately uncovers the nation's ambivalence. It is then torn between its interests as a North American nation and its filial sentiments as a child of Britain.

A serious quarrel between Britain and the United States is the ancient nightmare of Canadian statesmanship. When, in the Suez episode of 1956, the nightmare became a reality, Canada was inwardly torn in a fashion which no foreigner could understand.

Not by calculation, but by the oldest instinct of its being, Canada moved in on the two titans to end their quarrel. Acting Canada's historic role as honest broker between the new world and the old, Lester B. Pearson, Canadian foreign minister, flew to the United Nations and proposed a compromise which worked, for the moment at least.

That incident may be forgotten when these lines are printed, but it is worth remembering because it represented a classic demonstration of Canada's ambivalence; it revealed the permanent touchstone of Canadian foreign policy.

As in domestic affairs, Canada has always been compelled by its unique circumstances to rely on flexibility, agility, and compromise in foreign affairs. It is the most experienced middleman of international politics. In Pearson, Canada has produced its first great international statesman, but Pearson is great mainly because he has understood and expressed, with a deceptive grin and a certain boyish touch of genius, the nation's middle position, its absolute dependence on the comity of the English-speaking peoples, its overriding concern with American policies. Pearson succeeds, in fact, because he understands the British and the Americans as they do not understand each other, because he is trusted by both, and because their confidence gives Canada a power of persuasion out of all proportion to its physical power.

Such problems, domestic and external, raise questions about Canada's future that Ottawa cannot hope to answer. The answers will come not from Parliament Hill but from the people. As we left Ottawa I knew that no one now alive would be around long enough to hear the answer to anything of importance.

But, looking back at the Tower of Victory, I thought it would be here, the carillon would ring out over the river, the changeless face of the clock would register impartially, hour by hour, the passage of time, which cures all things.

The clock hung in the darkness like a minor moon against the northern sky. Its hands pointed to midnight. Dawn would soon be breaking on Canada's eastern coast. It was early evening on the Pacific. No single theory, no simple answer, could fit a land so vast and contradictory.

NORTHERN BOUQUET

*I*f he had kept that almost vestigial organ in repair, modern man's nose would lead him, blindfolded, across Canada. His sense of smell would tell him exactly where he was going.

The country reeks of distinguishable odors. It is subdivided by invisible olfactory lines as definite as the boundaries of its provinces, though more complicated. It has an unmapped geography and unrecorded climate of smell.

The sharper and sweeter scents of the land touch even the dull, civilized nose. Wild roses, the nation's tireless pilgrims, carry the innocent fragrance of childhood and nostalgia everywhere, increasingly strong as they move northward. All Canadians know the sensual emanation of syringa, the Balm of Gilead's overpowering night redolence by the creek bottom, the frail whiff of violet, currant, and lady-slipper, the genial stench of the yellow skunk cabbage, the green smell of swamps. But the great smells of Canada are more than brief local spurts of perfume. They are enduring, potent, and elemental.

First of all, the earth's own smell, the clean, masculine smell of dry prairie, baked clay rangeland, bunch grass and acrid sagebrush, of sleek furrows newly plowed, and in summer evenings the feminine aroma of hay newly cut.

Then the smell of wood. Alive, the forest exudes a ceaseless symphony of smell in two major themes, evergreen and deciduous, with countless subthemes and nuances, from the soft, mild flavor of the hardwoods to the harsh, resinous breath of cedar, fir, hemlock, and balsam, the spicy tang of juniper. Dead, the forest exhales the smell of new boards and oozing pitch, the old, unmistakable sawmill smell of the lonely road, the hidden valley, the great lumber towns.

Always, alive or dead, the wood smell is mixed with the aromatic smell of wood smoke from a mill burner, a campfire, or a forest fire darkening the sky, stinging the human nostril a hundred miles from the flame.

The brave smell of stone is here, too, but few men pause to savor split granite, mountain cliffs of moss and lichen, glacial boulders sweating in the sun, and slimy rocks long salted, encrusted, and matured by the sea.

And finally the sea itself, the fumes of salt, kelp, fish, storm, mist, ice, and far-off places.

Upon these elemental odors men's cities all impose their distinctive essences. A blind Canadian should know when he has reached Halifax; its maritime smell of sea, cod, wharves, ships, and tar is as legible as a signpost. He should recognize through his nose the moldering stone of Quebec; Montreal's mixed smell of traffic, coal smoke, and French cooking; Toronto's smell of business, the dank effusion of finance in Bay Street, and even, perhaps, the last faint reminders of York's original bog; the smell of railways, river mud, and grain in Winnipeg; in Vancouver the Pacific smell of rain, ocean, forest, and prosperity.

Alas, the Canadian nose, like the civilized nose everywhere, is blunted and benumbed. It has lost the concord of sweet smells. It no longer senses the full, pungent bouquet of the north.

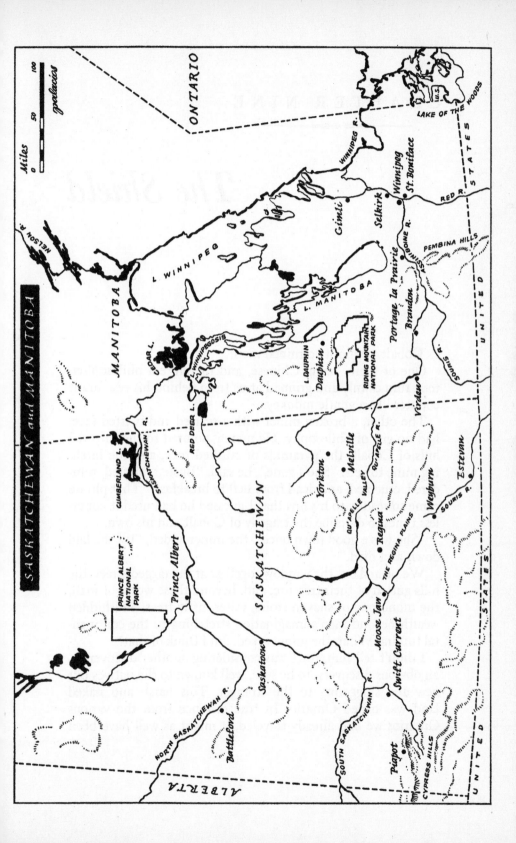

CHAPTER NINE

The Shield

In Cobalt we met two ruined men.

One of them, being Chinese, and therefore a philosopher, took ruin calmly and grinned at us from behind his restaurant counter like a gentle monkey.

The other, a broken miner with a scarred and twisted face, had no gift of philosophy. He merely pointed to the tortured hills of Cobalt, the pyramids of crushed rock, and the lurching mine towers. "She's gone," he said. "Busted, blasted, murdered, crucified, and dead from hell to breakfast." That phrase came so readily to his lips that I guessed he had used it countless times to describe the tragedy of Cobalt and his own.

"She was a good town once," the miner added, "till she laid down and died."

We peered out the window together at the ragged street, the hills gutted of their treasure, and, beyond these works of man, the monotony of shaven stone, water, little trees, and hidden wealth beyond man's imagination stretching to the continental tundra. What, the miner asked, did I think of that?

I didn't tell him, for I was considering another discovery—an obvious discovery, to be sure, well known to the natives but new and staggering to the stranger. This harsh and naked land was called Ontario. In true distance from the various Ontarios we had already traveled, it might as well have been within the Arctic Circle. It was, in fact, within another circle, or, rather, the semicircle of the Canadian Shield, that vast stone horseshoe which lies across two thirds of the nation, from Labrador to the Mackenzie River.

On entering the Shield, hardly a hundred miles north of Toronto, we had begun to see that not only the land but also the people had changed. The people of the Shield are of many races, by national definition. They are all one race by the definition of environment and by bent of mind.

On the other side of the Shield, men's eyes are turned southward to the central river system and, beyond it, to the United States. Once the line of the Shield is crossed—and that crossing is marked as clearly as any international boundary by the sudden eruption of rounded glacial rock—you find human life turned forever northward and bounded on the south by the awesome Pre-Cambrian dike.

North of the stone rim, human life is numerically small. Most of the Canadian people live south of the rim, about seventy per cent of them within one hundred miles of the American boundary. That pattern may shift somewhat, but not much. For the Shield is arable only in a few jagged trenches, and it can never support the population of an agricultural land. Its mining towns doubtless will always be widely separated specks on the empty Arctic slope.

At all events, the Pre-Cambrian line is decisive. Yesterday we had walked the cozy streets of Ottawa and, a few days earlier, the lush orchards of Niagara. Now we seemed to have landed on a different continent. This was no longer Ontario, whatever the map might say. It was not the real north either. More than half the girth of Canada lay beyond Cobalt. Nevertheless, we had crossed one of the sharp internal borders and spirit lines of the nation. Of which division the two men in the restaurant were unconscious markers and mileposts.

The Chinese proprietor—speaking in an odd mixture of English and French—told us that the fatal mistake of his life had been to settle in Cobalt. His restaurant in Montreal had employed eight French Canadian waitresses (those girls, he said, were good-lookers, *trés jolie*) and had earned him a modest fortune, now lost. Here he was his own cook, waiter, and dishwasher. He had been trapped in Cobalt. Still, he rather liked it. The people were so nice, so *gentil*.

"Pay no heed to the Chink," the miner said. "He's nuts. Say, when I first hit this town she was the best damn town in the north. Thirty-five mines, ten thousand people, and whisky two drinks for a quarter—and not watered down, like now. We was rich on a dollar and a half a day. That was nineteen-seven. Now she's dead. Two mines, two thousand people. And me too old to work."

Why didn't he leave Cobalt for an easier climate in the south?

"Hell, man," he shouted, "you can't leave the north. Once you're in it you can't get out." Why? His battered old face took on the deeper wrinkles of cerebration, and finally he explained everything. "It's the north," he said. "That's all. The north."

So he, too, had trapped himself in this diminished town. Cobalt! It was a word of magic fifty years ago. When Jim McKinley and Ernie Darragh picked up a hunk of pure silver beside Long Lake, on August 7, 1903, these humble timber-cruisers had unlocked the Shield and given Canada a new dimension. Out of Cobalt surged the great Ontario mineral boom which is just getting nicely into its stride today. But it has left Cobalt, its birthplace, far behind, almost forgotten.

Though the country northward was far outside our route to the Pacific coast, we decided to make a little detour and see at least the edge of the boom. Evening had come before we escaped from Cobalt and headed into the empire of the Shield.

The straight, smooth road bore no mark of man's passage in an hour's travel, save countless corpses of porcupines crushed by his wheels. A yard from the pavement the Shield, oldest solid substance on our planet, and mother of all things, rolled in mammary swelling to a hard northern horizon under a dome of gunmetal. The northern twilight, like the rock beneath it, was flecked with precious mineral. Gold dust danced in the long sunset, and the air carried the old, tantalizing Canadian smell of wild rose, acrid spruce, Balm of Gilead, and damp muskeg—a smell sweet and bitter with boyhood memory and a man's vain regrets.

Suddenly the silence was shattered by a thundering frog chorus, daylight died grudgingly with a last scarlet tear, and to the northward the lights of Kirkland Lake glowed like a false dawn. As we neared the town we could make out a red neon cross against the black fringe of the world and then the ghostly mine towers floating in the moonlight.

It was after twelve o'clock when we reached the brassy main street of Kirkland Lake, but on a Saturday night no one had yet thought of going to bed. We could hardly find a place to park our car. Every restaurant was crammed. Store windows blazed with displays of refrigerators, washing machines, electric gadgets, new automobiles, women's lingerie, evening gowns, and all the essentials of civilization, more than a hundred miles from nowhere.

The townspeople saw nothing strange in this little patch of light amid the dark void of the Shield. To us the town looked as unreal as a stage set erected half an hour ago, to be dismantled and carted away at daybreak. Of course it wasn't really a town at all, for all its solid business buildings, modern homes, and shiny new cars; it was a miners' camp.

We could not hope to sleep in the stifling cubicle of the hotel. The Diamond Drillers Convention, or some such festive company, had taken over the town and would be drilling enthusiastically with a clink of glasses until dawn at least. So we went for a walk. No one else was walking. Kirkland Lake seems to travel exclusively on wheels and boasts the ownership of more cars per head than any other place in America. Yet a block from the glaring main street we found ourselves on the lip of wilderness and limbo.

The cold northern shoulder of the earth sloped downward to the pole in a hush punctuated here and there by the tick of men's machinery, in an opaque darkness pierced by his few pale winks of light. He can bore a few miles of tunnel into the body of the Shield, smelt some fragments of its ore. His camps—called towns or even cities—leave hardly a bruise on a surface little changed since it rose from the steaming liquid of creation.

The houses of Kirkland Lake clutch the bare rock faces. The rough floor of the Shield cuts through the back yards. Sidewalks sometimes reel six feet above the road, and the road is level with the next row of roofs.

Some thrifty householders have managed to grow a tree or two, a bed of flowers, or a patch of lettuce in a square yard of soil. The rich have made a few ambitious gardens. But this town remains physically and spiritually a camp. Perhaps there can never be anything but camps upon the Shield, whatever they call themselves.

We inquired our way to the office of *The Northern Daily News* and found the editor, a blonde slip of a girl, working late. She said that, after her home town of Galt in the Ontario farm country, she had been overpowered by the glacial boulders of the Shield. Then, going home on a holiday, she had found that the south was no longer home. The north had got her. It gets everyone.

The mystery, she intimated, lived in the land and in the people. The land was the most beautiful she had ever seen, once she adjusted her urban eyes to its stern contours, and the people were the best she had ever found in Canada—generous, candid, and neighborly as no other people.

The symbols of their life, she said, were the mine towers, understandable only if you looked at them in moonlight or against the dawn. A stranger might find only ugliness in these crooked steeples of metal and wood, but after a time they began to appear beautiful in their line and angular composition, like a good painting. They were the marks of men's occupancy, his title deeds to the Shield. And down below them, deep down in the substance of the Shield, men were working day and night. That, said the girlish editor, made you think. She advised us to take a second look at the towers.

We took a second look, but to us the towers were just black exclamation marks, clumsy and ill-shaped, punctuating the bright alphabet of the stars. A sensitive girl from Galt might see in these poor wooden sheds the cathedral spires of England or the minarets of Baghdad. The men who had made them and now labored in secret runnels far below had penetrated a mystery too deep for us. We were only southern Canadians, suddenly overcome by a sky that hung in spangled ceiling over emptiness and instantly cut us down to size.

Retreating from a sky and an earth too large and brutal to be borne, we pushed our way through the crowded doors of a restaurant at two o'clock on a Sunday morning. Naturally another Chinese philosopher, the universal Canadian, the same man who wears slightly different masks from St. John's to Victoria, presided over this establishment. A second universal Canadian was present also, the miner who has followed the rainbow all his life and found no pot of gold. At the moment he was a little drunk and meditated a duel of honor.

The cause of this feud evidently went back a long way. As it was no business of ours, we turned discreetly to a loathsome mess of bacon and eggs—Canadian restaurant food being almost universally loathsome—while the miner, his hard-rock face convulsed in rage, informed a tipsy youth that he would meet him outside, at leisure, and destroy him with his bare hands. The youth tottered to the door. The miner forgot the quarrel and undertook to educate us in the history of the north.

We were in luck. We had stumbled upon a rich ore body. For the next hour that man drilled us with an eye like a diamond drill and recited his private Odyssey. It was the story of his kind everywhere.

Yes, he'd known them all in his time. He remembered Harry Oakes and W. H. Wright, who staked Wright-Hargraves and Lake Shore, filled Kirkland Lake with sludge, built a town on this foundation, and began the Golden Mile of seven mines.

"And a lot of good it did Oakes," the miner said. "They murdered him somewheres down in the West Indies. You seen it in the papers? Well, he should of stayed up here where he belonged. And Wright, he went to Toronto and bought a newspaper and race horses. Too bad."

He even remembered, or said he did, the fabled Fred La Rose, a blacksmith, whose mine was the first producer in Cobalt and the start of the great rush.

"Why," he affirmed, wagging a bony fist under my nose, "when I first come in—I was only a kid then—they was hand-cobbin' the stuff, just breakin' it up with a hammer and shippin' it in gunny sacks, it was that rich. Pure jewelry."

His eyes were glazed with drink and recollection. "The Porcupine!" he muttered. "Sufferin' God, the Porcupine! Say, have you ever heard tell of the Porcupine? There was a guy from Klondike, name of D'Aigle, only knew placer, you see, and started drillin' and never saw what he had and went away and Benny Hollinger and some other guys come along and flipped a coin for the claims and that was the Hollinger. Can you beat it? Then a guy by the name of Preston fell down a rock and landed on a vein. That was the Dome."

So the great names, the facts and fables of the Shield drifted through his talk, together with items from his own adventures —the hopeful strike, the promise of opulence, the disappointment, the endless trek from mine to mine. Others had struck it rich, and he had ended where we found him, in a grimy Chinese joint.

I repeated the question I had asked in Cobalt: why didn't he leave the north? Of course I got the same answer.

"Once you're in," he said, "you can't get out. And who wants to? Sure, the big boys in Toronto get all the gravy. They don't even come up here to see us work, not them. Might get their shoes muddy. But they miss all the fun down there. What do them pansies know about minin'? They only own the mines."

He permitted himself a bitter little laugh and stretched his hands across the table for me to see the callused palms and crushed fingers.

"That," he said, "is minin'. Fifty-three years of minin' and still broke. But, hell, it's okay. This country's only beginnin'. They haven't even scratched her yet."

His long recital and much coffee had sobered him considerably. Remembering his quarrel of honor, he proposed to settle it outside and return after he had destroyed his enemy. I never saw that dauntless old face again. No doubt he is still following his rainbow to the end.

It was after three o'clock now, and revelers still surged through the restaurant. They were of every breed, look, and language. Though they spoke in English, French, German, Polish, and tongues beyond recognition, all of them bore the unmistakable mark of the north: not physically, but in the texture and slant of the spirit.

An assortment of diverse breeds had merged here in the single, unvarying breed of the miner. These men, and their women, too—the chunky, laughing women who followed their mates wherever the trail happened to lead—might seem to settle down in a comfortable camp like Kirkland Lake, but they were not settlers. They were rovers. They spent their money as fast as they got it, on cars, on trips, on a good time, and then moved on to the next camp.

Their talk was of neighborly affairs, of baseball, movies, fishing, and the minutiae of the small town anywhere. Yet it was not the talk that you would hear south of the Shield, for it exchanged the family news of the universal miner—the price of gold, silver, lead, and copper, rumors of a new strike to the northward, tales of sudden wealth in the uranium fields, and shrewd, detailed discussion of the big mining companies' annual reports.

They knew their craft, from the deep tunnels to the stock market, and they spoke against a background of caste tightly established in the hierarchy of the mine executives, the engineers, the businessmen of the town, and, at the bottom of the heap, the miners working with their hands.

Now they were assembled in this nighttime den as lonely men always assemble, as the Indians squatted around a campfire, to escape the loneliness and the dark. They had come to find some light, some company, and perhaps some drink after the labors that mainly enrich other men far away in the boardrooms and clubs of the city. But by the irony of all things, the working people, as the old miner had said, seemed to have more fun than the owners of the stock certificates. Here a new car is a king's ransom, a tarpaper shack is a castle, and a glass of beer is the poor man's champagne.

Thus through the restaurant there ran that invisible but inviolate line between the boisterous, restless, rootless northern folk and all the settled folk south of the Shield—men of wilderness and rock, men of city and cultivated field.

The short northern night of summer had died when we reached the street. The mine towers, robbed of their mystery, stood up stark and hideous against the pink sunrise, their machines still clanking and grinding on the Sabbath. The main street, after the night's glitter, was silent and deserted. The town had shrunk to a few yards of pavement, a huddle of buildings, a minor blotch on the bosom of the Shield.

That mighty horseshoe pressed down on more than half the nation was not what we had expected after seeing it only at night or, in daylight, from trains and airplanes.

We had pictured an unbroken and uniform sweep of badland, Christmas trees, and glassy puddles. We found the Shield varying from mile to mile as the rock welled up into little mountains, sank into swamp and muskeg, parted to hold big lakes or circular inkwells, disappeared under a fur of black spruce, and opened now and then into lush meadows for man's plow.

The fertile belt of clay, the rich fields, big barns, and sleek cattle around the dairy town of Earlton, about one hundred miles within the Shield, looked almost unbelievable after the sterile rock north and south of it. A young French Canadian farmer said most of the people hereabouts came from Quebec and were doing fine. The ancient civilization of the St. Lawrence had leap-frogged across the stone dike and prospered in this remote pocket of agriculture. Plenty more land could be cleared, this man said. Life was good and everybody friendly, also bilingual, as they should be.

We picked up another French Canadian, a forlorn and soiled figure who had been hitch-hiking his way to the prairies, had been robbed of his valise and money at Timmins, had slept by the roadside without food for two days and "lost his courage." Now he was beating his way home to Montreal with a "broken heart." For once the westward march of his people had ended in retreat.

His spirits picked up, however, after he had breakfasted on the remains of yesterday's picnic, and he entertained us with French songs and nasal imitations of Maurice Chevalier until we came to North Bay on Lake Nipissing.

There he turned east and we turned west into still another Ontario, which is rapidly becoming a racial suburb of Quebec. Sturgeon Falls, for example, a town built by the electrical power of the raging Sturgeon River, prints its street signs in English and French. We heard little English among its people.

To the westward a combination of minerals, timber, and water power is making a series of industrial centers in the most unlikely places. Probably nature never intended man to live here, but around the smelter town of Sudbury he has improved on her work of desolation.

The fumes of his acids, in the process of extracting most of the world's nickel, have killed every blade of vegetation, stripped the rock of its thin disguise, and produced a fair replica of hell or Hiroshima. One might be traveling, for several miles along the highway, on the surface of some dead planet. Sudbury crouches around the belching Moloch of its smelter. It rears new mountains of slag. It builds a city in a vacuum of aching stone, and looks from the distance like a casual outcrop of gray ore.

As the heat gushed out of a stone oven at a hundred degrees Fahrenheit, we staggered into a little store for a bottle of cold pop to discover, behind the counter, the stately figure of Colonel Blimp, speaking in the Colonel's accent. I suspected that this English gentleman might be oppressed by the mixed population of Sudbury, and asked him obliquely if there were many foreigners in town. He bridled at my question.

"What do you mean, foreigners?" he demanded. "This, sir, is an international city. No people are foreigners to us. They're all people."

Thus rebuked, we sped westward on a busy highway at the customary local speed of eighty miles an hour.

It was too hot to pause at Blind River, a name as magical today as Cobalt was half a century ago. This village is surrounded by perhaps the largest treasury of uranium yet discovered, and confidently expects to be a leading Canadian city. A smiling old priest was greeting his parishioners at the steps of his church, but by this time such a pleasant rustic scene can hardly have survived a potential metropolis of the atomic age, an unlikely seed scattered by the first nuclear bomb.

Soon we were in a region of hill, forest, lake, and river. It is cooled by the refrigerating apparatus of Lake Huron and is perfectly designed for the camper, fisherman, and painter. Now we began to understand why those pioneer Canadian painters, the distinguished Group of Seven, had gone gently mad in such surroundings. Their reckless brush strokes seem extravagant only to those who have not beheld their model.

That night we camped beside Lake Huron, in such an amphitheater of terraced green rock, wild flowers, tufted islands, wheeling gulls, and dancing fireflies as the Group of Seven has never quite captured.

An early start brought us to Sault Ste. Marie for breakfast. The Sault is a town, to be sure, a town prettier and better built than most on a single main street several miles long, so that a businessman must take a taxi to visit his neighbor in the next office. But the Sault is something more important than a town. It is the nexus and hinge of North America.

French *voyageurs* found that out long ago. Here, on June 4, 1671, Sieur de St. Lusson proclaimed, by musket fire and a ceremonial sod raised on his swordpoint, France's lawful claim to America entire. Though events worked out otherwise, nothing could alter the Sault's place as the fulcrum of continental geography.

Beside the canal locks that drop Lake Superior twenty-two feet into Lake Huron, we fell into talk with a handsome gentleman in seaman's blue serge and peaked cap. His face was dark and finely cut, his mustache was fierce, his eyes were gentle. He might have been a descendant of those old *voyageurs*. In fact he was, on the maternal French Canadian side of his family.

He gave us a gruff reception at first, like a captain long accustomed to the discipline of the bridge, but we surmised, from his attachment to a mongrel named Mike, that he had a softer side. When I ventured to remark that the locks appeared interesting, he reproved my ignorance with a cold look.

"If," he said sharply, "one hydrogen bomb dropped right here, America would be paralyzed."

That was hardly an exaggeration. The largest single tide of continental freight flows through these locks in the holds of some two thousand Great Lakes ships.

Having registered those facts, the captain mellowed somewhat and invited us to the snug cabin of a tugboat, the command of his later years, to examine certain relics. He showed them to us in an offhand fashion, but we could see that they were precious.

Adventures incomprehensible to anyone except a lake navigator were recorded in old charts, photographs of forgotten ships, newspaper reports of wrecks, collisions, and fires, portraits of many gallant seamen drowned in some of the world's worst water.

The captain had gone to sea as a boy (for the Lakes are indeed a terrible sea of fog, storm, and short, wrenching swell). In those days, he said, some of the older ships were still made of wood. Even on the newly built "whalebacks" a seaman must slither over an open deck between bow and stern. A skipper navigated by whistle, experience, and instinct. Today life afloat was much easier and safer. Enclosed passages reached all parts of a modern lake ship. It was protected by radar and connected with shore by telephone.

"They even have good food," he added. "And no bedbugs! But in this water it's no cinch and never will be. Often it's easier to take a ship across the Atlantic than down the Lakes —more room and a longer swell. I've done both."

No, he'd never lost a ship. His luck, he confessed, had always been good. Still, he'd come uncomfortably close to disaster a good many times. Take the memorable storm of December 11, 1936. That was a corker, all right. He'd wallowed into Fort William with decks awash, ship half sunk, and rigging turned into one big icicle. Some skippers, not so lucky that night, had joined uncounted companions in the bottomless cold of Lake Superior.

Well, it had been a good life. The captain fingered the photographs and clippings, his eyes full of memories, but made no attempt to communicate them. This unique race of fresh-water seamen who have survived the Lakes and revised the economy of a continent can never communicate their adventures.

"Sometimes she was kind of tough out there," he admitted, and fell into the silence of his craft. What more could be said to a landlubber?

We returned to the wall of the Canadian lock, empty at the moment, and watched a steady march of vessels stride from Lake Huron into the MacArthur lock on the American shore. They loomed up vaguely in the mist, announcing their arrival with a scream from their whistles. All of them looked alike to me. The captain knew the name, dimensions, and freight capacity of every ship at a glance.

To the westward, in Lake Superior, other ships awaited their turn, each a silhouette of high bridge in bow, funnel in stern, and nothing between but a black pencil line. The captain named them for us at a distance of two miles and explained the evolution of their design through nearly two centuries of experience since the days of birchbark canoes.

These were floating machines, automatically loaded and unloaded. One of them could carry, in 600 or 700 feet of hull, the grain of 40,000 prairie acres, the freight of 200 boxcars, and the material for 60,000,000 loaves of bread. I thought them efficient and ugly. The captain reproved me again. They were beautiful, he said.

Some fishermen dangled their lines idly in the tailrace of the St. Mary's River below the powerhouse, doubtless forgetting that Frenchmen had portaged around these wild waters not long ago and the fur men of the North West Company had dug a ditch twenty-five hundred feet long and eight feet wide to carry their canoes and bateaux. A model of the little lock on that first Sault canal—it was built at a cost of "up-wards of £4,000" in 1798 and destroyed by the Americans in the War of 1812—has been installed amid a sweep of lawn and flowers to remind Canadians of their fathers' work.

Nobody seemed to notice the reminder that morning. And how many Canadians or Americans outside the Sault know that Charles T. Harvey, an imaginative salesman of household scales, built the first ship canal, on the American side, in 1853, at a cost of $999,802.46, forty years before the first Canadian canal, which cost $34,000,000?

As the Transcanada Highway had yet to be built along the bluffs of Lake Superior, and the only available Canadian road lay far to the northward, we made an American detour south-ward through Duluth and, turning back across the boundary, came upon an astounding picture.

The grain elevators of Fort William and Port Arthur rise, lean and lonely, beside the indigo pool of Thunder Bay like the towers of Carcassonne. The Canadian towers seemed to us more impressive than the French. Besides, the elevators, in the simplicity of their functional design, are genuine and orig-inal, whereas self-conscious Carcassonne is an overprimped reproduction of another age.

Clarence Decatur Howe, who built these concrete columns, is usually accounted only an eminent Canadian politician and businessman. At the Lakehead he had unconsciously qualified as one of our leading artists.

His work, seen at a distance in clean vertical line, is our nearest approach to Egypt's Pyramids, England's Tower of London, or India's Taj Mahal. At any rate, it expresses exactly our grim and practical northern life. All the labor, the silence, the loneliness and stern beauty of our land broods in these gray cylinders, rank on rank astride the blue metal of the lake.

The visiting spacemen of the future will make nothing of these colossal structures, will probably ascribe their upright sproutings to a religion which worshipped strange and savage gods. In a way those future antiquarians will be right. Canada worships the gods of commerce. The engineer is its idol; the production and movement of material things are its constant fascination. Those elevators of the Lakehead contain our tribal deities.

They contain much else unknown to the passer-by. From the outside a terminal elevator is a motionless bin, supposedly filled with grain. Inside it is a workshop of whirling machines, conceived by Disney and operated by his Seven Dwarfs, very hot and dusty from their work.

The boxcars roll in from the prairies. A pair of mechanical hands grasps them, upends them, and shakes out their grain; or if this latest unloading gadget has not yet been installed, two muscular men, masked against the dust, wade waist-deep into the cars with squares of board attached to cables. As the cables drag the men and their boards out again, the grain comes with them. It is caught on belts moving perhaps sixty miles an hour and carried in a brown ribbon to the "leg," which lifts it in an endless chain of buckets to the upper stories.

There it is automatically weighed in gigantic tanks, poured out through movable chutes, cleaned on vibrating screens, and passed under a magnet to extract any metal scraps from some farmer's machinery out west. ("Watch out for that magnet," said the elevator boss. "Get too close and it'll pull your watch out of your pocket, or maybe your gold inlays.")

At last the clean golden stream is pouring into the belly of a ship and oozing slowly through the many separate holds like thick syrup. A man beside every spout flicks samples from the stream with a tin dipper, and in an office near by the final verdict on the farmer's work is quickly rendered.

The grader, a great man in the hierarchy of the elevator, spreads a handful of grain across a tray. He looks at it, rubs it between his fingers, and, within two minutes, must say whether it is Number One Northern or maybe fit only for cattle feed.

How does he know? He cannot explain. The color tells him something—this rich red stuff is obviously of highest grade—but his fingers tell him more, and, after a moment's doubt, his experience tells him everything. Not only experience but also affection. He fondles the grain as a miser fondles gold.

This stuff is, of course, much more valuable by proper measurement than the almost worthless gold of the financial myth, and it is moving out of the Lakes to the river, to the great canals, to the ports of foreign lands and the stomach of mankind. It will soon be a loaf in some London housewife's oven and served up with sticky jam for an English workman's afternoon tea, or it will be eaten by brown children or yellow in the forgotten byways and lost villages of the world.

The gaping decks of the grain ship were battened down. The captain climbed aboard, telling me that this was a dull trade and he wished to God he'd become a dentist or an insurance salesman in some warm house ashore. He blew a farewell toot of the whistle, and the long black vessel, low in the water and pregnant with her living freight of seed, wallowed out into the lake.

The townsman of Fort William who had us in tow boasted that the suction pump of the Lakehead handled more grain than any other port on earth. He showed us the paper mills, the torrent of iron ore paralleling the torrent of grain, and a dozen other industries that make Fort William and Port Arthur, beside it, two of the busiest towns in Canada and the home of forty racial stocks. ("In our champion hockey teams," our guide said, "half the names are always foreign.")

This place has come a long way since two roving rascals, Groseilliers and Radisson, first sighted Thunder Bay, since Du Lhut started buying furs here, since the Nor'westers founded their Fort William and Lord Selkirk captured it by force of arms for the Hudson's Bay Company.

Alas, the soil of all that rousing history is buried under the railway tracks. But Fort William takes its past seriously, maintains a fine museum of antiquities, and worships its legends—especially the legendary Indian maiden Green Mantle, who led her captors over Kakabeka Falls and died with them rather than betray her tribe.

An obvious question must plague every visitor. Why these two separate, well-built, and handsome towns against the blue lake, the elevators, the ships in ceaseless shuttle, and the square shoulders of Mount McKay? Why should a community organically one be divided by an imaginary municipal line and by a mental line much more visible and profound?

The natives spoke obliquely of this division and hurried on to something else, as a man may hint at things unseen and not intended for human sight.

Rudyard Kipling, pausing here for an hour or two, grasped, as usual, the inner facts. The Twin Cities, he wrote, "hate each other with the pure, poisonous, passionate hatred which makes towns grow. If Providence wiped out one of them the survivor would pine away and die—a mateless hate-bird."

We did no inquire too deeply about these things. One does not question the mysteries of the tribal deities who brood in the concrete temples. It was clear anyway that the Lakehead belonged to Ontario only by provincial statute. Its eyes are turned to the west, where the grain comes from. The people of southern Ontario and the people of Thunder Bay are as unlike as Canadians can be—a settled society and an impatient band of pioneers.

As westerners we were prejudiced in this old folk argument. We like a breed of western men who can casually build an industrial complex five hundred miles from anywhere, blast mountains, toss the grain of the prairies into the conveyor belt of the Lakes, plan to make a province of their own someday, throw up their own colossi and endow them with spirits, while moose and bear wander into town.

Yet how minute and pathetic are all these works upon the dark infinitude of the Shield! Walking the busy streets of Fort William and Port Arthur, a man feels the security of human habitation. The Shield seems far away. From an airplane he looks down on a Lake Superior which is no more than a bowl of dark blue porcelain flecked with white soapsuds. The largest grain ship is smaller than a pin. The elevators have become gray pebbles at the edge of a black ocean undulating, wave on wave, to the Arctic.

It is quite wrong, however, to imagine, as most Canadians do, that the Lakehead, surrounded by barren rock and squat forest, must always live on the manufacturing and transportation industries. As we soon found, on driving west, the stone desert of the Shield contains here a huge oasis of agricultural land. It should become one of the nation's major farm areas when it is cleared.

A swarthy young giant of Polish descent, whose father had cleared a fine farm now waving in hay and grain, told us that this was the best farm country in Canada.

We asked him if he ever grew tired of hard labor and thought perhaps of taking a job at high wages in the industries of Fort William. "Not me," he said. "I'm a farmer. This is good land, and there's still miles and miles of it to clear."

He and others like him were pushing back the forest far northward to the edge of the Shield. We left him at his gate, a happy man, a symbolic figure of western Canada, the portrait of the pioneer. Though the prairies lay far ahead, we knew we were already in the west.

GOLDEN DAYS

*S*ome night in late September the steady trickle ceases on a
lip of mountain rock. In the morning the rock shines with a
new and solid coat. A white film clings to the edge of the
upland pond, melts by noon, but advances again in the darkness. A bear, a deer, a gopher, or even a man sniffs the air and
knows that summer has begun to die.

Every Canadian understands those faint signs of the great
change. Better perhaps than any other North American, he
knows autumn. It is peculiarly his by long experience in a
northern land.

Since the white man's first year beside the rock of Quebec,
when Cartier and his shivering crew watched ice seal the St.
Lawrence and cut the road to home, autumn has touched Canadians not as a season but as a warning; not as a mere lapse
in summer but as the first tentative stride of winter; not as a
relief from labor but as the time of desperate preparations.
The cold will soon come down from the north.

The Canadian countryman hastily stores the last of his
crops, drives his cattle from the hills to the winter range, hauls
up his boats, chops his wood, and battens down his house. The
largest city must install its storm windows, fill its oil tanks,
overhaul its snowplows, light the furnaces of its offices and
factories, fit out its children in warm clothing, and protect
its communication lines from ice, snow, and the mad Artic
gales. These golden days of autumn will not last long.

Nature's preparations in this latitude are infinitely larger
and more complex than man's. Canada is no place for Keats's
female figure, drowsed by the fume of poppies. Here autumn
is purely masculine, a workingman. His rough male kiss can be
felt on frosty dawns. His labors are sensed through eye, nose,

and skin. His hurried chemistry must recolor the land in brief seasonal exhibition before all colors are expunged overnight by a single daub of white. His strong muscles must drain the sap of every tree, unload the summer freight of foliage, coat the lakes, dam the streams, and slowly build the Gothic architecture and glistening gargoyles of the ice.

Though these are not quite the energies of life, they contain a kind of sublife, inorganic, senseless, but more potent than any organism. A force not unlike life solidifies at one touch the liquid of four million square miles. The counterpart of spring's explosion arrests the growth of all vegetable cells. The power of freezing and expanding moisture convulses earth, splits rock, and gradually shatters mountains. Man is not immune to this process. A change in physical climate changes, with rude shock, the climate of the human mind.

A Canadian feels the autumn in body, mind, and most of all in memory. He sees it with the eye and with the mind's eye, the racial eye, surveying the autumns of three hundred years. It is the same autumn that Cartier knew, for all men's inventions have hardly touched it beyond the city's streets.

Maples turn to cool flame on the Laurentians, the tamaracks of the Shield to rusty red, the central plains to yellow. Poplar leaves whirl like gold coins and spill down the Rockies' slopes. The coastal forest drinks deep of rain after the summer's thirst, deciduous foliage falls, and evergreens stand black against a monotony of gray mist.

Down the flyways of coast and interior the waterfowl move south. Salmon swim into the rivers from the sea, lay their eggs, and die. Apples swell and redden in the valleys of Annapolis, Niagara, and Okanagan. Wheat pours into prairie elevators. The last ships race from the Lakehead to the St. Lawrence. A spicy smell of pickles engulfs the farmhouse kitchen and penetrates even the apartment kitchenette.

No man knows better than the Canadian this season's magic and its melancholy. All men in Canada watch, with joy and foreboding, the hot blue skies of noon, the cold, spangled skies of night, the crisp mornings of frost. All men know what lies ahead. A chill wind is blowing, leaves are falling, and a white specter is striding out of the north.

CHAPTER TEN

The Hub

THE Pre-Cambrian Shield ended as suddenly as a prison wall. Like prisoners released through a stone gateway, we entered the central plain of North America.

No stranger can fail to recognize that formidable fact of geography. It hits him straight between the eyes like a physical blow. He will not guess, however, that he has entered a distinct compartment of a plain trisected by invisible lines. This compartment is named Manitoba; it is a sovereign province, but it is much more than that. In a subtle fashion known only to the natives, it is a civilization and, by Canadian standards, an old one.

Far to the westward a pillar of smoke and a faint smudge against the horizon marked the capital of Manitoba's civilization. As we crossed the floor of the prairies—as horizontal as if they had been laid down with a spirit level—Winnipeg slowly emerged in an upended slab of basalt upon the circular brink of emptiness.

We had known and loved it so long that this town, whether glistening in winter frost or beaded in summer sweat, always welcomed us like an old friend. At last we had reached the hub and crossroads of Canada, the beating pulse, the very heart, halfway between the oceans.

But Winnipeg had changed. By the estimate of the old-timers, it had deteriorated.

The change was not apparent in the city's affluent exterior, the wide noisy canyon of Portage Avenue, the spreading suburbs, the well-kept, thrifty, and peculiarly boyish look which has always illuminated this place and its people. Nevertheless, a fundamental shift had altered the economic, political, and, more important, the mental gravity of the central plain. Winnipeg no longer ruled it from the lakes to the mountains. John Wesley Dafoe was gone.

The Manitoba Club, that genial haunted house on Broadway, boasts a certain leather chair, scuffed and torn by long use and seldom occupied nowadays. No one, I suppose, can ever truly occupy it again. This is Dafoe's chair, the vacant throne of a dead age.

Remembering Dafoe as the greatest Canadian of his time, I entered the club with reverence. The familiar chair still stood in the reading-room among the chairs of the old monarch's vanished privy council, known in the folklore of Winnipeg as the Sanhedrin. The room was vacant. Doubtless the younger men in the club had never seen the Sanhedrin in session and could not grasp the full meaning of its disappearance. The old-timers know.

When reclining here at ease, rather like a tired lion, Dafoe said little. If he spoke, it was usually in the farmer's antique idiom acquired in the Cumbermere Valley of Ontario or at the tough hamlet of Bully's Acre. Mostly he listened and laughed, his huge body shaking in silent convulsion, his strawstack of hair sprawling across his ruddy face.

He was always thinking, though, and his thoughts were soon transferred by the stub of a pencil from the Sanhedrin's throne room into the classic English style of the *Free Press* editorial page to shake the nation.

In those days he and his newspaper represented a solid, concentrated, and potent force in the nation's affairs. They spoke for the entire west from its undisputed capital of Winnipeg. They stood for the old-fashioned Liberalism of the Manchester School, the simple, farm-based democracy of Jefferson, the economics of Adam Smith, the distrust of centralized government and mass mind, the theory of the sacred, individual person.

Now Dafoe was gone, and his era with him. Its ideals of individualism had been replaced by the seemingly new and actually age-old ideal of collectivism and big government. The Sanhedrin was dissolved. Winnipeg had become the capital of Manitoba only. The prairie citadel of ideas had fallen before the mass march.

Manitoba, where prairie civilization began a century before the rest of the central plain was settled, had lost its dominance, not merely in terms of population, business, and politics, but also in a far deeper sense. The whole climate of opinion which surrounded Dafoe's era and made him Canada's ablest prophet had changed. His world had been repealed, his western kingdom shattered.

Still, if Winnipeg's former sovereignty has decayed, I find it on every visit a bigger, busier, richer city than ever. It is still our strongest and most coherent Canadian community. It is filled with our liveliest folk.

This I can say with a fine impartiality, since I detest the outside look, the flat terrain and cruel climate of Winnipeg, but respect its soul just this side idolatry. Once I belonged to Winnipeg, in a journalist's capacity, but Winnipeg never belonged to me. That was the trouble.

Winnipeg cannot belong to anyone, can never be understood by anyone or perhaps endured by anyone except its natives, an exclusive brotherhood. For the Manitoba cell of the prairies, outwardly a part of the west and closely joined to Ontario by geography, is inwardly disjoined from both, is practically watertight and leakproof, even in the mass age, and Winnipeg is the hard nucleus of this cell.

But some of Winnipeg's inhabitants, as I soon discovered, were rather worried about its future. The reason for this worry, and much else, can be discerned in the Manitoba Club, if you remember its departed elders and what they stood for.

This hushed and stately institution may resent an invasion of its privacy. It cannot begrudge us a western history shared by the nation. Much of that history was planned and enacted in the club, or in an area of half a square mile around it.

A few yards off stands the last remnant of Fort Garry, a stone-and-wooden arch through which passed the *voyageurs* from every river of the west, Canadian and American.

Near by, the Hudson's Bay Company, once the governing power of the whole west, administers its far-flung commercial empire from a modern office building, but maintains there, with honorable nostalgia and jealous care, the documents, the relics, and the proud spirit of its unique sovereignty.

Just beyond Main Street flows the Red River, carrying a cargo of events older than La Vérendrye, the first French Canadian to burst through the Shield; events as old, indeed, as human life in the center of the continent.

A block or so to the south, the Assiniboine merges with the body of its parent in the nodal point of the prairies where human events were entered for so long in Indian times.

Across the Red lie the bones of Louis Riel, the mad Métis rebel and forgotten father of Manitoba.

Naturally, therefore, on such a site, the club became in later times the spiritual node, forum, and nerve center of the west.

I was not surprised to meet here a survivor of the great days who lamented their departure with much eloquence and soothing drink. Not long ago, he told me, Winnipeg had been the entrepôt of the west and its only real city. Now its long monopoly, dating back to the fur trade of Fort Garry, was broken by vigorous competitors in Saskatchewan and Alberta. Edmonton, he said, would outstrip Winnipeg in the lifetime of the present generation, but happily he would not be alive to see that catastrophe.

These were the visible and calculable facts. As the old Winnipegger explained, they were not the important ones. What, I asked, would he consider an important fact? Without hesitation he replied: "The Grain Exchange is closed."

He spoke like a messenger announcing the destruction of a shrine and the murder of its vestal virgins. No Canadian beyond the prairies can understand it, but something of that sort —tragic, unnatural, and insane, as they think—has happened to the men who used to trade wheat by auction, whose hoarse voices in the pit could be heard daily and hourly from here to Chicago, Liverpool, and Moscow. If Adam Smith's infallible Market and his species of purely economic men had reared a temple and enshrined a priestcraft anywhere, it was in Winnipeg. The Grain Exchange was the temple. The traders were its priests.

By closing the Exchange, my friend affirmed, the Canadian government had not merely changed an established trading mechanism and undertaken to sell all the western wheat through a government board, but had closed an epoch that started with Lord Selkirk's first Scottish settlers on the Red River nearly a century and a half ago. It had canceled Winnipeg's power to fix wheat prices by auction and transferred that power to an organ of the state.

There, said the old-timer, was a local fact comprehending all the larger facts of our age. He meant, of course, the swing in society everywhere from individualism to collectivism. When even the rabidly individualistic farmers insisted on selling their grain collectively and pooled their profits, something profound and incalculable had happened to the west. At the same time the west, once a united force, powerful and often decisive in Ottawa, with Dafoe as its regnant voice, had gone into voluntary political liquidation by splitting its votes among four splintered parties.

This process symbolizes in one farm area and one city built by farms another organic change in Canadian society at large. The nation is moving from the farm to the city. Some ten years ago twenty-five per cent of the Canadian labor force worked on farms. Now the farms support only fifteen per cent, and will soon support less.

As in all industrial nations, the metropolitan age has concentrated people in a few huge clusters like Winnipeg or in the smaller towns around it. The rural population of the prairies has been dropping rapidly. Fewer hands in the fields produce more crops by the use of machinery. Cities like Winnipeg are swelling with grave symptoms of dropsy.

Having considered the latest figures and many rousing memories, I left the club to take a good look at a town which had long been my second home.

The lavish width and reckless pedestrians of Portage Avenue; the rundown look of lower Main Street, whose day has passed; the City Hall, that incomparable masterpiece of pinnacled and leering ugliness; the parliament buildings in whimsied mixture of miscellaneous architectures and topped by the Golden Boy, a civic idol; the pot-bellied curve of Wellington Crescent and its double line of rich men's castles, many shaped like high-class penitentiaries; the older streets of broken mansions beside some new business block; the trees laboriously planted and faithfully tended in garden and boulevard until only a few spires prick the green ceiling of summer; the savage winter winds around the Fort Garry Hotel and the sparrows roosting for warmth on the light bulbs of the porte-cochere; the roomy park where they grow bananas and tropical blooms in a vast conservatory while the demented blizzards dance out of Hudson Bay—all these things were as familiar to me as my own back yard.

I also knew a little of the North End, on the wrong side of the C.P.R. tracks, an enclave of foreign languages, almost a separate city, and the oldest Canadian melting-pot.

Sometimes I had been admitted to the big houses of the rich and watched with admiration the speed, hunger, thirst, and spacious talk of Winnipeg's upper social set, a proud aristocracy within Canada's most democratic town; to the homes of those modest scholars who make Manitoba University one of Canada's best; to a hospitality unknown elsewhere and handed down, without dilution, from the smoky parlors of Fort Garry.

In short, I knew Winnipeg to be our strongest community because it is alone in the terrifying vacuum of the plains, must think its own thoughts, invent its own pleasures, and do its own work. Surrounded by a waterless sea, it builds its own island, battens down against the perpetual storms of cold, heat, and river flood, flashes from its lighthouse an indomitable ray of courage, and, in a voice never quiet day or night, shouts its defiance at the darkness of midcontinent.

But it is for natives only. Not many Canadians are strong enough to sustain its climate or its pace. Why, there were winter mornings when I walked half a mile to the *Free Press* office in an advanced state of rigor mortis, and I have sat all day in a cold bath when the wind came in blowtorch blast from the south.

Human life here duplicates the restless weather which has become the pride of Winnipeg and the jest of the nation. Only natives can keep track of all the teeming people's enterprises, the indigenous ballet, the symphony orchestra, the clubs, societies, charities, celebrations, campaigns, concerts, theatricals, athletics, and so much debate, local politics, and bewildering civic adventure that the visitor reels out of town, exhausted after one week-end.

Considering its circumstances, Winnipeg must be accounted the most prodigious growth in Canada. Prodigious and altogether different in kind from any other Canadian community. It is not glamorous and sinful like Montreal, nor obese and smug like Toronto, nor scenic, brassy, and *nouveau-riche* like Vancouver. It has no glamour, no scenery. It is too busy for sin. It moves too rapidly to grow obese, and must struggle too hard ever to become smug. It is too old to be *nouveau-riche* and, besides, it lacks the means.

Winnipeg is closer than any other Canadian city to the earth, to harvest and common things. The civilization at the junction of the Red and the Assiniboine is flavored with the strong juices of early Canada, but it contains a hidden paradox.

Though it stands alone, it has become our least provincial city with the single exception of Montreal. Compelled to mind its own business and build a metropolis out of Red River mud, it shaped itself to fit the wide world. Collecting the prairie grain and selling it at the far ends of the earth, Winnipeg must know, in the ordinary course of business, what crops are ripening, what markets fluctuating, what governments rising or falling everywhere.

Moreover, many of its people came from those far places, and Winnipeg has taken a daunting race problem in its stride. It welcomes immigrants into its professions, appoints a Ukrainian to its provincial cabinet, a Jew to its courts. Precisely because it is so conscious of race, it abhors racial discrimination.

Go to Montreal, Toronto, or Vancouver and you will hear men talk of money, minerals, timber, oil, gas, transportation, and factories. Go to Winnipeg and you will hear them talk of grain, moisture, frost, hail, rust, foreign markets, and foreign politics.

A businessman here may never have lifted a pitchfork, but he knows how grain grows. He knows that the livelihood of the prairies hangs on a thin margin, a few inches of rain, a few degrees of temperature, a few days more or less of growing weather. He is, indeed, a farmer *in absentia*, and his character, molded by these natural forces, makes the character of Winnipeg.

It is made also by a history which few Canadians remember. Manitoba is an old country, as age goes in Canada. Selkirk's settlers walked to the Red River from Hudson Bay, their Scottish bagpipes skirling, in 1812. They found that the Métis, mixed offspring of French Canadian *voyageurs* and Indian women, already had built a society, almost a nation, around the river junction. A Manitoba character had been established seventy years before the C.P.R. crawled westward out of the Shield.

When the railway brought its first passengers to settle on the prairies, they were of solid rural Ontario stock, not adventurous immigrants, discontented folk, and often radicals from Europe or the United States like most of the settlers farther west. They were established Canadians of unalterably conservative mind. They made Manitoba perhaps the most conservative province in Canada except Quebec.

This story is written legibly at the nexus of the two rivers. The old days are more palpable here than in any other Canadian town since Winnipeg is closer to them in spirit. Here the dullest man can see, as pictured in Whittier's verse, "the smoke of the hunting lodges of the wild Assiniboine" and hear, from the great basilica across the Red, "the bells of the Holy City, the bells of St. Boniface."

Yes, and a sensitive nose can still detect, even amid the

smell of these city streets, the old smell of buckskin, Indian campfires, horses, pemmican, and rum; then the smell of musket fire as Cuthbert Grant and his half-breeds massacred the Red River farmers at Seven Oaks, and again as Riel seized Fort Garry and ruled his brief republic in frock coat and moccasins; then the smell of smoke as the first stern-wheelers paddled down from the States; the smell of steam as the first locomotives lurched out of the badlands; the smell of printers' ink and coal-oil lamps in a log shack as the first weekly newspaper came off its hand press; and finally the clean smell of wheat pouring in from the west as bearded immigrants in sheepskin coats drove their plows to the barrier of the Rockies.

All these men have left their several marks. Their trail along the Red River is Main Street. Portage Avenue winds in the curving path of their oxcarts bound westward for Portage la Prairie. A corner of their fort yard is a little garden around the crumbling gate. The bloody grove of Seven Oaks is a park where children play and old men blink in the sun. Their first locomotive glistens in honorable retirement beside the main line of the C.P.R. Across the river the towers of the basilica identify an older French Canadian sub-island within the island of Winnipeg.

I walked across the bridge to St. Boniface, a town of French speech, a distant suburb of Quebec, and stood for a moment observing the gravestone of Riel. After his second rebellion in Saskatchewan and his execution in Regina, his friends brought his body home in a freight car and on his grave planted a ring of lilac bushes. Not many people pause to note the resting-place of a man whose death, by turning the French Canadian race against a Conservative government, altered the whole political history of the nation. Yet the rebel, martyr, or madman of the west could say truthfully to the jurors at his trial: "I know that, through the grace of God, I am the founder of Manitoba."

And what a name he gave it! When the emissaries of his Métis republic wrung their own terms of union out of a helpless Canadian government, they told Macdonald that Manitoba meant, in some Indian dialect, "The God that Speaks."

It continues to speak in many strange tongues, but how many of Manitoba's present rulers remember the meaning of its name? And how many Canadians from other provinces, crossing this region by train or airplane and seeing it only as a flat checkerboard of farmland, realize that the cultivated prairies are only a small corner of Manitoba?

Two or three hours of driving southeastward from Winnipeg, on the old Dawson Trail, brought us to a woodland of big evergreens, rushing streams and innumerable lakes that drain into Hudson Bay. A few miles farther lay Winnipeg's fashionable week-end resort, the Lake of the Woods, just over the Ontario border, and filled, so a native told us, with forty-eight thousand islands. We didn't try to count them, but took him at his word.

Northeastward from Winnipeg, we found the Winnipeg River, Vérendrye's highway to the west, dammed for power in a few places but still foaming in untamed rapids as he must have seen them on his first voyage.

Then, straight north from the city. we followed the muddy Red through the sleek acres of Selkirk's settlement. The churches of golden stone, built by the Scotsmen after their march from the Bay, are oddly mingled with the later onion-shaped domes of Russia. Central Europeans have taken over most of the Scotsmen's farms and brought not only their own church designs but also those mud-plastered and gaily colored log houses which were first built on the Danube and the Russian steppes. These, in turn, have given way to modern houses, convenient and ugly, but in the fields of black earth the peasant women still wear bright kerchiefs and billowing skirts as they kneel beside their mile-long rows of vegetables.

Presently we discovered the stone battlements of Lower Fort Garry, which the Hudson's Bay Company built to guard the river from the Americans if Fort Garry ever fell. No invader reached the Lower Fort. Its three-foot walls, narrow loopholes, and ponderous gates heard no shot fired in war.

Fortunately they have been preserved to offer a cool oasis

of greenery and flowers on a hot evening. The cellars are so deep and cold that we hugged the blazing fireplaces though the prairies around them were limp with heat.

Few cars stop at the old fort. Most of them are going to the shallow inland sea of Lake Winnipeg, where the city week-enders can wade a mile from shore. We hurried through the crowded summer resorts and drove on to Gimli, the Icelanders' fishing town. Their big lake boats, their nets drying on every fence, the blond fishermen (handsomest men in the nation), the women of powerful frame and calm face, tell the happy ending of the Vikings' Canadian saga.

As we approached Lake Manitoba to the westward, it seemed to lie at least ten miles away, a thin glint on the sky-line behind a fringe of trees. We stepped from our car to find a canoe awaiting us beside the road, half hidden in rushes. A muskrat-trapper of silent habits pushed the canoe into a passage hardly three feet wide, and a moment later the world had disappeared.

Even this man, who had spent his life on the swamp, would have been instantly lost in an unmapped maze without the stakes planted here and there to guide him. We saw nothing but the solid wall of reeds twice our height, an occasional acre of open water, and everywhere myriads of ducks, gulls, and pelicans. They rose in a cloud, with deafening cries of anger, and blotted out the sun.

We were still within shouting distance of the shore and could have been on a distant ocean. I asked the guide how he expected to find his way home. He only grunted and twisted his canoe like a needle through a rumpled cloth of green until we came at last to the open water of the lake.

It was late afternoon by now, and we wondered if we would ever step on land again. That trapper knew his swamp. He followed his guideposts, drove his needle back and forth in jerky stitches, and when we seemed as far from shore as ever, the canoe grounded, a ruddy moon beamed on the prairies, and to the west a flock of ducks floated across the scarlet page of sunset like black notes of music.

Yet most Canadians think of Manitoba as a field of grain beside a railway track. And even as we watched the dying glimmer on the lake, we remembered that most of Manitoba —the forest, the rivers, the lakes innumerable, the mining towns, the stony Shield, and the Bay—still lay far to the northward. There such projects as a huge new nickel refinery are giving this farm province a broad industrial base.

But one need travel only a few miles from Winnipeg to leave every trace of civilization far behind. We hired a launch in the middle of the city, ascended the Red River, and in half an hour were lost on a minor Amazon. The sluggish stream of brown water looped in the repeated letter S. On each bank stood an impervious jungle, unmarked by any trail, untouched by any ax. The sky was a mere slit of blue. We suffered from acute claustrophobia not five miles from the corner of Main and Portage and not half a mile from the plowed prairies.

Then we drove southwest of Winnipeg and beheld the flat plains heave, like a squall at sea, into the Pembina Hills, sink into lush valleys of grass, and end in a chain of unsuspected lakes. Americans from Dakota were joyfully catching a hideous sort of fish under the impression that they had penetrated the farthest wild west.

The railway traveler sees only the dismal villages of the main line, the whistle stops around a wooden grain elevator, a skating rink, and a garage. In southern Manitoba many charming towns sit astride some nameless stream, snore peacefully under the shade of great trees, and look almost like the blessed towns of Ontario.

Despite all his machinery and household conveniences, the life of the average farmer in this country is still hard. Of itself it explains the current change in the politics and thoughtways of the prairies, the decline of the old laissez-faire economics that once flourished here, the emergence of collectivism in the grain industry.

We stopped one night for supper in a farm kitchen and found it replete with all the electrical gadgets, plumbing, and chromium furniture of a modern city house. But the woman who cooked the supper was not a city woman (she made better pickles and pies, for one thing), and the wizened man in mechanic's overalls could never be anything but a farmer.

"All we want," he said, "is a little security, same as folks in town. But no. The town folks want security for themselves, and they tell us to take whatever the market says and be damned to us. They get paid regular. We're supposed to gamble."

He was not a radical or a socialist. He belonged to perhaps the most conservative group of Canadians in Canada's most conservative province. He was, in fact, a small capitalist—"too small," he said wryly—but he and his kind were determined to get a fairer share of the nation's income as the labor unions had got it in the towns, and to get it regularly.

His wife compelled us to eat a third piece of pie and sent us off with a big jar of her pickles. The farmer went back to his barn and began to reassemble his tractor. He had another hour of daylight and didn't intend to waste it.

Down the road a piece we met a gaunt figure leaning on his gate. His face was red-hot from the prairie sun, but it had settled into lines of permanent melancholy. He admitted that he was just an old-fashioned sort of fellow and didn't hold with contemporary notions.

"The prairies," he said, "have run right off the rails. Everybody thinks you can tinker with the market and stop the law of supply and demand. Well, you can't. Trouble is, people aren't thinkin' any more, not on the right things anyhow. They're thinkin' about cars, movies, sex, sensation—God knows what all. In my time when we stopped for lunch on a threshin' gang we used to argue about the tariff, or Laurier's speeches, or maybe religion and the preacher's sermon on Sunday. You won't hear that kind of talk today. We've lost our way somewheres along the line."

Human life was changing, but nothing, he added, would change the life of wheat. As he spoke of wheat the farmer's gloomy face lighted up. Wheat wasn't as simple as it looked. It needed a dry spring to drive the roots a yard into the ground for moisture and make a strong plant. Then came the danger point of early summer, when rain was vital; and after that, wheat must have a hot August to ripen the seed before the early frost.

For a good many years that perfect combination of weather had yielded big crops, but the farmer remembered the earlier drought years and predicted their return. The Canadian boom wouldn't go on forever. It wasn't in the nature of things.

We drove through Portage, whose main street, the end of the old wagon road from Winnipeg, is wide enough to carry the traffic of New York, reached the solid, well-groomed streets of Brandon, crossed the deep canyon of the Assiniboine, and drove north over the plains toward one of nature's wildest aberrations.

Ahead of us a perpendicular cliff burst from the prairie like a single mountain, perhaps an extinct volcano. Presently we were climbing a steep road through a forest of evergreens. At the summit we looked out upon a misplaced chunk of the Rockies, a long lake of clear water, a woodland glade, and, within it, a herd of sulky buffalo.

Such is Riding Mountain National Park, the most improbable park in Canada. Here the prairies, undulating eastward from the mountains, make a sheer drop, a single dizzy step down to the level of Lake Manitoba. From the eastern flank of this queer eruption we could see the farmland all around neatly squared in tints of violent green and yellow, exactly like the interior of France as painted by Van Gogh.

Next day we started westward again and blundered upon yet another unlikely little niche in Manitoba's life. The shabby town of Virden was filled that Saturday night with men obviously not farmers or tourists—men in jumpers, greasy overalls, the high, buckled boots and the raffish slouch hats of their craft. A migratory North American race of oil drillers had paused here for the moment.

These men did not have to announce a new oil field. It announced itself by the noisome stink of crude oil in the middle of some farmer's field, by the steel skeletons of the oil drills and the miles of shiny pipe.

Already the first pumps were waving their arms in rhythmic

gesticulation, as well they might. They announced the biggest
news on the prairies since the first locomotive whistled here.
But the big oil fields and the continental sub-basement full of
natural gas that will soon revolutionize all human life on these
plains still lay far to the west. There being no vacant room in
Virden, we decided on a forced march into Saskatchewan. It
was a lucky decision.

In all Canada we had found no sight to equal the prairies
softened and almost liquified by the twilight and oozing in
the transparent water-color wash of sunset.

The horizon lay in a taut circle. The circle was cross-stitched
by the silver thread of railway tracks and cleanly cut by the
straight diameter of the road. Euclid himself had drawn this
design in pure geometry.

To the westward, geometrically barred by the picket fence
of telephone poles, the sun hung like a red billiard ball in a
steel rack. Night crawled across the prairies, and the lights of
Regina glowed dimly under a mock mountain range of cloud,
on the far side of a dark sea.

COWBOY FROM HOLLAND

The he great myth of Canada and the essential ingredient of
the nation recently hurtled into my garden on a tricycle. It
was ridden by a golden-haired boy of five years just out from
Holland. I do not know his name. He has yet to master the
English language. But he has learned the first word of the
myth. The word, of course, is "cowboy." He shouted it though
my gate, brandished two toy pistols, and whipped his three-
wheeled horse over my flower beds.

Though my young friend knows little about Canada, he has
hit unerringly on its true content and oldest instinct. He has
joined that long procession which started out of Europe in the
first days of the seventeenth century, crossed an ocean and a
continent, and marched westward to another ocean. He has
grasped, by the deep wisdom of childhood, the primal force
forever driving the Canadian westward against the wilderness.
After the trim postage stamp of Holland he has seen the limit-
less space of a new land. He has breathed the west and become
a cowboy. We are witnessing in our neighborhood the birth of
a Canadian.

The other day the carefree cowboy got down to the serious
business of Canada. He became, by hereditary impulse, a
farmer. His father, who had long cultivated the soil of Holland
and acquired a Canadian farm only a month ago, gave the boy
a set of tools, a little tin spade, rake, and hoe. Immediately
the horse and pistols were laid aside.

As I drive down our country lane, the boy was digging up
the roadside, smoothing it with his rake, and preparing to sow
his first crop. There, in that small figure, was the genius of an
ancient farm people transplanted across ocean and continent.

He shouted at me, in his own tongue, to observe his labors. They didn't amount to much beside his father's long spring furrows near by, but they were a beginning. The seeds of Holland would germinate in the Canadian soil, and the seeds of Canada in the boy.

Soon, I suppose, he will forget his native land and his father's language. Within a year or so of entering a Canadian school he will be indistinguishable from other young Canadians in appearance, speech, and mind. Yes, but he, and other boys from foreign lands, carry with them certain invisible baggage that no customs inspector will discern. They carry, like the first French Canadians, the English, the Scots, the Irish, and the rest of us, a fraction of the old world. It is of such fractions, mixed together and smoothed by environment, that Canada is made.

Yesterday some boys born in Canada jeered at the Dutch immigrant and trampled his new seed bed. When he sought refuge in my garden, I tried to tell him that the Canadians were only demonstrating, by a perverse method, their pride in Canada. They acted, I said, like boys everywhere and much like the world's statesmen.

I tried to tell the immigrant about another boy of his own age who reached Upper Canada in 1820, the son of a Scots storekeeper with a habit of unprofitable speculation and an addiction to strong drink. That boy seemed to have less chance in life than the boy from Holland. Yet he died as the first prime minister of Canada and the idol of his people.

John Alexander Macdonald, as I attempted to explain, was an immigrant. So were the French before him and the Indians before them. All Canadians were immigrants a few generations back, and so diverse in blood that no racial stock could now claim to be a national majority. We are a nation of immigrants and minorities, slowly combining and issuing in what we call the Canadian breed.

The Dutch boy listened, but he didn't understand. Repeating the only Canadian word in his vocabulary, he said he was a cowboy. Well, that would serve well enough for a start. He had begun to get to the root of the matter. And today I observed the next chapter in an old story—the native Canadian boys were teaching an immigrant the art of baseball, the secret of a robin's nest in an apple tree, the green mysteries of a swamp.

CHAPTER ELEVEN

The Big Farm

In crossing the western political boundary of Manitoba, the traveler supposedly is crossing also a line of ideology. He has entered the only large-sized political unit of North America which calls itself socialist and has repeatedly elected governments of that label. But at the first sight of Saskatchewan in the dawn our eyes were too filled and our minds too staggered for mere political speculation. If this was like no other land in Canada, what exactly distinguished it?

Size, of course—size unbroken, unimaginable, overpowering in a soundless void. You can see farther here than anywhere else in the nation, breathe deeper, and, we began to think, feel better. Size on this scale might even expand the dimensions of the human being. That was only a stranger's conjecture then. As we soon discovered, it happened to be true.

The flooding rivers and oozing sloughs of a wet spring had increased the illusion of distance and smeared a transparent water color of blue, green, and yellow across some ten thousand square miles.

Ducks paddled lazily in roadside ponds that might drain into the Arctic Ocean, Hudson Bay, or the Gulf of Mexico. Crows meditated on fence posts like professors in black scholastic gowns. The burble of meadowlarks did not break but only seemed to enforce the silence of this vacuum, and a cleansing wind carried all the perfumes of Eden.

As the day retired reluctantly from the earth, an army of clouds, white banners streaming, marched across the western sky. Then the banners, as if reversed, glowed in folds of crimson. A surge of flame set the planet alight from pole to pole.

In all that infinitude there were no men, only men's minute works. Broad-shouldered grain elevators stood in a solemn circle of dwarfs on the ultimate boundary of space. The largest barn looked half an inch high. A train of freight cars crawled like a brown caterpillar, and its frail whistle was drowned by the croak of a frog. No men were in sight because the machine had replaced them.

At last we found a man. He was mending a fence with hammer and staples—a tiny speck of human life against the void of land, water, and sky. His roughcast face seemed to offer a sculptured likeness of the Canadian west, cast in bronze and glowing in the sunset. Rodin could have modeled that man and exhibited him in the Louvre.

He kept hammering when I addressed him, but admitted, in some guttural foreign accent, that it had been a bad spring, a hell of a spring, and half his farm too wet for seeding.

Not as bad, I ventured, as some springs he must have known. No, he agreed sullenly, not as bad as that. There couldn't be anything as bad as the dry years. Had I seen the prairies in the big drought?

I said I had seen them. I had seen the dust heaped up in gray windrows along the fence lines, the thistles tumbling among the half-grown wheat stalks already dead of thirst. I had sniffed the smell of drought and the sour smell of poverty. Yes, and felt the universal presence of those times, the specter of dumb human hopelessness from the lakes to the mountains. Now the land was sleek with the surge of healthy grain all the way to the horizon.

"If you was here," the man added, "you seen what it was like, eh? No crop, no money, no nothin'. Kids with no shoes to go to school. Everybody on relief. Half hungry all the time. That was it, all right—drought. Now look at it!"

He pointed to a circular wooden bin, his private granary.

"Full up," he growled. "Can't sell it. And another crop to come. A big one." Then, bitterly: "And the papers still talkin' about a boom!"

Wasn't this better than drought and no crop at all?

"Better," he answered doubtfully, "but still no good. It's one way or the other, too much or too little. You can't win."

What did he think of Saskatchewan's socialism, which baffles the rest of the nation? The man stopped hammering and flung out a memorable judgment on life.

"It don't matter none," he said, "what a man thinks of politics. That's his business. What's he think of kids and women and dogs and whisky? That's what matters."

To nail down his personal philosophy, he hit the fence post a blow like a full stop at the end of a sentence. Having punctuated the sentence, he said no more. Our first reception on the farmland of Saskatchewan was depressing and quite misleading. That bitter man, as we were to learn, could not have been less typical of his kind.

We left him still hammering in the painted twilight, and undertook with some misgivings a siege of the socialist citadel in Regina. After all the mean things I had written about socialism, I expected a chilly reception.

Well, I should have known better. No one ever received a chilly reception in Regina even at forty below zero, a common winter temperature. This town's heart is an unfailing furnace. It keeps the human temperature thermostatically controlled the year around, at exactly the right level, for resident and visitor alike. And it is no hyperbole, it is a simple, statistical fact, to say that Regina is our most successful Canadian town.

Other western towns faced the same terrible climate, but they were built with nature's aid. Winnipeg, Saskatoon, and Edmonton, for instance, found navigable rivers at their doors, the original highways of travel. Calgary had the warming Chinook wind and, at no extra charge, the backdrop of the Rockies for decoration. Regina had nothing but a Pile of Bones to fasten its earliest name, as a buffalo-hunters' camp, on the mapless prairie.

It is entirely man-made. It is built against nature's clear intent and ferocious opposition. Man has won that long contest. After flattening his town under the tornado of 1912, nature withdrew, defeated. Man cleared away those ruins and made a habitation perfectly suited to his needs, physical, spiritual, and even, perhaps, political. I call that success.

Wide business streets and clean-cut buildings declare Regina's youth, prosperity, and unlimited expectation. A shady square of trees and flowers in the middle of the business district suggests a rare civic sense of proportion, an instinct of communal beauty.

Near by, a causeway arches across a little prairie creek, cunningly dammed and widened until it looks like a miniature Thames. An art gallery and museum of fine, simple lines smiles with stone dignity upon a park of blossom that man has learned to grow in this harsh weather. Finally, a swamp has been enlarged into a lake of clean water and reflects, like a mirror, the chaste body of the legislative building and its formal gardens, a corner of King Louis's garden at Versailles.

These are the title deeds of Regina's success. If they are artificial, they are by no means unnatural or temporary. The concrete bulk of grain elevators and a thick spiderweb of railway lines around them anchor Regina in the reality of the plains.

Wandering about the streets on a Saturday night, we felt at home for the first time since we began our journey. Regina has a warm, intimate, homelike quality. It seems to belong, as few towns do, to its people, to the farm lads with tanned faces and big hands in town for an evening's fun, to the comfortably stout farm women in their best clothes, to the immigrants with fierce whiskers, to all that potent mixture of peoples, histories, and accents who are making a new breed on the prairies.

In the streets, cafés, and spacious park there is none of the hurry, impatience, and stuffiness of a city. There is still the relaxed, neighborly spirit of the village common and the country store and the first furrow ever plowed across the Saskatchewan soil. Regina is still young in heart. May it never become a city.

Such a town could be built by the ordinary skill of men's

hands even on this worst of all possible sites. Something more than skill and the hope of profit was required to build the community within the town.

A first hint of mysterious inner elements appears in the palatial, almost unbelievable grandeur of the government offices. They might be occupied by socialist governments; they were designed to house the kings of the earth, the dynasts of the Saskatchewan farm.

These corridors, galleries, apartments, and chasms of marble must surely be the work of an unusual race. It disregards climate, economics, and every rational calculation to raise up here, in proud defiance, its testament to a boundless hope. As I had suspected, the dimensions of geography expand the dimensions of men's minds.

At any rate, it was in Regina that the fertile womb of the great North American depression bore Canada's first socialist party in 1933 and the Manifesto of the Co-operative Commonwealth Federation, which promised an imaginary socialist state but was watered down, two decades later, because a capitalist state had meanwhile been changed into something else entirely and seemed to be working very well.

It was in this legislative building that the first Canadian socialist government took office in 1944, but its theoretical socialism soon melted under the rays of the Canadian boom.

How, the traveler may well ask, did socialism first gain office in this most improbable corner of America, by the votes of the fiercely individualistic farmers of Saskatchewan? In answer to that obvious question a distinguished member of the socialist hierarchy told me a moving little tale.

Not long ago, he said, a certain Saskatchewan farm beside a rutted country road turned on its first electric light. No newspaper recorded the event, but it was important just the same. The humble story of that farmhouse is, in essence, the story of Saskatchewan from the beginning.

Consider, said my informant, what had happened to these nameless folk on the solitary farm. Since 1903 their house had been lighted by kerosene. The farmer and his wife had watched by dim lamps the procession of life and death, of happiness, heartbreak, and common things that make every house uncommon and fill it with secrets. There had been no running water, no refrigeration, none of the luxuries considered essential in any city house.

Then at last, after half a century of waiting, the wires were installed. A vital current, the energy of civilization, the power to drive tools and ease human labor, was flowing into the house, and its owner prepared to push the magic button.

He was an old man now, nearly a hundred, his bearded face like a saint on a church window. His son stood beside him, and he was old, too, and bent from arthritis, the penalty of his life's toil; and the son's two sons, now in middle age, and their sons and daughters, a noisy band of great-grandchildren. Four generations of that house awaited the wonder of electricity.

The great-frandfather pushed the button. The house, the barn and barnyard blazed in light. All the younger men exclaimed, the children squealed, but the great-grandfather watched with puzzled eyes and said nothing. When you have sowed and reaped more than fifty harvests on the same land and left three generations to carry on your work, there isn't much to say, even if you watch a miracle.

Not much to say, but much to think about—a whole epoch of Canadian life and a unique adventure on these plains compressed beneath the aged man's finger as he pushed the button and saw the light.

That, said the so-called socialist, was the story of Saskatchewan and the answer to my question. The answer, I confessed, was not clear to me. What sort of people had turned a parched prairie of buffalo grass into our largest Canadian farm to produce half our cereals, equipped it with every kind of machinery, and finally brought electrical power to the solitary house on the rutted road? What had turned a band of stubborn individualists, alone among Canadians, to the experiment of socialism?

My friend smiled tolerantly. Couldn't I understand that socialism was only a modern label for a process under way here since the first plow reached Saskatchewan, a process quite different from the early settlement of other provinces?

Those older provinces had been settled slowly by a few pioneers in primitive times, before Macdonald built his transcontinental railway. Here in Saskatchewan the railway had suddenly dumped a horde of settlers, many of them immigrants from Europe, upon raw and hostile earth.

They had no money, houses, plowed land, or knowledge of the frontier. In a common dilemma they found that a man could not survive here when Saskatchewan must be changed almost overnight from a frontier to a farm. Every man needed his neighbor's help to raise a barn, dig a well, thresh a crop, or fight a prairie fire.

Learning that need not by theory but by hard experience, every man became a co-operator; co-operation produced the farmers' huge co-operative wheat pools and then collective marketing. Finally old-fashioned co-operation devised a new label. It emerged in a new doctrine called, or miscalled, socialism, and in such things as a government power line down an isolated side road.

That, my socialist friend assured me, was the whole meaning of socialism in Saskatchewan. A few government-owned industries of little account and a handful of real socialists could be called socialism only in a headline or a political speech. The existing system, if it could be termed a system, was only the expression of a way of life established long ago by environment. It was not an ideology but an instinct.

That man was right, I think, in saying that if the Co-operative Commonwealth Federation of the Regina Manifesto had been elected only in Saskatchewan and failed of election in every other province, it had been in fact an extraordinary success. Its ideas, appropriated by the great political parties, had infiltrated, colored, and altered the whole society of Canada.

In Saskatchewan social change has been more profound than in most provinces. A government expert gave me such a bewildering mass of figures, such a detailed accounting of new oil wells and refineries, gas pipelines, mines, America's largest uranium reserves, forests, and expanding industries of all sorts that I forgot all the details and saw only a vague picture of

Saskatchewan, the great grain province, becoming an industrial province, a rural people deserting the farm for the city, a population rising after ten years of decline.

The smattering of theoretical socialism looked pretty thin upon the surface of the industrial boom, especially when the government was ardently wooing the investments of wicked capitalists.

As it was useless to note down statistics that change daily, my host led me to the provincial archives and presented a changeless exhibit.

There stood the long table used by the Fathers of Confederation at their Quebec Conference. Somehow it had found its way to Battleford, then capital of the Northwest Territories, and later into a Regina secondhand store, its length much reduced by a clumsy carpenter.

The Fathers were careless of a mere table. Saskatchewan guards it jealously. I suggested that such a national property should be in Ottawa, but the provincial politician indicated that a civil war would break out if anyone attempted to move Saskatchewan's heirloom. Macdonald, I thought, might be scandalized to see his workbench in the hands of wild-eyed socialists. However, if he met these genial men in person, doubtless he would understand.

Saskatchewan is peculiarly conscious of its brief history as a province. In little more than fifty years not many places have accomplished so much. No wonder that these people hoard and polish their past until the story of every town and hamlet begins to look like an epic. Figures unknown to Canada at large swell into titans. Many local politicians already are immortal in their own land.

After hearing the government's explanation of its policies, I set out to learn how they suited the farmers. Soon I was sitting in a cool shed of machinery, far off on the edge of the Regina Plains.

The man who sat beside me there, on a monstrous new swathing machine, looked strangely unlike a farmer. He wore a Panama hat, somewhat battered but obviously expensive, an immaculate white shirt, khaki trousers of excellent cut, and shoes fit for a drawing-room. Yet he had just come from his fields, where he was working literally day and night to plant the sodden acres as they dried out.

His tanned face, set in lines of serenity, might have been the face of a successful businessman or an academic. Actually he was both. In the summer he managed the complex business of his farm and in winter he often lectured to the university students of Saskatoon. But he remained a dirt farmer by choice and a portent of agriculture's new age.

When he had finished his college education, he said, the farm of fourteen hundred acres required the labor of twenty-five men at harvest time and twenty-two horses. Now he and one hired man sowed the whole crop and reaped it. The big horse barn was empty, the machinery shed full of gadgets worth a substantial fortune.

Why, I asked, did a man of his sort choose to farm though he could live comfortably and practice a learned profession in the city? He turned on me a bantering smile. "Because," he said, "I like it."

He had found no life so interesting as the life of his own farm, nothing to equal the glory of these Regina Plains. We went outside and looked across a country as flat and smooth as a well-laid floor. On three sides a faint blur separated sky from earth. On the east an idle finger of smoke pointed down at Regina, which lay below the horizon line, like a ship far out at sea. Only the top of a grain elevator, the ship's turret, was visible behind the curve of the world.

Even a mountain man like me could see the fascination of this naked distance and understand why a recent English visitor to the farm had sat out all night alone to watch the stars and the dawn. But what was the fascination of farm work?

"I suppose," the farmer replied, "it's the new challenge every year. I mean the job of raising a crop on this dry land and beating the weather. That, believe me, takes a lot of doing."

A lot of doing on a dry land. Not long ago this man had rowed in a boat five miles around his flooded fields and, with luck and labor, day and night, he had managed to sow six hundred acres as the water subsided.

"You see," he explained, "this country's so dry most of the time that you can't even get water in a well."

He had to haul domestic water in a tank truck from the outskirts of Regina; he saved every drop of rain from the roof of his house and pumped more water from a dugout near by to irrigate his grove of trees, lawns, and flowers.

I inquired about his current crop, and his answer struck me as final definition of prairie life: "Oh, we always have a crop at this time of year." There might be none, of course, by autumn, but it was useless to worry.

My inquiries about socialism only amused him. Not one farmer in ten, he said, was opposed to the collective marketing of grain, and not one in a thousand was a socialist.

I risked one last question: what was the use of his education in this style of life? He thought about it for a moment and said he guessed education gave him a deeper interest in the scientific processes of agriculture.

That was only half an answer. The other half could not be put into words. This man and his kind are totally involved, physically and spiritually, in the greater process of the earth, of growth, harvest, weather, and fundamental things of which politics, in Regina or anywhere else, are only pale shadows.

The farmer went back to his fields, where he would work most of the night, with headlights, to drill the last possible grain of seed into the soil while there was yet time for it to mature before autumn frost.

We drove northward and down into the green glacial trench of the Qu'Appelle Valley, and then, on the far side, through so many towns, villages, and crossroads hamlets that we might have been in crowded France. Most of Saskatchewan is an empty land, but it is sprinkled with innumerable clusters of habitation, far apart. Less than half its people live on farms.

These towns are not so far apart that their people feel isolated from one another. They are linked by seventy-five per cent of all the roads on the Canadian prairies and by a busy private grapevine. They talk lovingly of their local affairs and brave civic hopes, of great names overlooked by the nation. Each huddle of houses around an elevator is a metropolis in its own eyes. Everybody in, say, Weyburn seems to know what is happening in the distant city of Moose Jaw (which is thoroughly modern despite its old Indian name), for these are essentially a social folk, all members of a tightly knit society, and they are also the most political folk in Canada.

Why, you can hardly strike up a conversation anywhere before you are enmeshed in a political argument, the chief indoor and outdoor sport. Nowhere else do Canadians take such a direct, earnest, and partisan interest in their public affairs. Nowhere else, I dare say, do farmers finish their milking early in the winter afternoons, hurry to the kitchen, and turn on the radio to hear the debates of the legislature, the most popular program on the air.

After countless talks, in countless towns, with quite the most intelligent people we had met in Canada, we came by easy stages to Saskatoon. It surprised us.

Beside its brown river and soaring bridges, Saskatoon has an antique, almost a European, look, though it was built only yesterday. Half close your eyes and observe the tower of the Bessborough Hotel across the river and you can imagine yourself in a provincial town of western France.

Or stand among the honest Gothic stonework of the university—the supreme monument, I suppose, to the urgent spirit of Saskatchewan—and you might take this quad for a detached portion of Oxford, only awaiting the growth of trees to confirm its antiquity.

As a college town, Saskatoon is yeasty with academics, who usually look as if they had come originally from the farm. We asked one of them to define the special character of Saskatchewan, and he told us a queer little tale.

Recently, he said, the taxpayers of a town not far away had met to decide whether they should build a new school. They argued all evening about the expenditure of a few thousand dollars while a swarthy man of Polish blood, a farmer much respected in this district, sat silent in the back row. At last, as the meeting seemed hopelessly deadlocked, this man shuffled to his feet and, reddening with embarrassment, spoke in a thick foreign accent.

"School," he said, "I don't know much about it. Never went to school, never learned to read or write. But I come here and see this is good, big country. I see school is good, too. I want my boys should go to school and do better than me. So let's build the school, build it big and good just like this country."

That speech sounds banal in print. The reader will wonder why I have quoted it. But let him imagine the group of farmers in their hall, the illiterate peasant from Poland pronouncing in clumsy sentences his own discovery of Canada. A school is a good thing, so let us build it. No socialism here, no theory of politics, just the instinct of a simple man who has learned to work with his neighbors, who pays his share and wants a better life for his sons. The farmers built their school.

"There," the professor said, "you have Saskatchewan. We moved in here from all over Canada, the States, and Europe with no fixed ideas, no ideas at all, except land hunger. We were poor and just did what we had to do. We need a school, a university, or something else, so we build it. They call this socialism nowadays. No, it's just Saskatchewan."

The former principal of a village school told me another story of these people. In his young days he had taught a class composed entirely of immigrant children. They were shockingly poor. Some had no shoes. Most of them could speak only a few words of English, and all looked shy or terrified when the teacher entered the room.

Thirty years later he came back and the same kids seemed to be in the school. It was uncanny. These were the children of his old class and so resembled their parents that he could guess almost every family name.

"But," said the teacher, "there was a difference. These kids spoke good English. They had boots and warm clothes. And they looked me straight in the eye. They were Canadians."

That, too, was Saskatchewan, a land of many racial stocks

and many separate regions. We soon realized, in fact, that
there were four distinct Saskatchewans lying in distinct layers
from the American boundary almost to the Arctic.

A few hours of driving northward out of Saskatoon brought
us to the second layer. The level plains ended suddenly. The
land began to roll. To the north we saw a blue haze like a
distant seacoast. Approaching it, we found an unbroken
band of rustling poplar trees and squat spruce. We were entering the parkland.

The farmers of the parkland have cleared big farms and are
still clearing. Their newly broken earth is gray-brown and
tangled with roots under the first breaking plow. Huts of
poplar logs and sod roofs remain beside the newer houses.
But even at Prince Albert, a pleasant, well-built town aslant
the muddy North Saskatchewan, we had reached only the
southern edge of the north.

Not far beyond Prince Albert the layer of parkland merged
into the third layer: thick spruce forest, much of this wood
large enough to make good lumber, the rest capable of support-
ing large pulp industries. At nightfall we were dining beside
the clean lakes of Prince Albert National Park and walking in
a virgin wilderness.

The sun went down, a disk of burnished copper, beside the
black margin of the lake, only to pop up again a few hours
later. The summer days are long up here, the darkness brief,
but we were not far north after all. Above us lay the fourth
layer of Saskatchewan, where the forest dwindles to mere
sticks on the stone welter of the Shield.

The country around the park is inhabited here and there
by pioneers leading, except for a few machines, the lives of
their grandfathers. Some of them reveal, in their dark faces,
the blood of their Métis ancestors, who, south of here, on the
Saskatchewan, enacted their misguided second rebellion and
heroic tragedy.

By some lonely road you may see white children and Indians
walking to school together, tin lunchpails in hand, or riding
a horse, three small riders on its back—the unchanged country
child of one hundred years ago. Or in a bluff of poplar and

spruce you will come across a half-built shack and a few acres roughly broken, the beginnings of a farm, the old story of the prairies repeated.

A new pioneer of this region—a grim-faced young man in his middle twenties—thumbed a ride to Prince Albert and dropped a clanking gunny sack on the floor of our car. Some part of his tractor had cracked and he was taking it to town for welding. He sure wished he could buy a new tractor to cut the wild hay of a swamp which supplied his winter cattle feed.

How many cattle did he possess? He blushed as he admitted that he had only eight. "That is, so far," he added.

Eight head. Four young steers, three old cows and a bull, fed on wild hay. They were his capital and his hope. Oh, yes, he would do all right after awhile on his quarter-section and, with luck, would soon buy the quarter-section next to him. He had cleared only fifty acres, but this land—"jumbo," he called it—was rich. It sometimes yielded sixty bushels of wheat to the acre.

Eight head, fifty acres. That may seem a small accomplishment in a nation accustomed to reckon industrial development by the billion. I thought it a prodigy of one man's labor on a total income of $1,500.

What cared this fellow for the Farm Problem, for Socialism, the Gross National Product, or all the jargon of the economists and politicians? He dropped off at Prince Albert to get a month's work there, if he could, any kind of work, to pay for the tractor's repair and a few acres' more clearing next autumn.

We drove southward to face the shattering heat of the prairies and, toward evening, dropped without warning into the deep hollow that holds the unlikely town of Swift Current. I call it unlikely because Swift Current is no farm town like the many we had seen that day. It looked like a cattle town straight out of the old west, or Hollywood.

The antique lobby of the hotel was occupied by unmistakable cattlemen and retired stagecoach-robbers wearing leather complexions and thick, pendant mustaches. They tilted back on their chairs in the immemorial posture of their craft, glared silently out the window, and doubtless saw strange sights, long forgotten. An astounding bellboy, surely the comedian of a western movie, was old enough to be my father.

On the streets most of the male pedestrians were garbed either in ten-gallon hats, tight overalls, and the high-heel boots of the cowboy or the greasy jumpers and buckled boots of the oil driller. Both cowboys and drillers had come to town in automobiles of the latest model. The cattle and oil industries evidently were doing all right.

Next morning we drove west by an endless, dusty detour, through a land of sagebrush range, scowling beef cattle, grim towns with such whimsical names as Wild Horse, Seven Persons, Chin, and Piapot, demented railway lines leading nowhere, and freight trains evidently lost in the desolate Cypress Hills.

At noon of a blistering day we slid down a clay canyon into a handsome little city, entered a palatial hotel, and discovered that we were in Medicine Hat.

Yes, Medicine Hat. That name alone invokes the whole splendor and magic of the west. And I record here, in admiration and some wistfulness, a national fact of some importance: among the townspeople gathered for lunch sat the most beautiful Canadian woman I had ever seen. In Medicine Hat, mind you.

"And why not?" my wife asked with a judicial air.

Why not, indeed? We had crossed the line into Alberta, where anything, absolutely anything, can happen, and soon would happen to us.

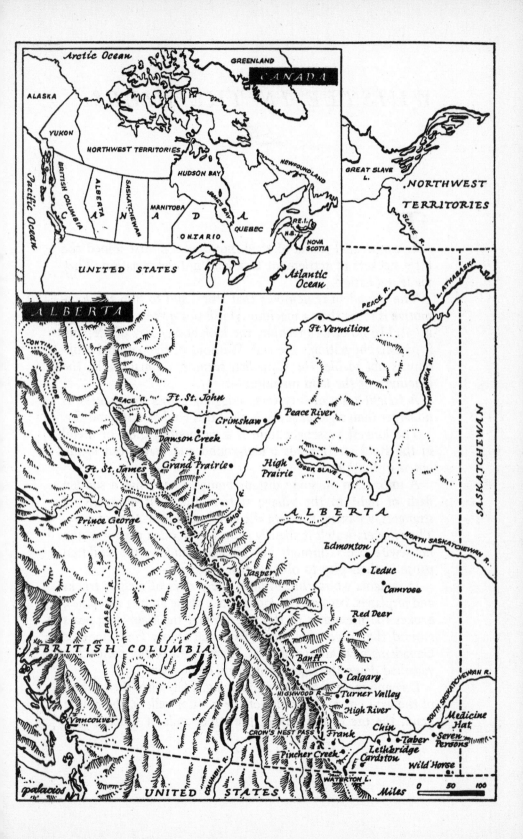

WHISTLE IN THE HILLS

*T*wo parallel shafts of steel, nothing else, first joined the little pockets of settlement in a land not yet a nation. They made it a nation.

The Canadian remembers that story, and to him the locomotive is more than a machine. If it is not quite a living thing, it has, like no other machine, the look and energy of life, and it propels the nation's lifestuff. Without it, the national economy is not viable, the Canadian scene is unimaginable, the loneliness of the land unendurable.

A freight train of fifty cars, wriggling across the prairies, is no larger than a garter snake against this void of earth and sky.

The longest passenger train is a momentary glint of metal in the Rockies. It bores underground and crawls out again, but is instantly lost.

A milk train on some distant branch line brings a sudden flash of light to the village station, the brief company of strangers, a passing flavor of the city, and a little ache of envy. The villagers watch it silently from the wooden platform, the housewife peers through her kitchen window, the children pause in their play to observe this wonder.

It remains wonderful, even in these days of freight trucks and airplanes, because the locomotive, alone among machines, evokes the memories of the race. When the train disappears around the curve, the village faces the empty land alone as Canadians have always faced it. A fragment of the nation has vanished down the tracks, but it will come again.

Day and night the trains are moving. They carry the timbers of the west coast, the apples of the interior valleys, the prairie grain, the ore of the Shield, the paper rolls of Ontario and

Quebec, the fish of the Maritimes, and the manufactures of the cities. The nation's labors will be useless, the nation itself must die if the trains ever cease to move.

In all weathers the trains must be kept moving. They move through summer heat and the blizzards of winter, the locomotive double-weighted with ice, the brakes frozen, and the boilers chilled. Avalanches of snow, rock, and soil roll perpetually over the mountain tracks. Rivers rise in flood to crush the prairie bridges. Frost heaves the ties and drops them again in spring thaw. Yet they are the lifeline of Canada. The trains move, and must always move if the nation is to live.

Managers, labor unions, economists, politicians, and engineers argue the economics of the railways from day to day and year to year. No problem of business is more important to the nation. But to the Canadian in the lonely places the train is not a problem. It is a friend, a messenger, the bearer of portents from far away, the sure proof that the nation is alive and never idle, day or night.

The Canadian listens from his bed, and hears in the locomotive whistle the old frontier music of his fathers, the authentic Canadian sound, the shout of the living nation. Whenever the whistle screams and echoes through the dark hills, all men understand its message. The locomotive, as if it, too, were living, utters the password of the race.

CHAPTER TWELVE

———◆◆———

The Big Dreamers

THE TRAIL ahead, if it could be called a trail, zigzagged across a slide of broken rock. I looked down a sickening drop at the Castle River. It gleamed through the timber no wider than a knife's edge. Behind it rose the serrated wall of the Continental Divide, reef on reef to north and south, the largest substance in America.

James Riviere, our guide, dropped off his horse. He was an experienced mountain man, his six and one half feet of muscle were encased in durable rawhide, but even this veteran of many trails would take no chances here. He began to lead his horse over the slide. We followed on foot, suddenly aware that we had reached an elevation of nearly ten thousand feet.

It was painful to breathe this thin air. We staggered, puffed, and sat down to rest after a dozen steps. Riviere also rested, watching us out of the corner of his eye. He wondered if the greenhorns could make it to the other side of the avalanche. The pack horses heaved as if their lungs would explode. It was no place for lowland animals. Yet we could see, not far off, a mountain goat grazing serenely on perpendicular rock.

The avalanche ended at last in a narrow funnel between the hills. All the winds of the world were sucked through the funnel. Our horses leaned drunkenly against them and lurched down the cliff to the eastward. Half an hour later we were setting up our camp in fairyland.

Yes, I know that word is used too loosely nowadays, but it was valid here. A little meadow of grass lay within a ring of pungent spruce. A jet of ice water shot out of a pink grotto with a merry tinkle, to disappear instantly underground. All around us, carved and shadowed like the walls of a cathedral, the Rockies cut a perfect blue circle from the sky.

Two grizzlies had lumbered off at our approach, grunting their displeasure. Elk had left new tracks by the stream. A mountain ewe eyed us anxiously from the side of a symmetrical basin, decided we were harmless, and continued to provide her lamb with a liquid dinner.

The night came at one stride. With it came a moon of swollen size and exaggerated brilliance. The mountains turned to polished silver. Presently the Big Dipper wheeled up and slid down over the rim of the planet. It left us alone in a black pocket. No man had passed this way for twenty years.

Horse and rider had sweated on the hot, upward trail. Now our buckets froze. We huddled about the fire and drank a mixture of boiling water, whisky, and sugar (Riviere called it Mountain Milk, which he considered a good temperance beverage). After shivering in our sleeping-bags until dawn, we arose and consumed four frozen pancakes. They improved our outlook.

Here, surely, we had escaped from men's affairs and the Canadian revolution? Riviere offered no comment on that question. He took me up a hillock and handed me his binoculars. I stared down at the green floor of the southern Alberta prairies that seemed visible in this clear atmosphere all the way to the Great Lakes. Then I saw what Riviere meant. A luminous pinpoint glistened on the plain. It was the newly built refinery of Pincher Creek. Natural gas would soon be flowing from there to Montreal. We could not escape the revolution.

As we rode out of the mountains and descended into a wooded glen, where his family's homestead had once stood, Riviere reined in his horse to show us the grave of his father. "Frenchie" Riviere, a celebrated figure in Alberta's mythology, had been buried, according to his instructions, on a hillside far from any habitation. But only a hundred yards away the largest oil rig in Canada had started to drill noisily through the substance of the Rockies. The revolution would not let the old pioneer sleep in peace.

James, his son, looked grimly at the grave and oil rig. There was nothing he could do about it. There was nothing anybody could do about the Alberta boom once man had bored down and found the Canadian treasury of oil and gas.

At the moment, however, James had no time to brood on these things. Urgent business called him home to his ranch in the foothills. About a dozen young trout had lost their way in the spring flood of Carpenter's Creek and, when the flood subsided, were imprisoned in a shallow pond.

James (no one called him Jim), his hired man, and I spent the next two days trying to catch those fish. They must be put back into the creek, James said, or they would die of drought and starvation. Most of them eluded us while the work of the ranch was ignored. I began to perceive for the first time the gorgeous lunacy of the Alberta breed, Canada's great-hearted madmen and darlings of the boom.

The cattle sale at Pincher Creek necessitated, of course, a general holiday. We drove into town with Riviere, listened to the singsong gibberish of the auctioneer, watched the hard-faced buyers fixing the nation's beef prices with raised finger, and saw the steers hurried into the railway cars. Pincher Creek has been a cattle town for a long time, but its hopes are fastened on the gas industry.

"You haven't seen," said a resident who wore a beard like a flaming gas well, "what's underneath your feet. More damn gas down there than anywheres in the world, enough to blow the lid off hell. When we get fixed to sell it, just watch this town grow!"

It is growing already, but some traces of its boisterous beginnings remain. We sat in a restaurant beside an aged Indian who might have arrived that day with Sitting Bull's Sioux. His hair hung in black braids down to his waist. His eagle's face was finely shaped and terrifying. The withered woman beside him wore a cotton dress, a blanket over her shoulders (though the thermometer stood at ninety), and moccasins up to her knees.

We drove north to High River, knowing its fame (no Canadian town is more famous) but not its contents. These began to reveal themselves as we entered the office of *The Times* and discovered Mrs. Hughena McCorquodale, so far the greatest discovery of our travels.

She was simultaneously reading proofs, answering a telephone, and rolling a cigarette. I use the word "rolling" in a loose sense, as loose as Mrs. McCorquodale's handiwork. For in truth, after forty-five years' vain experiment and much coaching from expert cowboy rollers, she builds her smokes like birds' nests blown and tattered by Alberta's Chinook wind.

They and their maker have become one of High River's many legends, well worthy of Bob Edwards's town and, like the newspaper which made his reputation throughout Canada, an Eye-Opener. Naturally, in such a storied place, we had called first on Edwards's successor because she represents— in her insatiable appetite for life, her reckless romanticism, shameless nostalgia, and corrosive wit—a fundamental strain of Alberta's nature. The lady facing me across the littered desk was an unrepentant maverick in Canada's maverick province.

She looked up from her work to warn us sharply that there was someone we must see right away if we wished to understand her country. "Wait a minute," she said, "till I finish these damnable proofs."

You will note that she said "damnable." She didn't say "damn" or the more fastidious "damned." She said "damnable" because she is a stickler for accuracy in everything except her gruesome and bulging parcels of tobacco.

Observing our interest in that native landmark, she added: "Oh, yes, we all look crazy here. It's the altitude. It's Alberta. But you'll get used to us."

There was no need to reassure me. I had fallen in love with her at first sight, with her town and her country. Despite age and white hair, Mrs. McCorquodale was still a beautiful woman, but I didn't know then that she was also a character waiting, quite unconsciously, for a novel to grow about her, probably from the pen of her celebrated literary neighbor, Bill Mitchell.

Meanwhile she led us down the street to one of western Canada's most notable and least noted men. I had expected from her enthusiasm to meet a stern personage in buckskin like Buffalo Bill or Gary Cooper. The man who greeted me at the door of his little bungalow was short, dapper, and mild-mannered. He had shaving lather on his face and a Scottish burr on his tongue. Yet this was the fabled Billy Henry, last of a unique species and adventurer extraordinary, whose life is too improbable for fiction.

Henry sat me in his neat parlor, finished his shave, and un-covered a face of well-worn saddle leather. That face had looked often at danger. It was the aging but dauntless face of Alberta's youth. The embodied myth—no, the reality—of this land stood before me and protested in quiet tones that his experience really didn't amount to much.

When Henry, a boy from Perthshire, came to High River over seventy years ago, southern Alberta was reputed the toughest region of the North American frontier. Not long before that the American whisky-traders of Fort Whoop-Up had debauched several Indian nations, Sitting Bull and his war-riors had fled here after their victory of the Little Big Horn, and a handful of Northwest Mounted Police had tamed these desperate fugitives without firing a shot.

Now, at the age of eighty-nine, Henry was alone in his tiny house, his wife gone and all the partners of the old Whoop-Up Trail hardly remembered in the province made by their hands.

Henry remembered. How could he forget the great days, the open range, the Indians, the cattlemen, the herds moving across the American border? This migration fixed upon Alberta a special quality of mind, a certain spaciousness and buoyancy, the instinct of the gambler, which still tinctures life today. Henry was the spirit of the great days incarnate.

"Ah, well," he said in his Scottish accent, "it wasn't like the movies, you know, and the books. They were big men, but they were kind. Never tough."

He groped for the right word to describe his vanished company and added: "They dreamed big."

They dreamed big. The old man's eyes glistened with moisture at the memory. Yes, they dreamed big and lived, on their boundless, unfenced acres, a life that the world will never see again.

"Oh, sure," Henry mused, "they'd come into High River on a Saturday night shooting off their guns and making a bit of noise. I've seen the dust popping all over the street from their bullets. But it meant nothing.

"They were," he repeated, "kind men. Make no mistake, though. They meant what they said. If they warned you off their range, it was their last warning. And if a stranger came up from the States in a hurry, you asked no questions. What had happened to him down there was his business."

They dreamed big, and one of the biggest dreamers was an ignorant man of commercial genius named Pat Burns. In his early days he could not read or write, but as he bargained craftily for cattle he would scrawl endless figures on a piece of paper to impress the vendor. Burns, the man of business and later one of Canada's chief enterprisers, was smart enough to see in Henry the man of action.

Thus began a strange partnership which sent the junior partner and a herd of cattle to the edge of the Arctic. Having heard rumors of this incredible feat, I asked Henry if it could be true.

"Oh, it was true, all right," he said. "But nothing out of the ordinary."

Nothing out of the ordinary, you understand. Only the story of a young cowhand, then in charge of 26,000 cattle at a handsome wage of $75 a month, who is asked by Burns to take 150 head to the Yukon gold rush.

"Well, yes," Henry agreed with some reluctance, "it was a long way and hard work. Loaded them on a scow at Vancouver, towed them up to Skagway, and drove them over the Pass. We had a little trouble in the mountains. Lost the trail. Ran out of feed and winter coming on. So I killed them and froze them and built a barge and floated them down the

Yukon and sold them in Dawson for a dollar a pound. Big money then. Pat Burns did well. A great man, Pat, but a little light on wages."

That was all. He had driven his cattle to the Yukon and sold them at a handsome profit. No, not quite all. A year or two later Burns had heard of another gold rush to Atlin, in northern British Columbia, and Henry, with 75,000 pounds of feed and freight, had driven twenty-two beef cattle inland from the coast through jungle, swollen rivers, and five feet of snow.

"There was no trail," Henry explained, "and the snow made it a little awkward. I'd never seen deep snow before, and I had no guide. First I drove an unloaded sleigh ahead to break trail, then a loaded sleigh or two, and finally the cattle. Dug out a kind of cellar every night and bedded the critters down. They came through fat. Never lost one. And we took in some stoves and butter and sold them to the miners like hot cakes."

Anything else? Ah, well, since I asked, he had made a second trip to Atlin and none of the cattle had died. Still, he didn't think he'd want to do it again. He preferred southern Alberta to the north, even though the farmers' fences had closed in the range and cowboys moved about in automobiles and carried their horses behind them in trailers.

"Why," he remarked with a chuckle, "I mind the time we'd ride a hundred miles a day. Easy, if you don't take the guts out of a horse in the first twenty miles."

His memory sharpening, he recalled his friend Slick, a respected bootlegger from Montana, who used to pack kegs of whisky across the border and cache them in Henry's corral if the Mounties weren't around.

"Slick made five trips a year," Henry said, "and always gave me a gallon. Good stuff, too. Ah, a fine lad. Never sold to Indians."

After telling me many tales of drought, blizzard, frozen cattle, prosperity, and ruin—"it was all the luck of the game"—Henry recalled one living man as good as any of the old-timers.

I shook hands with Henry at his gate and knew that I would never meet his like again. At least I had seen in the flesh the original character, grain, and flavor of this country. I had seen one of the big dreamers. The problem now was to find Henry's spiritual successor, who was lost somewhere in the hills.

Bill Mitchell offered to find him. This major Canadian novelist and creator of the "Jake and Kid" saga on television can find anybody in Alberta, though he is usually himself lost in some big dream. He drove us westward from High River toward the Rockies and the biggest dream we had ever encountered.

Beside us the foothills rose and fell in placid ocean swell of green. Everywhere bands of portly cattle stuffed themselves on the new grass of summer. The Highwood River chattered through caverns measureless to man. Like a stage setting of pasteboard painted crudely by a child's brush, the teeth of the mountains pierced the western sky, too gaudy to be true.

We skirted Turner Valley, its oil pumps and torches of surplus gas, and stopped at a crossroads store to confer with Mitchell's old friend Pete Dixon.

This Indian of lofty stature needed only a feather bonnet to make him a twin of Sitting Bull. He had come out of the hills to buy a cowboy hat for his grandson, a pretty boy with soft, brooding eyes, but more important matters were worrying Pete that day.

A fellow tribesman, notorious for his skillful peculations, was on the loose again. Fifty of Pete's newly cut fence rails had disappeared. This theft already was a *cause célèbre* about here, and no doubt would have been a killing matter not long ago.

Dixon took it calmly enough, though there was a chilling glint in his eye. He would get satisfaction in an affair of honor (and probably provide some excellent copy for Mitchell).

I judged that we were now a long way from the main road, not by distance but by time. A few miles distant white men, supposedly intelligent, were accumulating fortunes and ulcers in the oil industry. Here an Indian chief and a Canadian novelist were debating at length the theft of fifty fence rails. They renewed my faith in human sanity.

At last we found the man whom Henry had nominated as the only true heir to the great days. Bert Sheppard received us in his bachelor's quarters, a rambling house among the outer vertebrae of the continental spine. I must say that, at first glance, this silent, middle-aged person fell below Henry's description. The first glance was misleading. A second informed me that we had not come some fifteen thousand miles in vain. Here was a man.

Bert's face was lean, bony, darkly tanned, and drawn taut. His shirt was of spotless white, his overalls blue and faded from frequent washing, his high-heel boots of the best cut, his manners as shy as a schoolboy's.

We had been told that he was the best horseman in Alberta, but when we asked him about his craft, he looked fixedly at the ground, his head tilted bashfully to one side, and agreed, with some doubt, that he had ridden a little in his time.

To escape further personal questions, he led us into his barn. A dozen sleek horses, fully saddled, were eating lunch amid that sound of grinding teeth on crisp oats which is one of earth's immemorial tunes, as the smell of a barn is one of earth's sweetest emanations.

Half a dozen cowboys had just dismounted after their morning's work—tall, gaunt fellows, shy and silent like their boss. They greeted us with the instinctive dignity of their kind, gripped our hands in a crushing vise, and, according to their custom, called us by our first names. These, too, were men.

An apprentice cowboy entered the barn with a broken nose and a half-broken horse, obviously effect and cause. He allowed, blushing crimson, that both nose and horse would be all right in a day or two.

Bert advised us privately that this youth would make a top hand after a few more seasons. Many years were required, he said, to educate a cowboy, as distinguished from a mere rodeo rider, for whom he indicated a cattleman's disdain. To know what cattle would do in a pinch, to foresee their next move on a drive, to understand their minds—that was a skilled trade not to be learned under half a lifetime.

But few men nowadays were ready to undergo such an apprenticeship. The craft of the cowboy was dying and would soon be dead, Bert thought. The industrial boom and its high wages were taking all the youngsters into town, the big ranches were being cut up into small spreads that one or two men could manage, and the revolution had not spared the range.

Bert sighed. He expected to lose all his cowboys in the autumn, and then what? He guessed he would have to retire, this horseman who had started life by breaking other men's horses for six dollars apiece, six of them a week, and now owned one of Alberta's historic ranches.

After all, he said, ranching must be considered only as a business. That was the only lie Bert ever told me. For ranching was no business to him. It was a passion. This man, like his predecessors, dreamed big.

Maybe, he suggested apologetically, we'd like to see his chuckwagon. It was a fine chuckwagon, in perfect order, gaily painted and quite useless on a modern ranch. He had mounted it in a separate shed as his own monument to the Alberta myth. We asked him (knowing the answer) why he bothered to maintain this obsolete equipment. Well, he guessed the chuckwagon reminded him of old times and life on the range.

Nearby he had refurbished a rotting log cabin and set it on concrete foundations merely because it had been used by the Mounties long ago. Yet this man tried to tell us his ranch was a business!

Bert's little monument has been well placed. Southern Alberta was the first hunting-ground of the Royal Canadian Mounted Police. They marched across Canada in 1874— three hundred men in scarlet tunics—to police the whole plain between the lakes and the mountains. They established their western headquarters at Fort Macleod, not far from Bert's ranch; they enforced the law with such fair treatment of white man and Indian alike that the Canadian west escaped entirely the wars of the American frontier; and they built an institution that still polices most of Canada today.

They no longer ride horses except in parades, and their modern quarry is usually the urban criminal, drug-peddler, and foreign spy. Yet their tradition of integrity and equal justice remains an essential part of the state's foundation.

Tourists photograph these men in ceremonial uniform. Hollywood caricatures them (with Technicolor and the best intentions). Writers of fiction weave improbable tales about them (no stranger than the actual record). But Bert had seen through the fiction and erected his own little testimony to a solid Canadian fact.

We adjourned to his house for a discussion of history and a bottle of Scotch. The discussion started slowly. Bert crossed his legs and arms in an invariable pose, tilted his head, and turned his eyes upon the floor. Each sentence, in answer to our questions, seemed to cause him acute physical pain.

The answers became less painful as he got to know us better. Soon he was chuckling quite shamelessly and his eyes met mine in quick, mischievous dashes. Had I ever heard of Miss Eleanor Shackerley? (This with a sudden giggle which started me.)

Why, everybody knew that Miss Shackerley, an aristocratic English spinster, had come out here to keep house for six brothers, all of them killed in the first war. She used to invade the stores of High River wearing antique London fashions and carrying a gunny sack for her parcels.

Another giggle from Bert and then: "She was taking a bath one day. Very fond of baths. English, you know. A slew of visitors turned up at the door. Didn't like to keep them waiting. Came to the door with a bath towel held in front of her. Big woman, small towel. Told the guests to make themselves at home. Turned and left the room. Still holding towel in front. No towel behind. Quite a sight."

Bert was thawing out. He positively squirmed with internal convulsions. Had I ever heard of Dan Drumheller? Quite a guy, Dan. Best rider and runner in this country seventy or eighty years back.

"Was captured by the Nez Percé tribe south of the border. Ordered him to race on his black stallion against the Indians' best ponies. Partner told him, Dan, let the Indians win or they'll scalp us. Dan says, yes, he'll let them win, but can't stop the stallion. Wins easily. So Indians make him race on foot. Promises not to win, but can't stop himself. Wins easily again. Thrown into a teepee with a band of young squaws. Stallion turned into corral with Indian mares. What's up? says Dan. Indian chief says, stallion in corral, you in here, because we want fast colts and fast boys."

What came of that experiment Bert didn't know. Horrified to realize that he had told such a tale before my wife, he blushed again and announced abruptly that we'd better be getting along. Had something else to show us before lunch.

We started out in his car, the Highwood's canyon on one side and the Rockies floating on the other like icebergs in a green sea.

Bert remembered some lively tale at every curve in the road.

Right down there, he said, in that gorge of reddish stone, a German rancher had taken his life with German efficiency. Drank poison and hanged himself. No use. Shot himself in the head. Then jumped into river. Complete job.

Over there, in that log house, a Yankee denned up with a Spanish lady from Mexico who had absent-mindedly extinguished her husband. Comfortable arrangement, but didn't last long. Yankee married a Snake squaw. Very happy marriage. Used to say he was the only man who'd lived with a Snake for twenty years and never got bitten.

Everybody around here, Bert guessed, was friendly. The Duke of Windsor's ranch lay just beyond that range of hills. Nice fellow, the Duke, and Duchess, too. Queer thing happened one day in High River. Newspaper reporters asked Duchess the measurement of her bust, waist, and hips. Gave them the figures without turning a hair. What did I, a newspaperman, think of a thing like that?

Didn't think anything. Was dizzy and punch-drunk from scenery and legend. In my small way was dreaming big.

A long drive on a narrowing road and a rough trail brought

us to Bert's hideout, where the Rockies fell, vertical, into his back yard. He led us to a neat house of logs, and in half an hour was serving us steaks from his own cattle and fat trout from his mountain stream. Then, after some hesitation, he produced a document of historic importance.

All his spare time, for the last ten years, had been used to compile the record of every ranch in the Highwood country. The whole procession of the great days was there—the spring and autumn roundups of a hundred thousand cattle; the men who never saw a house all summer and often died of winter cold; such figures as Soapy Smith on his way to crime and a gunman's end in Alaska; Big Jim, the blacksmith, whose victims were buried in quicklime; the Sun Dance Kid, a fleeing American bank-robber fated to die violently in Brazil; and Old Martin, the English gentleman, with a gallon of whisky and another of water always tied to his saddle.

That manuscript contained the essential stuff of future Canadian history books and one of the nation's tallest tales, which happened to be true.

Not many old-timers and genuine cowboys were left, Bert said, but he could show us two specimens. We went to a house near by for dinner. There an astounding man of seventy years—nearly seven feet tall and as wide as a door—lived with his third wife and a new baby, the hopeful beginning, he said, of his third family.

He had fought as a boy in the cattle-rustlers' wars of Montana (as proved by a bullet crease across his bald skull); had fought also in the prize ring; had often been rich and more often poor; had lived all the previous winter with wife and child in a tent; and now was herding cattle for Bert.

He'd been a strong man once, he admitted, and could live for two weeks on nothing but whisky, after which, he told us as a surprising fact, you must have some solid grub. Now he wasn't much good. His neck had been broken. Twenty-four hours in the saddle tired him plumb out. Appetite gone, too. He dandled his baby on his knee and consumed enough food for three men. Undoubtedly he could have strangled a full-grown steer with his bare hands. Bert winked at me. This was the genuine article.

Beside him sat another genuine article, less than half his size. This man's name, Casey Castleman, was known and respected on every Alberta ranch. He had worked on most of them and, though old now and grizzled, could still outride most of the young hands. His seamed face puckering with memory and merriment, this born humorist held us fascinated until Bert intimated that we had another call to pay.

It was close to midnight and a mountain cloudburst had turned the road to glue when we drove through Dave Diebel's log gate. I could see by the massive construction of the gate and the log house beyond it that their builder was a craftsman in wood. He turned out to be also a master of horseflesh and machinery, a skilled judge of cattle, and the best rifle shot in the country.

He wouldn't tell us about these things, of course. Speech did not come easily to this tall, lank, and deceptively soft-voiced man. His wife, a handsome woman who wore overalls or city clothes equally well, mentioned that Dave had once killed a grizzly with a club. He immediately corrected her. It was only a black bear, and not a very big one. He had been compelled to use a club, lacking a rifle, because the bear was killing his calves. The skins of many grizzlies killed by his bullets covered the log walls of the parlor.

There was more important business to consider that night. Bert and Dave conferred at length about an old Indian named Jonah, who seemed likely to starve somewhere in the hills. Couldn't get to town because his car had broken down. Mrs. Diebel would pack a hamper for Jonah right away and Bert would deliver it. Dave would haul the broken car down to the ranch and repair it in his workshop. All this, mind you, half a day's drive from the oil-rich metropolis of Calgary.

My recollections of the Highwood Valley are confused, for we came back here again, in the autumn, when the poplars spilled their gold across the foothills, the wheatfields were golden also, and the sky was flecked with southbound ducks.

I recall, however, a week of glory at Dick Machin's Stampede

Ranch, its huge museum room of antiques, its customary six meals a day on a revolving table, the hot afternoons of riding on the range, the cold nights beside a log fire.

We were the only dudes present in the slack season, but a pair of big oil operators arrived from Calgary to spend a week-end out of doors and, locking themselves alone in the parlor, gambled at cards, without a moment's interruption, for twenty-three hours. Then they drove back to the city, much refreshed. They live it up in Alberta.

Not far from the Stampede stands a peak which the natives call Old Flat Top, a landmark for miles around. The Diebels took us up there one hot autumn day, eight thousand feet above sea level, and on this unlikely plateau we found an oil drill poised like a black numeral against the horizon. It was the latest statistic of the Alberta boom.

A cutting wind blew out of the glaciers to the westward. The bare rock was streaked with veins of ice. Yet a crew of men, who lived in a village of trailers, had replaced the original inhabitants of this waste, the sheep and goat, and were boring straight down through the stone spires of the continent to its underlying pool of oil.

I remember also a shoot with Mitchell, Davie, and Bert beside a prairie slough, and the ducks' black calligraphy on the sunset, and those white geese, the waveys, descending suddenly out of the north like big snowflakes. Then dinner in a millionaire's country mansion, replete with servants, family plate, and vintage wines. (Anything can happen here.) And finally a big night at the house of the Mitchells, in High River, that memorable night when Myrna's prize horse and a disreputable pinto broke out of their pasture, set the town by its ears, set the Mitchells galloping in all directions, overwhelmed the local telephone exchange, trampled the neighbors' lawns, and committed what Mrs. McCroquodale described as "errors of toilet."

Most of all I remember a summer dawn when I walked about the streets of High River in my slippers and pajamas to behold, as on the morning of creation, the splendor of the plains, the mountains, and the big sky.

The town slept under its rustling cottonwoods. The birds shouted their matins to another day. The air was loaded with the smell of plowed earth and young crops. The Rockies were flushed with sudden pink. A dawn to remember. I cannot tell you why, but in this climate, in this lovely town, and among these people, a man finds ten years at least cut from his age.

It was in the spick-and-span little city of Lethbridge, later on, that we received some expert instruction on these matters.

Harold Long, then editor of the excellent *Herald* and a rich depository of the Alberta myth, was preoccupied at the moment by a complex business deal. An Indian named Wolf Child had offered to pay an old debt in the currency of hand-sewn moccasins, yet to be made, and I could see by Long's expression, as he answered the telephone, that he had been pondering this offer deeply. Nevertheless, the great editor of Alberta—a man whose creased and weathered face is the face of the southern plains—set aside the afternoon and most of the night to explain the mysteries of his maverick province.

The adventurous, gambling spirit of Alberta had arrived here, he said, with the original American whisky-traders, and soon afterward with the American cattlemen. On that first sedimentary layer the later waves of immigration from the States, eastern Canada, and Europe had deposited new layers of varied and often heretical ideas. (Less than half of southern Alberta's people are of Canadian stock.) But Long was inclined to think that the climate must be the greatest human fact of all.

He went on to boast that the climate was the most violent in the world. If the weather took to Chinooking, the temperature could rise by eighty degrees in a few hours. Hail might dent or puncture the roof of an automobile. Why, a year ago he had driven to Calgary on a hot June day and returned next morning behind a snowplow.

Such climatic violence, he thought, produced a certain violence of the human mind always clearly visible in Alberta's maverick politics and in the strange financial doctrine hopefully named Social Credit. Anyway, Alberta had produced in

Long a great Canadian editor and in Lethbridge a fine town.

The abundant wealth of this countryside grew directly out of the earth, once water was applied. Only a few years ago several acres of bunch grass were needed to support a single beef animal. East of Lethbridge we found ourselves on a baked and withered range and then in the vast irrigated garden around the canning plants and sugar factories of Taber. Half a million acres sprouted peas, corn, beets, and other vegetables, all set in geometric lines.

We drove west again toward the Rockies and noted some further evidence of Alberta's varied life. The magnificent Mormon temple at Cardston; the Hutterite communities of bearded men in black shirts and women in billowing petticoats; the occasional cowpuncher on that obsolete machine, the horse; the pumps and pipes of the oil fields; the thin shimmer of Waterton Lake like a tear in the wrinkled eyes of the mountains; above all, the sunshine, the cloudless sky cut by nothing but the mountains' white teeth, the intoxication of the clean upland air—these things all shouted the wealth, beauty, and inherent excitement of this land.

Who could be depressed, normal, or even quite sane in this electric enivronment? A little drunk on the free wine of Alberta, consumed by the eye only, we reached the narrow Crow's Nest Pass. The Rockies rose up before us in a solid rampart of frosted rock. Presently we were in Switzerland. At least, it could have been Switzerland—cultivated fields at the mountains' base, a river of milky glacial water, cataracts of pink penstemon bloom gushing from every bank—if it were not for man's work.

A Swiss would have decorated this gorge with toy villages of cuckoo-clock chalets, sold and resold the scenery, and grown rich on the tourist trade. More practical Canadians have scarred and blackened the pass and deposited on the rubble of their coal mines some of the most hideous towns in the nation. The natives seem to like their mines, their rows of unpainted houses, and the miner's harsh life. They have grim memories of explosion, disaster, violent death, and heroic rescue, tragedies that bind them together. You can still see at

Frank the split side of Turtle Mountain and the avalanche of boulders, as large as freight cars, that rolled down one night in 1903 to cover the entire town. The road winds through the debris of the slide and over a collective tomb sealed forever.

It was now time to creep up on Calgary. As we approached it between a double rank of garish motels, I felt like the logger in the old American tale who said he was going to Bangor, Maine, to get drunk and, oh, how he dreaded it.

Calgary has always bewildered me. Since my last visit it had become more bewildering than ever; far larger, too, richer and more extroverted. It is the beamish boy of fortune, the wonder child of the west, the temple of the world's greatest Stampede, the inner shrine of the Alberta myth, the unbroken colt among Canadian towns, and our wildest maverick.

It was built, like Rome, on many hills, and is cut by its own Tiber, the Bow, and the Bow's child, the Elbow. Another Rome, superior to the original, could have been reared on this plump flank of the Rockies, but Calgary is no Rome, in body or in mind.

Its body sprawls, undulant and sensual, in the sun. Its mind is the mind of an overgrown cowtown. (I say that with no disrespect, for I can think of nothing better than a cowtown and a race of cowmen.)

The jolly aberration of these urban dwellers—they wear cowboy hats on every ceremonial occasion and like to think themselves true western characters, though they have never felt a saddle between their soft thighs—is refreshing, guileless, and valuable in a prosaic nation.

No one can be here half a day without feeling invigorated, young, and rich. This is the town of youth eternal, and it revels in youth's strength, folly, uncertainty, and glory. All the adventures of the great days have issued here in a town of lofty buildings, crowded streets, and homemade millionaires.

Thus, you will find a rich man's Cadillac parked before a store which sells secondhand saddles, broken bridles, and rusty spurs—the reality and the myth. The bellboy in the hotel will ask for market tips on the latest oil stocks and offer you some of his own. If you enter one of the new skyscrapers and the office of an oil tycoon, you will think you are in New York or Hollywood.

Where else, for example, except in Texas, would you find a man like Frank McMahon? He was a poor diamond driller not long ago, but became overnight one of the richest and most powerful men in Canada when his famous Atlantic No. 3 well blew in at Leduc, caught fire, and was controlled, after six months, by an underground injection of wire bales, golf balls, and chicken feathers by the carload.

From there McMahon and men of his sort went on to pump oil and gas from northern Alberta to Vancouver and the Northwest States, from central Alberta to the St. Lawrence. They bought themselves mansions, race horses, airplanes, New York apartments, and Broadway shows. In their oil-and-gas industry they have revolutionized Alberta's finances, its society, and its mind, turning it into a second Texas.

Now they are undertaking to tap the world's largest known supply of oil in the Athabaska tar sands up north. And they are only beginning to make Alberta Canada's largest source of fuel, power, and, perhaps, wealth.

Calgary may be, as its residents affirm, the most American town of our most American province. Three separate waves of American immigration have rolled up here to pause at the foothills. The first came on horseback some seventy years ago. The second came by railway in the real-estate boom of 1912. The third arrived after the last war by Cadillac, on visitors' permits, to bore for oil.

This latest influx is so large, friendly, and rich that some early Calgarians—a fine old buckskin aristocracy—wonder if the original spirit of the place can survive.

We spent an evening of civic lamentation among these folk on an eminence once known as American Hill, then renamed Mount Royal, to assert Canadian autonomy, and given such patriot street names as Frontenac, Montcalm, Levis, and Carleton.

Alas, said our hosts, the Americans were capturing the hill again. They lived mostly among themselves in a foreign enclave, regarded their stay here as a brief tour of foreign duty, and yearned for home. Some thirty thousand American visitors to Alberta, most of them in Calgary, had drastically changed the town's ways, raised wage scales, filled the shops with luxury goods far beyond Canadians' means, and set a dizzy social pace that Canadians could not hope to equal.

We drove north across some of America's fairest farmland and over the invisible caldron of oil and gas beneath it. Nothing marked that treasure except a few drilling rigs, some shiny tanks, and those birdlike pumps whose beaks peck rhythmically at the ground. Ahead of us the towers of Edmonton's oil refineries and chemical plants stood out suddenly like the funnels and spars of a navy at anchor.

Edmonton is a fine town, but how much finer it could have been and never will be! It bestrides the deep trough of the North Saskatchewan on a site exactly like that of Budapest, which it does not otherwise resemble. That, of course, is not Edmonton's fault but the fault of North American civilization.

Making all allowances, the people of Edmonton could have done better on the majestic gulch of their river. They could have raised on its brink more than the single tower of the Macdonald Hotel and the pompous, fussy little domes of the Parliament Buildings, now overshadowed and dwarfed by some ghastly public buildings of glass and green bathroom tiles.

Nothing seems to matter here if it represents growth. For growth is Edmonton's pride, joy, and, an outsider may suspect, its mortal danger. Once the wealth of oil, gas, farm, forest, and coal mine, from central Alberta all the way to the Arctic, has been sucked into this entrepôt by railway, road, airplane, and pipeline, Edmonton will be the largest city between the Great Lakes and the Rockies. Unless it changes its ways, Edmonton will never be a beautiful city.

But it has its glimpses. The bridges hang like gossamer across the canyon. Every house has a brief summer garden of a brilliant hue known only in the north. The university stands above the river on a broad campus. The river, a few miles from town, churns through a ravine of rock, clay, and forest not yet spoiled by the march of subdivisions.

It was Saturday night when we drove into town. Hotel rooms were hard to find. Crowds swirled up and down Jasper Avenue as in a carnival. A ragged little man preached the Word of God at a busy corner, but could not attract a single listener and, having shouted his final predictions of hellfire, stamped off in disgust.

Edmonton had other things to think about, mainly itself. In all Canada there is no other town so pleasantly egocentric, so certain of Providence's special dispensation, so childishly happy about everything, so well aware of its own perfection. It is the self-worshipping Narcissus of the nation. Yet a friendly town, inhabited by generous folk who overwhelm you with hospitality and the statistics of growth.

Next day Alberta's erratic weather changed, all the accumulated liquid of the world's atmosphere was dumped by special dispensation on Edmonton, and we found ourselves staggering ankle-deep in the mud of a farmer's field.

Ahead loomed the black skeleton of an old drill. Cows grazed a few yards off, and wild ducks paddled in ponds of rain water. The drill was probing the inner contents of the earth without disturbing the surface. A new well would soon pour a black trickle of wealth into Edmonton but leave the old treasure of black topsoil intact.

We climbed up a ladder to a shaky platform. Four young men in crash helmets and oil-stained overalls huddled for shelter under a canvas tent. They watched an enormous revolving disk as it turned the drill and drove a shaft of steel, inch by inch, foot by foot, through some prehistoric forest.

The drillers were quiet, intelligent youths, nothing like the oil "roughnecks" of the movies. They shouted in my ear above the thunder of the machinery to explain, with scribbled diagrams, the various layers of the planet that their giant augur was penetrating. The sludge now pouring out of the pumps was powdered rock from the deep layer known as Devonian 2.

Like a trained gun crew, the drillers hoisted a steel column to the top of the tower, lowered it, fastened it to the disappearing column below, and set it in motion. The great disk turned again, the platform shook, the drill sank slowly into the earth. Next week the oil would pour out, the drill would be dismantled and hauled away. Only a length of red pipe, like a fire hydrant, would be left to mark this latest puncture of the planet's skin.

We had seen enough of Alberta's southern half to understand why many economists consider it perhaps the world's richest area. But we were not thinking of statistics as we started down north through the mud, dust, and endless distances of the Peace River Country. We were thinking of the unknown men and women behind Alberta's wealth. We were thinking of an old frontiersman and his memories, a rancher and his precious chuckwagon, some cowboys in a horse barn, an Indian in search of his stolen fence rails, a great lady with a monstrous cigarette.

COLD

❧

Midwinter long ago and the first white man's ship locked in the St. Lawrence ice. Midwinter in our time and the river frozen again, the Laurentians whitely bundled, the Quebec villages shining out against the snow like Christmas cards, the householders sawing firewood, the horses hauling logs from the forest.

Midwinter and the Lakes idle, a blue integument creeping across a thousand miles of water, the inland passage to Canada closed, the nation's economic lung choked, and in the little fresh-water ports the ships tied to some friendly wharf.

Midwinter and the prairie revolving outside the train's window like a milky platter, the soil solid three feet deep, as if it could never be warmed to grow another crop.

Midwinter and the dairy cows warm in their snug barns, the beef cattle huddle behind a bluff of poplar, the shaggy range horses pawing the snow for last year's bunch grass, their owners wrapped in two suits of woollen underwear, fur coats, and leather chaps, every ranch-house stove red-hot, the washing as solid as iron on the line.

Midwinter in Alberta and the Chinook suddenly blows its hot breath from the southwest, the snow turns to puddles, the muddy roads to dust, and animals sniff the false scent of spring.

Midwinter in the Rockies and the tracks of moose, deer, elk, sheep, and goat circle the lower hills in crisscross webbing, the spruce is coated deep with sticky icing, every stump bears a mushroom of snow, the train moves through walls of white, the nourishment of Canada's great rivers is poised for the spring thaw, and already the Fraser carries round wafers of ice like marshmallows.

Midwinter on the mild Pacific littoral and sea storms are tearing the limbs from the big trees, but the forest floor is strangely peaceful, muffled by a brown quilt of leaves, bracken, and sword ferns. Earth has become almost liquid. The coastal sponge is filling up to satisfy next summer's thirst, and the sound of its gurgle is like a boiling pot, stone-cold. High above, the woodwinds of the treetops and the drums of rain make contrapuntal cadence, and the foghorns of the shore add a rhythmic note in bass.

Midwinter and even the cities cannot escape the cold, that first great fact of Canadian life. Midwinter and half the nation's energies are needed to keep houses heated, industries working, communications open, and the thickening blood-stream of civilization in flow.

Midwinter—the supreme test, the economic handicap, the extra cost and annual adventure of a northern people. When the solstice is safely past, when the low-flying sun rises an inch each day and light lasts a moment longer in the evening, the Canadian yearns for spring's release. He curses, but secretly he loves his winter. Without it, this would be a different nation and we would be a different people. We might be better or worse, we might call ourselves by the same name, but we would not be Canadians.

CHAPTER THIRTEEN

———◆——◆———

The Long Day

A VAGUE rumor, nothing more, had brought us far north of Edmonton. At the end of this weary road—no one could tell us just where—a man and a woman, their names unknown, were said to be worth a long journey. That seemed improbable as we wallowed through a quagmire of peculiarly adhesive mud and then, by the shore of Lesser Slave Lake, staggered for miles on boulders as large as a man's skull, where road gangs had hastily tried to fill a bottomless muskeg.

But we decided to drive on. Though we didn't know it yet, this decision was the wisest of our travels. For we were about to make a memorable rediscovery of the human spirit.

Some weeks earlier the spring thaw had imprisoned scores of automobiles in what the local inhabitants called the "Great Impassability." Mud and muskeg had isolated the Peace River Country and revealed the sovereign fact of its life—its precarious tenure, its endless distances, its hopes long deferred, and its dogged courage.

The road ahead was an old road, perhaps the oldest in North America, and a strange caravan had preceded us here by some thousands of years. All the prehistoric hordes from Asia, men and animals, once moved, it is said, across the Bering Strait and down this rutted track into the heartland of the continent. They were followed, aeons later, by the Canadian fur-traders of the unequaled Athabaska peltry, by the settlers' wagons, and now by automobiles.

After that immemorial march we had no right to complain of a little moisture and a windshield blacked out whenever a car passed us in a splash of liquid clay. Besides, we were seeing a new and very ancient thing.

The protective dike of badlands ends at the gateway of High Prairie and a fertile plain begins. We had entered a distant annex of Alberta, the last farming frontier and possibly the most interesting region in Canada. It is an old region in our brief national history. Once it was decisive in continental affairs. It led the first Canadians to the western sea and their possession of the Pacific coast. Yet it had been peopled only yesterday, and it still felt the strong pulse beat of youth.

Here, in fact, was the final reproduction of a Canadian experience which had started three centuries before on the banks of the St. Lawrence. There will be no experience of this exact sort in America again. Hence, the settlers now subduing the northern wilds, as their ancestors subdued the south, are justified in using capital letters and naming their land the Peace River Country. It is almost a country, and may someday be a province. At any rate, it is unique.

That fact was intimated in a sudden flash. We rounded a blind corner toward nightfall to confront a staggering sight.

Below us, in its green trench, the Peace River shone like a braid of gold about six inches wide, and unraveled through winding coils to the northward. A swarm of black islands, no larger than waterfowl, swam in the current. Some white specks on the bank must be a town. Upstream, at the crooked elbow of the Peace, a rift in the hills marked the Smoky's deep ravine and Alexander Mackenzie's winter campsite on his voyage to the Pacific. With perfect timing an incendiary sun lighted a bonfire over the western hills in celebration of the summer solstice.

We coasted down the road's looping spirals. The river broadened out and turned from gold to Burgundy. Crossing the sharp borderline of twilight, we plunged into the dark shadow of the canyon.

Peace River town had escaped the day's rain. It lay under a brown dust, but fine gold dust hung above the river. A brave and noisy little street told us at once that this town was no part of the Canada we had traveled from Newfoundland to the Rockies.

It looked at first like a pioneers' encampment, a bivouac on the route of march, a temporary spark of life on the outer edge of things. Except for the automobiles solidly ranked by the sidewalk, Peace River seemed to live like a town of western Canada's beginnings, in a time lag of fifty years. But it is here to stay.

We shook the afternoon's accumulation of soil from our feet and entered the hotel through a litter of the natives' mud-caked gum boots. At the restaurant counter we sat between a blind Indian woman of noble bearing and a Ukrainian waiter from the beer parlor, who immediately recounted the story of his life and offered to pay for our meal. A group of young men, bearded and bronzed, conferred in whispers over a private table. These American engineers were searching the north for oil and, like all their craft, kept their business strictly to themselves.

Presently a burly man parked his truck outside, stamped into the restaurant, and ordered a double portion of ham and eggs. He had just hauled a load of wheat some three hundred miles, the shortest distance to the railway, from his farm at Buffalo Head Prairie. Yes, we were on the edge of things. We had found an almost forgotten species, the Canadian sodbuster on virgin land.

A good dinner fortified us for a walk about the town. It had a strident, cheerful, neighborly air, and evidently contained a variety of races.

Some of the farmers, who arrived in muddy trucks, had unmistakable Slavic faces and accents. Others spoke in French. A huddle of women before an undertaker's parlor lamented their own tragedy in a strange tongue. The undertaker—he wore an incongruous black coat and striped gray trousers—

soothed these customers as best he could in the English language, and they disappeared, like Ruth, into the alien corn.

Upstream a little way, the road petered out between some new bungalows and gardens of evening-scented flowers. There we watched the sunset casually ignite both land and water in solstitial explosion.

No one could observe this crimson pageantry without guessing why the Peace River people are fascinated by their Country and worship it as a religion. It lacks the conventional beauty of the Maritimes, the St. Lawrence, or the Rockies. Much of it is drab, and some of it ugly. In total it has a grandeur of its own, a haunting quality of size and emptiness; above all, the sense of virginity, of life in its salad days.

Most of its life as a settled community has been witnessed by men still living. J. D. Levesque, the richest merchant of Peace River town, knew it as a fur-trading post though he arrived here from Quebec as recently as 1913 with a wagon-load of trade goods and a secondhand circus tent, the germs of his fortune. This round-faced, placid little man admitted, in a faintly French accent, that he could live anywhere but would never move from the little town which grew under his eyes out of a dozen shacks on the riverbank. His feelings about the north were not to be put fully into words, of course. "Big," he said. "It's big and new and changing every day. That keeps a man young, eh?"

Certainly it had kept him young in his seventy-four years, but he had not forgotten the old code of the frontier. Though he did not tell me the story himself, the leading capitalist of the Peace River Country could have been observed, not long ago, in a log cabin cooking meals for an aged and sick Indian woman. This is the north more by custom than by geography.

Levesque had not come here by accident. His race, the French Canadian *voyageurs*, reached the Athabaska peltry and glimpsed the Rockies before the English of the Atlantic coast had crossed the central plains. Their descendants reappeared as farmers to build the farthest suburb of Quebec.

All this history was being recapitulated today in a curious

little episode. Peace River town was about to launch a ferry; not much of a ferry, to be sure, only a couple of wooden pontoons, a deck to hold automobiles, and a new type of jet engine. But to anyone who knew the record of the river its latest craft had an odd tale to tell.

Joint memories and a river instinct drew a crowd of townspeople to the beach that afternoon. Fred Gullion, son of a steamboat captain who had been called "the strongest man in the north," tinkered with the newfangled engine. It must have meant a good deal to him, for he had lived beside the river all his life and traveled it on a raft at the age of two. Charlie Maclean was there also, an old river hand and furtrader whose barges had been propelled by current and oars.

An Indian woman in a scarlet dress, accompanied by nine children and a tenth not yet born, had come to see the white man's latest invention. The throng included the undertaker, still wearing his black coat and gray trousers; the lady cook of the ferry-builders' camp, her bare legs cruelly lacerated by mosquitoes; a retired schoolteacher from Calgary, weak from excitement; a photographer from the Peace River *Record-Gazette*; a grave government engineer; and many clamorous small boys.

You might have thought, from the general mood of suspense, that the *Queen Mary* was to be launched by some royal sponsor. These people knew what they were about. They knew the origins of the ferry.

It was from this point that Canadians beheld the last continental mystery in the closing years of the eighteenth century. They had come thus far on their westward trek of nearly two hundred years, and they had halted here before the terrifying barrier of the Rockies. What lay beyond those shiny peaks to the westward?

Mackenzie paddled up the Peace from Lake Athabaska in the autumn of 1792, saw the very beach where the ferry now lay waiting, camped a few miles upstream, near the Smoky, and, next spring, lunged to the Pacific, the first white man to reach it by land north of Mexico. Fraser followed the same rivers to find his own. After him came Simpson, Little Emperor of the Hudson's Bay Company, a kilted bagpiper playing his pipes in the bow of the canoe. Then came the gold-seekers, and eventually the farmers about the end of the First World War.

A man required no great imagination to see that company of gallant ghosts moving past the modern town and dropping their paddles to stare at the ill-shaped ferry, successor to canoe, barge, and steamboat. From the paddle to the jet engine—that was the meaning of today's humble ceremony.

All was ready at last. A tractor lumbered across the beach and gently nosed the ferry's side. She started down the greased skids and stuck. The smiling undertaker looked professionally grave. The Indian woman and her brood watched, open-mouthed. Even the small boys stopped shouting, and in the silence thick clouds of mosquitoes buzzed like distant airplanes.

Another push sent the ferry splashing sideways into the current. Everyone breathed again. Having performed a familiar rite, the townspeople went about their business and we climbed the hill to the grave of Twelve-Foot Davis.

The folk giant of the north was, in life, a tiny man of sad face and drooping whiskers, but he had a superhuman strength. Tired of his job as a Boston pastry cook, he joined the rush to the gold fields of the Cariboo, in British Columbia, nearly one hundred years ago, and staked a claim twelve feet wide between the misplaced lines of two adjoining claims. His strip of Cariboo was wide enough to make him rich.

He moved eastward across the Rockies, carrying his customary pack of two hundred pounds, built a string of fur posts, and made himself the good Samaritan of every passing traveler. Illiterate, and blind in his last years, he became almost an uncrowned king. His loyal subjects included such notorious characters as Banjo Mike and Nigger Dan (the latter well remembered for his vow never to be "trod on by any man except Her Majesty Queen Victoria").

When Davis lay ill at the Anglican mission of Lesser Slave Lake in 1900, and an anxious nursing sister asked him if he was afraid to die, he uttered the valedictory of his kind: "No, miss. Why should I be afraid to die? I never killed nobody. I never stole from nobody, and I always kept open house for travelers all my life. No, miss, I ain't afraid to die."

In death the story of Twelve-Foot Davis slowly encompassed the whole north. The tiny man grew into a mighty myth. Another giant of his country, "Peace River Jim" Cornwall, moved Davis's body from its grave beside Lesser Slave Lake and interred it on the hill above the confluence of the Peace and the Smoky. And on a slab of concrete Cornwall inscribed a tribute fit for any king: "He was every man's friend and never locked his cabin door."

We stood for a little while observing the stark monument and the dreadful trench below it, then started north. The Mackenzie Highway ran, arrow-straight, through an almost unbroken sweep of poplar. A few farms had been hacked out here and there in an empire of good agricultural land. For two hundred miles on this bleak, monotonous plateau nothing stirred beside the road, no man or animal. Only the passage of an occasional freight truck, in a billow of dust, indicated man's presence farther north.

Somewhere along the way we picked up a tanned and sturdy boy. He was dusty, ill-clad, and shy, but he managed, in a few jerky sentences, to tell the story of his people, of a farming community hardly forty years old and already one of the richest in Canada.

His father had worked for many years in the Alberta coal mines to make a stake, and by 1944 had managed to acquire six horses. That was about all—six horses. He took up a homestead in this wilderness, built a cabin of poplar logs, and began to clear his land. The wife and two little sons helped him burn the brush. After a summer's work thirteen acres were cleared and yielded a crop of 120 bushels of oats to the acre in the following autumn.

Now, our passenger said, the family was well fixed. It had a fine house of spruce logs, a tractor, and even bicycles, which the brothers rode seven miles to school. All this had happened not in the early days of the west but in the last dozen years. The hundred thousand people of the Peace River Country are at the beginning of things.

I asked the boy what had happened to the six horses, the family's first capital. "Dad keeps them," the boy said. "They're too old to work and he has a tractor. We ought to shoot them, but we feed them all winter. Dad says he can't shoot his friends."

Late in the afternoon we turned off the highway that runs on to Great Slave Lake and followed a side road eastward until we came again to the oily current of the Peace. A dilapidated truck awaited the ferry at its flimsy wharf, and a squat man, unshaven and caked with dust, dozed over the wheel, having just hauled a load of grain three hundred miles down to the railway at Grimshaw. He told us he farmed around Buffalo Head Prairie, and added proudly that this was the most northerly farmland in America, or in the world, maybe. Yes, it was a long haul to Grimshaw, but a man could grow sixty bushels of wheat to the acre here. He had been lucky to get twenty-five in Saskatchewan.

"It's the long daylight does it," he explained. "There's only about a hundred growin' days between frost, but she grows twenty hours a day in the summer. No country like it."

All the north needed was a railway. (His face lighted up as he expressed the oldest dream of the pioneer.) Well, one of these days a railway would be built to the mineral zone of Great Slave Lake, and then life would be easy for the three or four thousand farm folks around here. He pointed to the puffs of smoke on the horizon—clearing fires on the newest farms.

A decayed raft (it would be replaced soon by the newly built ferry from Peace River) chugged painfully across the current. We contrived to get our car aboard and off again on the far bank. It was evening, but the sun still hung high when we emerged from the poplar forest into the single street of Fort Vermilion.

One row of ageless, weather-beaten buildings grew like parched vegetation from the brown soil and fronted on a wooden sidewalk, a dusty track, and the flat bank of the river. No human form appeared. The only living things visible in Fort Vermilion were some saddle horses hitched to a log rail. The village looked like a thin façade of scenery which someone had propped up here by mistake and abandoned.

At last a wagon moved along the street with a clank of empty gasoline drums, and rattled down the bank into the river. The horses stood up to their bellies in the muddy water, drinking deep. Their driver picked up a bucket and began to fill the drums. This was Fort Vermilion's waterworks. The householders paid half a dollar for fifty gallons, delivered at the door.

Yet this was no new town. Men had lived in it for almost two hundred years since the days of the earliest Athabaska fur-traders. Their life, entirely dependent on river travel, had not changed much until the road was pushed through from Grimshaw in 1947. Their town still remained a trade post. The old traders would have seen nothing to surprise them in this desolate street except our car and Ma Kidd's gas pump.

That venerable lady, as spry and chirpy as a robin, flew out of her store to refill our tank and announced in a shrill, friendly voice that the country around here was the best under heaven and, God knew, she'd seen a lot of the world.

"Why, say," she chortled, "when I came in 1917 the loneliness near smothered me to pieces. There was only two other white women then. The Indians didn't know yes from no. So lonely you could hear yourself think. But, then, I was always kind of timid."

Her timidity was not apparent to the naked eye. She had lived in Fort Vermilion when it could be reached only by stern-wheeler or barge, and often could not be reached at all. In her small way she seemed to have prospered.

"It's the land!" she shouted. "Grows everything! You just can't stop it."

She pointed to her garden within a neat fence. The vegetables looked at least two months old, but had been planted less than a fortnight.

"Daylight!" she exclaimed. "Daylight practically all night. Only trouble is mosquitoes. We used to keep a smudge pot on the tongue of the wagon for the horses—they'd go plumb crazy without it—and another by us on the seat. Well, we've got the mosquitoes licked now, thank the Lord."

Unconsciously she fanned the innumerable insects about her face. I counted half a dozen of them on each of my hands.

There was no hotel in the village, but a silent Scotsman kept a comfortable stopping-house, and his wife set a good table. After dinner we walked up the street in search of the two people whose reputation, a rumor only, had brought us all this way. We were not disappointed.

Dr. Julius Kratz welcomed us to his house. He was a handsome man of middle age, and he was very tired. In the morning he and his wife had performed a difficult surgical operation, and all afternoon their little office had been filled with Mennonite patients from the backwoods. For relaxation he had been reading Greek drama in its original text when we knocked at his door. Now his wife appeared, a medical doctor, the surgeon of this remarkable team and a powerful blonde Amazon. Like her husband, she was steeped in the culture of Europe.

How, we wondered, had such a pair wandered into this outlandish spot? Theirs was a tragic and triumphant adventure possible only in a disordered world.

Two young medical students had met in a German university and decided to marry. Dr. Julius already had found an honorable place on Hitler's list of intended victims. He was of Jewish blood. Dr. Hanna had publicly refused to give the Nazi salute before her class, and was warned that she would be arrested that same night.

The lovers hurriedly married, fled to Switzerland, then to England, then to Israel, and finally to Canada. Everywhere they had sought nothing more than the chance to practice their profession, but they had found it only in Canada—of all unlikely places, in Fort Vermilion.

Its hospital had lacked a doctor for years. Few doctors were prepared to endure the isolation, the hardship, and the poverty of this primitive hamlet. Because two courageous Germans, uprooted in the Nazi storm, were willing to face the unknown, Fort Vermilion received the medical learning of Europe.

Why had they come here instead of practicing comfortably in some Canadian city? Well, they liked their work, though it was hard, and, as we learned later, had gravely damaged their health. Besides—they said this without any pretension and certainly without expecting it to be reported—they owed a debt to Canada. It had given them their first chance of freedom.

Dr. Julius recalled with a wistful smile that, on reaching Canada, he had been asked to write down on an official immigration form how long he and his wife intended to remain. He had seized a pen and joyfully scrawled one word —"Forever." A lucky day for Canada.

We walked down the street to the hospital, a thoroughly modern and well-equipped establishment of the Catholic Church. As devout Catholics, the doctors found it congenial. I was not much interested, to tell the truth, in their operating-room, their X-ray and other excellent equipment, for I had encountered here of a sudden the most moving thing I had yet seen in Canada.

Three brown little Indian boys looked up at us from their beds with the frightened eyes of woods animals. Medical treatment had saved them from death by tuberculosis. In a few days they would return to their parents.

Dr. Hanna entered the room ahead of us. Those little eyes were no longer frightened. The boys stretched out eager hands to their friend. As she picked them up, one by one, and introduced them to us, they giggled but said no word.

There was a picture never to be described or forgotten. A defiant enemy of Hitler, a great woman in her own right and a skilled doctor by education, was holding in her arms an Indian child from the wilderness of northern Canada, a child rescued by her skill and her husband's. Or perhaps more by love than by skill. Mercy knew neither nationality nor geography.

No photographer recorded that picture. Canada would never hear of it, and these doctors did not wish it to be known. Enough that in their obscure outpost, and often driving through heat or blizzard to some distant cabin, in an area of forty thousand square miles, they could cure the sick, repay their debt to Canada, and enjoy their freedom. But it seemed to me that the debt was all on Canada's side.

The boys would go home next week and grow up with some dim memory of a tall, golden woman and a gentle, smiling man to whom they owed their lives. Even that memory would fade in time. Well, we would not forget.

Everybody in the hospital, nurses, housemaid, cooks, and patients, Indian and white, had taken on the spirit of the doctors. They seemed to be happy, almost as if sickness were a lark and its treatment a summer holiday. Sister Marcella, a little white bird of a woman, had managed the hospital for two years without a doctor, and she chuckled at the recollection as she fed us homemade ice cream in the kitchen.

We talked for an hour or two with the doctors in their parlor, amid the books and the few family ornaments brought from their lost home. Good talk it was, too, spiced by Dr. Hanna's strong European coffee and rich German cakes, talk of books, music, and history, the talk of civilized people on the side of a dusty road and a lonely river. When we left, we were proud to call this man and woman our friends, and though their strange destiny was to call them soon to another Peace River village far away, we would remember them always with those Indian boys in Fort Vermilion.

It was still light enough at eleven o'clock to read a newspaper on the street. The brown river had turned pink under the dying colors of the sunset. The air was heavily scented, almost oppressive, with the perfume of wild roses.

Now and then a horse clumped through the dust, ridden by some shadowy figure in a cowboy hat and chaps. From a hall half a mile up the river came the sound of music. The young folks of Fort Vermilion, mostly Indians, were starting their weekly dance at the conventional hour of midnight and would conclude at five a.m.

That day's oddities were not quite finished. The last light slowly faded and I found myself on the sidewalk learning the

historic origins of Communism from a swarthy and deeply
wrinkled little man. He wore a blue military beret and a
regimental badge and carried a soldier's knapsack.

An exile from the Russian revolution, he had fought with
the Canadian Army in the First World War, and evidently
had thought deeply about the world's madness. He talked at
length—his accent slightly foreign, his grammar perfect—of
humanity's doubtful prospects and the misery of his people
in Russia. I was not really listening. I was slapping several
million mosquitoes from my face and ankles and trying to
solve a riddle.

How was it possible that here, so far from anywhere, at the
farthest reach of men's plows, a broken warrior from Russia
could expound medieval history to a stranger while an Indian
of scarred and twisted face grunted his approval and, next
door, two doctors from Germany, suddenly summoned, were
about to deliver the child of a Mennonite woman?

These people, the river murmuring in the darkness, the last
speck of light in the west, the faint sound of music, the shuffle
of horses' hoofs in the dust, and the immensity of sky and
land told me one thing at least: neither I nor any other man
from the city streets knew much about Canada.

The sun was well over the eastern horizon three hours later.
By breakfast time the day had turned uncomfortably hot. We
drove southward, and by late afternoon were back in the
settled farm country, the rank green fields, snug houses, big
barns, and busy towns around their grain elevators. Presently
we met the canyon of the Peace again at Dunvegan, that
doomed site of fort and settlement which was to have been
the great town of the north, fit to bear the ancestral place
name of the Clan Macleod. Where the palisaded fur post
once stood, where Simpson used to pause on his ceaseless
voyages, where real-estate promoters promised to build a
metropolis, nothing survived those lost hopes save a stone
cairn, a few rotten log cabins, and a chuffing ferryboat.

The ferry took us across the river. We climbed out of the
canyon, passed through many bustling villages, and at nightfall reached the little city of Grand Prairie. There the in-

habitants were in a happy state of mind. Crops were good, the community was growing, and a new highway, replacing the dreadful road and Great Impassability around Lesser Slave Lake, would soon provide a fast short-cut to Edmonton.

Everybody in all the numerous towns to the northwestward seemed to be happy, and it was hard to believe that these people had settled here, cleared these farms, and laid this spreading network of roads within a generation.

At Dawson Creek, terminus of the Alberta railway, we were just across the British Columbia boundary but still in the Peace River Country, for it defies any political line. The first broad stretch of the Alaska Highway brought us to the Peace once more, its canyon spanned by a huge suspension bridge, part of an American wartime engineering miracle.

We were looking for another sort of miracle. And, sure enough, Ma Murray was sitting, as we had hoped, amid the glorious pandemonium of her office in the town of Fort St. John.

The editor of *The Alaska Highway News* had arrayed herself, as usual, in rustling silk, apparently for some important social event but actually as a symbol of her infatuation with the north, her flaming vision of the universe. Though her hair had turned a little whiter since our last meeting, the wrinkles a little deeper, she defied time. A torrent of sound and a vocabulary hardly known to the English language burst from her as she fell into our arms.

This meeting ended, of course, the day's business in the office of *The Alaska Highway News*. We paused only to examine the rusty hand press in front of the door—it is supposed to have served Mark Twain in California before it printed the first works of Jack London and Robert Service in the Yukon—and then set out for the Murray farm.

A tape recording of Ma's conversation over the dinner table would make a priceless morsel of pure Canadiana, a classic of horse sense, sheer fantasy, and genial mania. She wrote as she talked, in a slashing, shouting, frontier style which I had thought must have died with Twain or, at latest, with Bob Edwards. I skimmed surreptitiously through the latest issue of her paper and found, among other exhibits, this chaste pronouncement:

"We're skrissed here in this town with some of the smuggest, smallest, short-sightedest businessmen whose butternegg philosophy binds their vision and ideas up tight as boiled cheese. Many of 'em are wallowing in their own eye-wash and are afraid to face their shadows. We deserve the dirty end of the stick, too, if we don't grab t'other and go after somebody."

Ma was impatient, but Fort St. John's fight had been won already. A railway would soon link it with Vancouver. It would have a big plant to process the gas of the surrounding country—the biggest gas field, Ma said, "this side of Armageddon."

She fixed me with hypnotic eye and hoarsely proclaimed the future of her town.

"Listen, son," she shouted, "when they're bringing in one of those gas wells the whole earth quivers like raspberry jelly. Now, I'm telling you, son, it'll shake your hangover and make your hide itch from midnight to breakfast time. The east hasn't heard about it, but, then, the east doesn't know any more about the north than a pig knows Sunday. We'll raise hell, I tell you, and put a prop under it. . . ."

Reeling under her idiom of violence, we drove into the Rockies. Spangles of lightning hung over them as darkness fell. The lamps were burning in the windows of home.

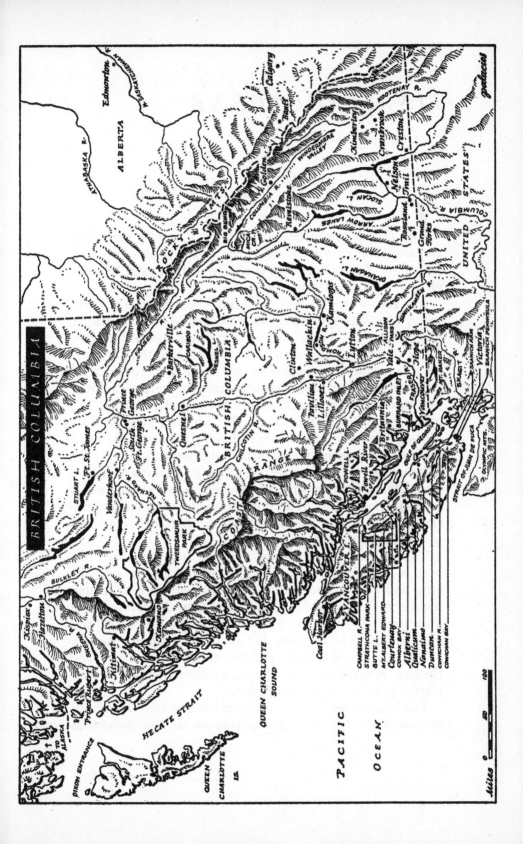

FINAL NOCTURNE

The swamp at the bottom of the hill yonder must have contained frogs since the early days of life upon our planet. Frogs sang down there when evolution had not even begun to glimpse the noble shape of man.

Just such a swamp once lay beside every Canadian settlement. The frogs' spring song was a recognized national anthem long before "O Canada" was written. Those bass voices of the big eastern frogs and the treble of their little western brothers became so much a part of human life in this land, such a familiar accompaniment of the spring cadenza, so universal a music, that we claimed the swamp singers as a special possession. We called them the Canadian Band. But wherever progress is advancing these days (and where is it not?) the boom of frogs is muffled by a human process of the same name.

In our swamp, at the edge of a growing Canadian town, you would think that the original inhabitants had established at least squatters' rights by an occupation of several million generations. Until this year no one challenged their unwritten title deeds in fee simple.

The generations of human children, playing beside the swamp, sailing toy boats, collecting tadpoles in jam jars, robbing birds' nests, and skating on the rough skim of winter, number only three or four since the Indians disappeared from these parts. As time is reckoned in a young country, that was quite a spell. The children, like the frogs, assumed that the swamp was eternal and, like children everywhere, they fondled the frog. A minute parody of man, a solemn humorist, a born plaything, he was every child's friend.

The swamp had its own regulated life and sure rhythm, its seasons of rest and labor, its nights of silence and thunderous sound. Months ahead of the tardy eastern frogs, our far western orchestra burst into spring crescendo at the Ides of March.

Last night the ten thousand massed musicians shattered the darkness without any advance notice or rehearsal. For private reasons of his own, every frog in the swamp just decided at the same moment to serenade the spring. We lay abed and listened to Canada's old, unchanging concert.

Human music is much better, of course, but it has not exercised any vital influence on the Canadian character. Canada would be inconceivable if frog music were stilled; and if we have lacked great poets and musicians, we hardly needed them so long as the native troubadours appeared at our doors every spring, on schedule.

In this rural neighborhood, however, we evidently took our swamp, like so many other humble things, too much for granted. We supposed that children would always play in the congenial mud and skate on the brief, cracked ice, that plovers would scream and wheel at hatching time, green mallards nest in the reeds, and frogs announce the winter's end. We expected too much.

Recently progress has put our swamp and its inhabitants on trial for obstructing the well-planned course of human events. The inevitable verdict is guilty. The sentence is death to the frogs and, as in the old tale, fun to their destroyers.

Residents on two feet have moved into new houses along the margin of the swamp. Streets have been laid out, trees cut down, telephone poles erected, and a higher jungle of television towers. All the advantages of civilization have sprung up overnight after futile aeons of evolution had made no perceptible improvement.

Now progressive men are draining the swamp itself. The little lake is shrinking to a puddle, and soon will disappear. Perhaps the frogs already find their quarters somewhat cramped. They must miss the dark, secret places where they went a-wooing and raised their wriggling families, but they are not equipped to understand here, or at the edge of any Canadian town, the triumphal climax of man's progress, the necessary end of the swamp.

Ignorant of their doom, the frogs perform a lively nocturne tonight and prepare for endless cycles of spring. Deaf to progress, blind to civilization, useless to the scheme of evolution, they are singing their last song. Next spring we shall have no more primitive balladry, only the superior music of the TV sets.

Man's boom no doubt is preferable to the boom of frogs. Still, the old-timers hereabouts will miss a precious particle of Canada and a fellow creature in the swamp of life.

CHAPTER FOURTEEN

——◆——

The Trail's End

BEFORE he descended his unknown river to the sea, Simon Fraser reached Stuart Lake, by canoe, in 1806. There, midway between the Rockies and the coast, he met an Indian chief and honored him with the name of Prince.

The grandson of Chief Prince greeted me at the door of his little cabin a few yards from the lake shore. Though he had reached the age of ninety-two and was somewhat stooped, he still stood well over six feet tall in his slippers and was the handsomest man I had ever encountered in Canada.

His face, molded in lean, angular planes, would fascinate any sculptor. The black, steady eyes, the sharp Roman nose, the closely clipped white mustache, and the air of gentle authority belonged to the portrait of some English aristocrat. Only the dark skin revealed the chief's origins, as the spotless white shirt and patched blue overalls revealed his poverty.

There being no second chair in the cabin, I sat on the edge of the homemade bed and listened respectfully to this oldest resident of the first permanent fur-trading post west of the Rockies. He asked me at once whether I preferred to use English or French. When I chose English, he spoke in the accents of an educated man.

"Of course," he said, "our family name of Prince was just flattery. Fraser was good at that kind of thing, you know. A prince is a big man and we're only a small people. But my father used to tell me that there were three thousand Indians here in his day. By George, things have changed!"

They had changed more than the chief realized. In his long lifetime he had seen, even from this isolated spot, something of the physical process which had transformed British Columbia from a gold camp into the flashiest exhibit on the entire map of Canada and perhaps the fastest-growing community on earth. The larger change, invisible on the lonely shores of Stuart Lake, was psychic—old-timers might call it psychotic—and already it had obliterated the British Columbia of my own youth.

"Yes, by George, things have changed," the chief repeated. "Everything is bigger, everybody is richer, but nobody seems to be as happy as in the old days. Why, I sometimes think most of us around here were better off when we had nothing but a flintlock gun, or maybe a secondhand rifle, with very little ammunition—it cost too much, you know—and a bow and arrow to shoot small game. Well, that's progress! Or so they tell me."

This was said without bitterness, with a certain cheerful resignation. Unconsciously the chief had expressed the thoughts of all that vanishing race, the British Columbia old-timers, Indian and white.

Through the window I could see the blue gash of Stuart Lake pointing like a jagged signpost to the westward. The same broad panorama of water and mountain confronted Fraser when he met the chief's grandfather. Some of the whitewashed buildings of Fort St. James still stood as their builders left them. But the British Columbia boom had penetrated even this unlikely place. A sawmill and a village had grown up since my last visit.

The chief followed my glance and read my thoughts.

"Everything changes," he said, "but the lake and the mountains. They never change. Only men change, by George!"

A little Indian girl, like a plump doll in a yellow dress, came shouting through the doorway, fell silent as she saw me, and snuggled into her grandfather's lap. He petted her with his trembling hands and whispered some Indian words. This child, he said proudly, had been baptized, like him, in the Catholic faith. I would find his birth certificate and hers properly recorded at the old church a mile up the road.

He inquired suddenly if I was a Catholic. I said I was not. Well, he hastened to add, any Christian religion was good, so long as a man observed it. What, I asked, did he think of the original Indian religion? "Oh, that!" he exclaimed. "Only a kind of dream, you know. It was nothing."

He told me many tales of his people, of Father Morice (a faded picture of that great missionary hung on the wall), of the hunt, the autumn salmon hordes, the sprucebark canoes of his boyhood. He had traveled far, even down the Peace River, on a raft, at the age of sixteen. Always his talk returned to the fame of his grandfather, Fraser's friend, around whose grave he had recently built a picket fence, hard by the lake. Well, he would be buried near by—quite soon, he supposed.

Yes, he repeated, everything had changed. The supply of game was depleted. His people worked in the sawmill, they owned houses and bought automobiles, but they had lost something—"and the white man, too, he has lost something, very big. By George, yes."

We talked for about an hour while the sky suddenly darkened, whitecaps rose on the blue lake, and I foresaw trouble for any traveler in the wilds of central British Columbia. As I prepared to retreat to a paved road, the chief got painfully to his feet, the once powerful limbs shaking, and bade me farewell. His handgrip was rough and strong. The black eyes searched mine for a moment. Then he said: "We shall not meet again, my friend. Not in this world. Adieu."

I looked back from a road now turning from dust to mud. The Indian who bore the name of Prince was watching me, erect and unafraid, from the door of a cabin as a prince might stand at the gate of his castle. He would not be there long. His British Columbia and mine already were dead.

A mountain gale and a cold summer rain soon made the road out of Fort St. James impassable. Some enterprising boy, with his father's tractor, pulled us through the worst mud-holes for a modest fee. We didn't know it then, but a cloud-burst over some half-million square miles was about to isolate British Columbia literally from the rest of Canada.

At the dismal village of Vanderhoof, almost exactly in the center of the province, we paused to reorient ourselves. That is never easy in British Columbia, for it is fractured, as no other province is, as by a convulsion of nature, by one sledge-hammer blow; is split into at least ten main compartments and countless minor cells whose separate pockets of human life are strangers to one another. But I calculated that, with luck, we might reach Vancouver, some six hundred miles away by road, in two or three days. As it turned out, we were actually distant from the coast by a detour of about two thousand miles.

Half of British Columbia, almost uninhabited, stretched north of us. To the west lay a lovely land that we had traveled many times before, a land of green valleys, mountains, lakes, and rivers, the storied hamlet of Hazelton beside the azure pyramid of Rocher de Boule, the decaying totem poles of Kispiox, the canyons of the Bulkley, and the gorge of the Skeena, leading to the port of Prince Rupert.

Not far from Vanderhoof the Nechako River had been dammed off from the Fraser and now flowed directly to the sea through a tunnel to spin turbines deep within a mountain at the aluminum plant of Kemano. The lakes of Tweedsmuir Park, east of the Coast Range, were rising to drown their timbered shores and swell into a new reservoir which nature had directed eastward and man had turned westward by a short-cut. Nowhere had Canada's revolution effected more rapid changes in the original substance of the continent.

But we had no time to meditate on these things. The problem, in this avalanche of moisture, was to reach the coast. Ignorant of our disaster, we pushed eastward to Prince George, one of Simon Fraser's fur posts which had grown into a lumbering center of some ten thousand people.

We had known it, not long ago, as a dilapidated main street and a few sawmills on the Fraser's muddy bank. Mr.

Peter Wilson, its veteran barrister, could remember it when the Grand Trunk Pacific Railway came through in 1914, when stern-wheelers still breasted the river's terrible rapids, when everybody expected to be rich tomorrow morning, and meanwhile the town's bread was made by a German baker, who kneaded it industriously with his bare feet.

Today Prince George was fairly bursting with population and civic pride, was becoming the capital and entrepôt of a virgin empire from here to the Yukon, but a few old-timers longed for the freedom, the poverty, the hope of wealth, and the gamble of the lost frontier. Though they used no such words, they knew, as I did, that British Columbia was paying for its boom with the loss of a special quality of mind, a spiritual climate, an inner tone which once distinguished it from all other provinces.

Its people necessarily were unique in Canada. They were the only Canadians who had penetrated the final barrier on the westward march. They had gone as far as man could go. Sealed off not only from Canada but also from one another in their mountain labyrinth, they were subtly united by their sense of separateness and their joint secret, the secret of British Columbia.

No mountain range could stay them. No land could satisfy their hunger until their feet were set upon the last margin of the continent. Now they stood at trail's end and shared a mystery. They alone had beheld the western sea and a world around them too big for their imagination, too beautiful for language, perhaps too rich for their own good. After that discovery they never looked back.

Once past the Rockies, they possessed the fairest or, at any rate, the most varied land in Canada, and they regarded it almost as a sovereign state, themselves as a chosen people. Their separate patriotism soon became the infatuation of a love affair—at times noble, at others mean and stupid, but always guileless, honest, and passionate.

As they lived in successive spasms of boom, from the boom of gold in Cariboo to the boom of timber on the coast, they came to expect, as their natural right, a superior place in

Confederation. By any material measurement they achieved it.

If they were more provincial, self-centered, and selfish than any other Canadians, their character was redeemed by a wild generosity among themselves, a largeness of view (so long as that view went no farther east than the Rockies), by a certain boyish credulity, by boundless expectations, and, most of all, by a boisterous, out-of-door life close to the earth, the forest, and the mountain.

They hardly understood the nation or their part in it. They never produced a national idea or statesman of importance, but they were faithful to their own ways, built their own civilization, worshipped their own land, and reared a miracle of sorts in its image. The lavish dimensions of their environment expanded their spirit while its size, beauty, and wealth blinded them to the still larger facts of Canada. In short, they were primarily British Columbians, and Canadians incidentally.

That pioneer British Columbia, as one could see even in Prince George, is being re-educated, tamed, and rubbed smooth by the massive influx of Canadians from other provinces, the conforming pressures of industry, and the sudden awareness of Canada. In the last quarter-century or so, no earlier, British Columbia has truly joined the nation.

That is a gain of inestimable value to the nation. Yet there is a loss, too. A loss of color, eccentricity, and grandeur, or at least comedy.

Prince George itself had produced one of the nation's classic comedies, and I recalled it now, almost in tears, as I bumped into an old friend on the street.

Some forty years ago, the local Board of Trade, seeking new industries, found that the only payroll available hereabouts was supported by an industry of pleasure a few miles downriver at South Fort George—an industry so prosperous that a railway contractor thought nothing of laying a thousand dollars on the bar to quench the evening's thirst of his workmen.

After lengthy economic research, the lady who operated the

leading enterprise of South Fort George built a palace of unexampled splendor at Prince George and invited society to a grand opening. All went swimmingly on a torrent of champagne until the police, allegedly under the influence of South Fort George, raided the new industry with fatal results.

"You should have seen," said my friend, a survivor of these events, "all those businessmen in dress suits diving through the windows. I went first, out of the second story. Well, that ruined our first industry. The proprietress shook the dust of Prince George from her slippers—they were gold slippers, as I recall—and abandoned her palace without a whimper. We made it into the first city hall. A good city hall, too. Some lady's first name was still painted neatly on every door."

We left the veteran of British Columbia's salad days and drove southward, only to find a flooded creek carrying the remains of a bridge and several shacks down to the Fraser. The whole north was cut off from the coast.

That little flood, perhaps twenty yards wide, told us more about British Columbia than any map. All human life here has hung from the beginning on a trail, a road, or a railway loosely glued to a precipice. In a land so splintered and partitioned a few inches of rain or a slide of rock in any one of a thousand places can segregate an area larger than any European nation.

There was nothing for it but to drive back through the Rockies to the Peace River Country, down the length of the Alberta prairie to the American border (all roads across British Columbia being closed by the flood), into Idaho, and thence by Seattle to Vancouver.

As so many times before, in summer heat or winter snow, we began to ascend the valley of the Fraser, for it is the central artery and economic aorta of western Canada, through which the nation's lifestream is pumped from the interior heartland to the coast.

This river, and its almost identical twin, the Columbia—both shaped like a clumsy letter S—alone impress some visible pattern on the chaotic geography of British Columbia. From his first arrival here thousands of years ago man's life followed that pattern and traveled the two rivers until airplanes could leap over the successive ranges of north-south mountains and the narrow intervening valleys.

Fraser reached the sea on the current of his river. The gold rush of the late eighteen-fifties retraced his steps to sift the river's sand bars and to build beside them the incredible Cariboo Road. Canada's first transcontinental railway, the Canadian Pacific, used this one practical breach in the Coast Range. But a stranger may travel a good hundred miles east-ward from Vancouver today without realizing what has hap-pened to the original road and to its builders, who, without suspecting it, were building a transcontinental state and, by a frail dike, were halting the northward surge of Manifest Destiny.

The broad Fraser delta on Vancouver's outskirts, with its green patchwork of dairy farms, looks much like the farm land of Quebec or Ontario, except for the high mountains around it, or perhaps more like Switzerland, except for its greater sweep.

Only a few mighty stumps in some farmer's field stand as decaying monuments to the old coast jungle. As the delta quickly narrows into the Fraser's black canyon, only a wooden cross here and there marks one of those little adventures of the gold rush that together made the national adventure of Cari-boo. Only yesterday it was still an adventure to drive into the Coast Range on a road not much better than the gold-miners' flimsy track.

The modern traveler, entering this jumble of rock and forest, driving a few feet from the Fraser's swirl, or observing it from some high place as a thin brown smear, will hardly be-lieve that steamboats once paddled these frenzied waters, that caravans of mules, oxen, and camels toiled along these dark bluffs, that Fraser crawled on hands and knees around the white vortex of Hell's Gate.

Yet there are certain signs and tokens to be read by the native. Those ancient cherry trees just off the main street of Yale were planted by the gold-miners and the builders of the C.P.R., and some of them worshipped in that little wooden church. An overgrown trail meandering in places near the

pavement is a lost particle of the Cariboo Road. The autumn
shoals of salmon, now swimming through the concrete fish
ladders of the Gate, have fed men since the Indians' arrival
here. The filament of steel at Alexandria hangs across the river
in the exact spot where Joseph Trutch and his workmen
fashioned the first suspension bridge, weaving its wire cables
by hand on the riverbank. And everywhere along the canyon
you can hear the voice that spoke to the first men, the growl,
the hiss and thunder of liquid force imprisoned here and
yearning for the sea.

Look down upon this scoured and riven trench, the mad
river, the ceaseless slides of rock and vegetation, the spark of
light from some lonely shack, the momentary flash of a great
train burrowing like a glowworm through limbo—then, if you
are a British Columbian, you can imagine the many passengers
of this last Canadian journey to the west, the Indians, the
miners, the road-builders, the railway-builders, and now the
whole constricted tide of the nation's business.

Suddenly, after the river has made its right-angle northward turn at Hope, geography, vegetation, climate, and human
life all change together.

The Pacific jungle of fir, cedar, and hemlock thins into
red-barked pine, black spruce, and stunted juniper. The dank
coastal reek is cut by the stinging medicinal whiff of sagebrush, the tantalizing scent of syringa and alfalfa, the rough
emanation of parched clay and hot stone, the clean smell of
new haystacks, horses, cattle, log barns, and saddle leather.
Soon the mountains begin to fall by successive steps into
round, kneaded hills of bunch grass. And coastal man, with
his life of cities, business, and fury, is replaced by interior man,
who lives, quiet and remote, upon the land, as his fathers
lived before him. This is the Dry Belt, another freakish pocket
in the rumpled garment of British Columbia.

At Lytton, where the Thompson's waters print a hard green
line across the muddy Fraser, most travelers turn eastward by
the main highway, but, by an old instinct, we sought the side
road to the sleepy village of Lillooet, followed the main
channel northward, climbed to the Indian hamlet and pre-

historic battleground of Pavilion, waved to the oldest inhabitants, Kate and Johnny, who sat blinking in the sun, zigzagged up the side of Pavilion Mountain, and dropped into an unlikely saucer of rangeland.

The Carson ranch in this upland hollow was probably the first cattle ranch west of the Rockies. Its founder discovered it on his way to the Cariboo rush and ruled it as a private kingdom. The surrounding pinnacles of blue and white, the green alfalfa fields, the drunken log barns, and the massive house of squared timber had been our second home for half a lifetime and, to us, the fairest spot in Canada. But we are prejudiced by memories of men, horses, campfires, feasts around a gigantic kitchen stove, and still winter nights when the stars hung low and the coyotes howled at the moon. Those days are gone. The Carson house, just a century old, is disguised under a modern veneer, modern barns have succeeded the lurching structures of log, and most of our friends sleep beneath a bare hillock and a single pine tree.

Having ridden so often about these ancestral acres with Ernest Carson, their master—and the master of farming, horsemanship, politics, road-construction, and life before his untimely end—we repaired with our memories to a favorite rendezvous on the lip of the Fraser's canyon.

The inverted icicles of the Coast Range gleamed to the westward. In the south the Lillooet mountains hung, transparent and insubstantial, like curtains of blue stuff. Straight below, in its brown ditch, the Fraser was a wriggling thread thin enough to fit the finest needle, and we could discern the rustle of its stitches. Even here, where we had always fancied ourselves free at last of mankind, we came again on the portents of the Canadian revolution.

On the bank of the precipice we met an old man, bearded and dirty, who flung out his hand and shrieked his solitary protest into the void.

"They're a-gonna dam her right down there!" he cried. "Sure as hell's a man trap, that's where the dam's a-gonna be. And then what?"

He glared at me under tangled eyebrows and awaited my

answer. As I could think of none, he added in a hoarse bellow: "I'll tell you what they're a-gonna do! They're a-gonna back her up a hundred miles, in a big lake, see, to make elec-tricity! What fer? Why, fer Vancouver, of course. They're a-gonna drowned half Cariboo to make elec-tricity fer Vancouver, and Vancouver's no good to nobody. Let 'em drowned Vancouver and leave us be!"

The revolution would not leave him be. Someday, perhaps soon, the Fraser would be dammed at Moran Rapids, directly beneath us, and the resulting lake would stretch northward one hundred miles or more.

British Columbia's largest resource and secret weapon of industry is water power. The Fraser's titanic motion contains one of the world's largest stores of unused energy. In the end every fall of water from the Rockies to the coast will be harnessed. The whole scheme of western geography will be wrenched into a new shape for man's supposed benefit. But these prospects did not impress the backward native of the Dry Belt.

"I'm agin' it," he said, and spat tobacco juice down two thousand feet with remarkably accurate aim. His protest thus recorded, he went his way and we went ours, northward across the broad interior plateau called Cariboo.

Until Ernest Carson rebuilt it, the old Cariboo Road, little changed since the time of its builder, Governor Douglas, curved around every rock, gully, and stump. Every curve had its story and every dusty inn its ghosts. Douglas, Begbie (the Hanging Judge who seldom hanged anyone), Amor de Cosmos (born plain Smith), Cariboo Cameron (who carried the bodies of his wife and baby daughter by sleigh, ship, and railway across America for burial in Ontario), Billy Barker, Ed Stout, Harry Jones, and all the old giants traveled this road, stopped at Clinton, at the Seventy Mile House, the Hundred, the Hundred and Fifty, and in their march to Barkerville gave British Columbia to the nation.

Who remembers them now? How many truck-drivers on this crowded highway, eating in some evil coffee shop, have ever tasted the Gargantuan dollar meals of Cariboo—as much as you could hold, no tips, all women strictly confined to the kitchen and men only in the dining-room?

The great days are finished here, as everywhere, but the Cariboo plateau is still the only place where the size of British Columbia can be glimpsed, where distance is not shut out and the next valley hidden by mountain or forest.

A soggy, lethargic coastal man like me fills his lungs with this dry upland air, regains his youth, and seems to need no sleep at night. After the metallic clamor of cities, his ears are soothed by the sound of gurgling irrigation ditches, of rivers murmuring in the night, of bawling herds, horses' hoofs on a muddy road, wind shredded through pine needles, and fire crackling in a drum stove.

The Cariboo breed, impregnated with the flavor and history of this land, is different from any other breed in Canada, but it is changing, and the land is changing, too, as both feel the first tremors of progress.

We could hardly find any remains of the old road beside the new pavement or recognize the busy lumbering town which has overlaid the drowsy village of Quesnel, on the Fraser's bank. The beloved Louis LeBourdais, Quesnel's first citizen, had been buried, as he wished, while the local band played "Don't Fence Me In." The jangle of spurs was heard no more on wooden sidewalks. No one seemed to remember the proud stern-wheelers that moved like white swans on the river, or even Cap Foster's leaky gas boat, the *Circle W*, which had borne me, more than thirty years before, down from Prince George.

Only Barkerville, in the mountains to the eastward, the ghost town and once the roaring capital of the gold rush, remains physically changeless or changes imperceptibly as its single street of shacks between the mountain and the tailings of Williams Creek molders under the weather.

Two survivors of the rush were still there when I first rode into Barkerville. Harry Jones sheltered me in his cabin beside the old diggings of Wing Dam. Bill Brown stamped out of Kelly's Hotel because a stranger was in town and he could never abide a crowd. Now the last argonaut of the sixties lies with his companions on the hillside above Cariboo Cameron's fabulous claim.

Nothing was left but a few ruined cabins in the Quesnel Lake country to remind us that from here four men moved northward in the fall of 1860 to hit the ultimate treasure of Williams Creek. Of the old inhabitants only the salmon remained. They swarmed upon the river sand, laid their autumn eggs five hundred miles from sea, and died before our eyes in the invariable cycle of their kind.

While we were watching those mysterious creatures end their lives exactly where they had been hatched four years earlier, a native of these parts joined us and uttered a queer remark.

"The salmon," he said, "know how to die. Once they've finished the job, they die right smack on time. Funny thing that a fish has more sense, and more guts, too, than a man."

On the west bank of the Fraser the enormous plateau of Chilcotin, the big ranches, the precious green specks of irrigated hayfield, the cattle, the cowboys, and, farther west, the badlands of stunted trees and swampy roads to the inner slope of the Coast Range, seemed to have resisted progress so far.

We drove southward again and eastward up the Thompson. No progress here either. The thirsty benches will become a rich farmland someday if water can be pumped up from the river, but now the last black skeletons of Wallachin's dead orchards confirm the decisive fact of vegetable life in the Dry Belt—its absolute dependence on a trickle of moisture.

Kamloops, the old fur post at the junction of the two Thompsons and the true nexus of the interior, looked so dangerously like a city that we fled northward to sanctuary. The North Thompson country is wedged tight between the Rockies and the Clearwater Range. It holds some of the nation's best scenery, a rain forest far from the coast and an assortment of improbable characters.

It was here, after a day's hard ride from any highway, that we first met Ted Helsett and knew we had found a man. On the pack trail or beside the campfire this blond Norwegian looked like some lost Viking god. Assuredly he had accomplished his own saga. Living on horseback all summer, on skis all winter, he had been trapped in forest fire and escaped by inches when the wind changed; had dropped a charging grizzly at a distance of three feet with his last bullet; had broken a leg in a blizzard far from home, had prepared to shoot himself, but, on second thought, had crawled two miles in two days, managed to light a signal fire, and was found, not quite dead.

Then there was Bill McGarrigle, a reformed professional baseball-player and talented comedian, whose cabin rescued us from rain, snow, and mud, and who showed us how to catch trout, on a fly, in an October snowstorm until our lines froze stiff.

At Dutch Lake lived Grace McGaw and Dorothy Bell, two reformed Vancouver newspaperwomen who, demented at the sight of a worthless bush farm, had made it over into British Columbia's happiest retreat. As their kitchen is by choice the happy end of our trail (for, thank the Lord, they have never regained their urban sanity), we tore ourselves away with difficulty and headed southward into the Okanagan.

There all sensible Canadians hope to retire someday, grow apples, and live happily ever afterward. The Okanagan's endless miles of orchard, frothing in spring blossom or reeling under the crimson weight of autumn, its three big towns, its snug houses, trim gardens, and air of affluence are all the work of men; for only half a century ago this was a bunch-grass range, inhabited by a few cattle.

In a province which can plow perhaps one per cent of its land, the Okanagan is a priceless piece of real estate. Still, the enchantment of the valley, known by hearsay all over the nation, is not to be found in its orchards, its towns, or even in the chameleon lakes that change, minute by minute, from blue to green to purple. Man's real achievement here is a perfect compromise between rustic and urban environment. A distinct method of life is so far uncorrupted. No blasphemer questions an indigenous religion and its ruddy local god named MacIntosh Red. It must be an agnostic of the wilder sort who questions the presence of a sea serpent named Ogopogo in Okanagan Lake.

The famous apples were ripening as we arrived, were moving by railway across the nation, and lying in crimson piles beside the road. Having purchased two boxes from a lively little man, a new immigrant from Germany, we started across the high Monashee Pass to the eastward and dropped down suddenly to the shore of the Arrow Lakes.

Now we were in the Columbia's watershed, on the river which is said to contain, in Canada and the United States, more electrical power than any other river on earth.

The Canadian share of these unequaled resources has yet to be harnessed, and is the subject of stubborn bargaining between Ottawa and Washington. The boom therefore had not yet arrived in the Arrow Lakes country. It lies silent, gripped by the mountains' vise and walled off from civilization except for a single road.

Silence and isolation will not last much longer. Soon a pulp industry will be built at the south end of Lower Arrow Lake, the hills will be logged, and civilization will march in. Already we missed the *Lady Minto*, that gallant old lady of the lake, who used to wallow up the rapids, her funnels belching black smoke, her feeble old body staggering, her whistle screaming defiance at the hills like an impoverished aunt, welcome at every man's door. Her whistle will never be heard again. "I cried like a baby when she passed my place the last time," a farmer told us.

Slocan Lake, in the next fold of the mountains, enjoyed its boom in the great days of the silver mines, and now sleeps with its memories. Someday, no doubt, Canadians will realize that this exquisite streak of water, which glitters like a vein of blue mineral, is an almost exact reproduction of Lucerne, and they will make it into a lucrative tourist resort. Nothing can save it from its fate.

Eastward, past the canyons of the Kootenay, I could no longer recognize Nelson as the town of my infancy. Yet, for all its progress, it remains quite unspoiled on the sloping side of Kootenay Lake, though I missed the fleet of stern-wheelers, those sprightly maidens of opulent bosom and shiny white flanks who paused at any beach if you waved a handkerchief, and the two fussy little streetcars that shuttled up and down the hill.

Perhaps an old man may also be excused one invisible tear in the lakeside park where he ate his first ice-cream cone (they were better then) and received his first intimation of progress in a circus tent.

We boarded the modern ferryboat, crossed the lake, and reflected that most of Europe's celebrated alpine lakes would fit into a corner of this blue basin. Few of them would rival its mountain setting.

Then we followed the sinuous road on the lake's eastern bank to the broad, diked grainfields of Creston—an incongruous chunk of the prairies, or perhaps a mislaid Swiss valley —and so eastward again through a black forest to Cranbrook.

A man may be pardoned for prowling through the streets of this town at midnight in search of a little house built by his father before there was any town here. The house still stood opposite the first church and above a swamp once full of wild flowers but now full of business buildings. (Alas, I could not find the mean hall in which *Uncle Tom's Cabin* was played every season by strolling players and several toothless hounds.)

Where we once drove in a buggy, paved highways led northward to the spacious Windermere Valley, the source of the Columbia, across the Rockies to Banff, westward to Golden, and around the Columbia's Big Bend to Revelstoke.

We took a long, hard look at the Columbia's upper reaches, for we might not see them again. When the master dam of this whole watershed, Canadian and American, is installed at Mica Creek, north of Revelstoke, the river above the dam will become a lake. Canada will have electrical power to support new industrial empires and to light Vancouver.

By now we had traveled most of inhabited British Columbia. Not without horror, we headed for the coast. While we could have driven straight west from Revelstoke and down the Fraser, we took a crazy circuitous route and found ourselves, for no good reason, beside the American boundary at the smelter town of Trail.

If nothing else had looked as good as in the old days, Trail at least had improved. The hills above the Columbia, once poisoned and stripped bare by the smelter's fumes, were turning green again. A grimy village had grown almost into a city. At night the hideous daytime shape of the nation's largest metallurgical plant looked like some Rhenish castle, every tower agleam and every light dancing in the river.

Few of Trail's people entertain such illusions. They are a practical, hard-working industrial people, tightly organized in labor unions, and, amid all the emptiness of the Columbia's stark valley, live an urban life. The revolution has established a distant but permanent beachhead here.

Years ago I had entered the inferno of Trail, had staggered past its miles of flaming furnaces and its lakes of acid, had penetrated the tunnels and underground city of the Sullivan Mine at Kimberley, source of the smelter's ore. One such vision of hell was enough for a single lifetime. So we drove up the hill from Trail to Rossland, that battered old eagle's nest which the miners fastened precariously to a perpendicular crag, and then, over two grisly summits, we came to the Boundary country at Grand Forks, yet another separate region nourishing another kind of people.

Once they were miners, as recorded by their pyramids of black slag. Now they are farmers in a hot, fertile valley, and are known to the world chiefly by the naked reputation of the Doukhobors, whose neglected orchards and square brick houses all of identical design, record the strange, violent, and often tragic story of the Spirit Wrestlers.

Next day, thanks to the fast new highway across Anarchist Mountain and down to the Okanagan Valley, we were driving straight westward through the Princeton Mountains, the autumnal gold of the Similkameen, and the high defiles of Allison Pass.

Twenty years earlier I had ridden a horse on Governor Dewdney's old trail, by narrow ledges and awesome cliffs, had waded the icy Skagit with Bill Robinson, the prospector (where was he now?), caught more trout than you will believe, watched mountain goat above the timber line, and thought this country beyond the reach of progress. Now a trail had become a wide pavement. I could find no trace of the old camping-places, the upland meadows where our horses grazed, or Bill's cabin on the turbulent Sumallo.

It was impossible to explain and useless to lament the glory of British Columbia's lost innocence. We paused in the mountains above Hope to share our lunch with a band of mischievous whisky jays and sadly descended to the Fraser. Presently we smelled the coast jungle, the Pacific's salty wind, and faced at last the corrugated silhouette of Vancouver at the river's mouth. There we heard the boom no longer as an abstract word, but as the audible drumbeat of Canada's march to the sea.

DEAD GIANT

A Douglas fir tree fell to earth last winter. For eight hundred years it had repelled the gales of the Pacific coast, and in that time had swelled to a girth of eight feet, one foot for each century. Now it lies among the living trees in a gulch of noonday twilight.

Under six inches of bark the dead giant contains enough clear-grained wood to build three houses. Though no man will cut or use that wood, it will not be wasted. Slowly it adds its compost to the forest's floor, and new trees will grow out of its fertility. For every tree that survives, ten at least must die in the dumb struggle for light and nourishment.

The forest lives on. It is not an assortment of separate trees, but a single organism, as interdependent, fragile, and delicately balanced as the society of man. And, better than man, the forest knows how to restore its society after destruction.

Close to the prostrate column of wood, man has been busy with his destructive work.

A typical coast forest stood here not long ago—gigantic, succulent, damp at midsummer, dark on the brightest day, impenetrable by any trail, forever hostile to man.

Its pillars supported the arches of a groined roof so tightly built that sunshine entered in straight, narrow shafts as it enters the nave of a cathedral. The bark of its firs was deeply wrinkled like the wrinkles of an aged face, the bark of its cedars woven in loose basket web, the bark of hemlock and balsam streaked with silver. Catkins of alder hung, in early spring, like drops of wine. Maple buds opened in cups of green-and-crimson porcelain. Currant bushes were heavy with earrings of ruby. Elderberries wore necklaces of scarlet beads. The sour fruit of Oregon grape and the sweet fruit of salal turned from green to purple and, in the fall, colored the droppings of bird and animal.

Deer drank in the forest's black tarns. Mink bred beside its streams and frogs in its swamps. Grouse drummed and hooted here, woodpeckers hammered, squirrels chattered, insects murmured in the nuptial flight of evening.

Today, for miles around, the mountains are stripped clean, the earth roiled by machinery. No single tree is left standing. Even the smallest weeds have been trampled into the mud. The loggers reaped their crop, burned their refuse, and seared the land. Over this enormous cemetery, where eight centuries of growth lie cremated or buried, black, worthless logs are scattered in myriads like broken crosses.

The forest will return. Only some of its members are dead. The organism is not dead. Already, in the space of twelve months, the earth is pushing up again its first tentative sprouts of unquenchable life.

Fireweed, the ubiquitous Canadian pioneer, has arrived overnight from nowhere to seize the old forest's vacant estate for a brief tenure. Its blossoms, in pink billow to the skyline and beyond, are the brave little flags of nature's countermarch.

Blackberries are crawling over the ravaged soil to hide its scars. Willows are rising also, and the thin spears of maple and alder from bruised stumps. A sword fern here and there, a tuft of bleeding-heart, a few dwarf stalks of salal lift their leaves to the unaccustomed sun and wait patiently for the new forest's merciful shade. Meanwhile their tiny parasols are ready to shelter the first conifer seedlings.

But the great work must begin underground. When the trees were cut, when the anchoring network of rootlets was broken and the soil began to drift in the rain's erosion, new roots knit up the raveled substance and with unseen stitches sewed together the particles of topsoil before they could slide downhill to the sea.

That work done, the conifers will soon appear, minute, hairy spikes of green, will gradually spread, and will finally engulf their deciduous protectors. In endless cycle of deciduous and coniferous growth, in proliferation of cell and annual ring of wood, in a process leisurely, mysterious, and unimaginable, the earth is held, replenished, and populated. The forest always returns.

Apparently immovable, it marches, seed by seed and sprout by sprout, from the mountains to the sea rocks. Blind, it knows its way. Mindless, it forever builds, falls, rises again, and accomplishes its sole purpose. Senseless, it feels the wounds of men's weapons and heals them. Voiceless, it speaks in the spring whisper of wind shredded through leaves and needles, in the tick and crackle of summer, in the staccato drip and tympanic beat of winter, in the organ wail of ocean storm. Handless, it clutches its shallow lodgment and seizes the works of man. It will digest them in its own good time.

CHAPTER FIFTEEN

———◆———

The Big Trees

In the great salt-water basin first discovered by the Spaniards and named for an Englishman, Captain Harry Burrard, a rusty ship was loading lumber. I could not decipher her dingy flag, but the men working about her deck were small, as spry as cats, and had dark Mediterranean faces.

A retired sailorman on the wharf—he was shaped roughly like a beer barrel, and his face was inflamed by its contents—advised me that these foreigners were Greeks.

"You know—Griks," he explained. "From Greeze." He wasn't sure where the lumber was going. "Probably," he said, "to the U.K. Or God knows where. What does it matter?"

It didn't matter. Every deep-sea ship afloat comes eventually to Vancouver and takes its merchandise God knows where.

The ports of the Great Lakes and the St. Lawrence would be freezing up at this late season. The port of Vancouver would be open and busy all winter. That reliable old nurse, the Japan Current, was maintaining the even temperature of Canada's Pacific littoral with hot-water bottles filled weeks ago at the equator. Slings of square Douglas fir timbers rose from a barge and dropped into the Greek ship's hold against the sunny blue background of the North Shore mountains and the recumbent forms of their twin Lions. The wind bore a sappy, summer smell of newly cut wood and oozing resin.

As always, the forest was moving from Vancouver across the seven seas. Here were timbers from some tree which had grown for several hundred years, to a girth of perhaps six feet, far up the coast, or on Vancouver Island, or on the distant Queen Charlottes. Another ship carried paper from Powell River. The grimy fish boats in Coal Harbor had just finished a season among the salmon and herring shoals from here to Alaska. In the railway yards near by a trainload of shiplap and plywood was starting its journey to the prairies, Ontario, or the southern States.

All the potent organism of the metropolis, all the offices, factories, and homes, had been built primarily on the forest, and, without that extra ring of wood added every year to every tree, would die of starvation. Just as certainly, Vancouver would become what it was not long ago, a small sawmill and fishing village, if the Fraser's canyon were closed and the umbilical cord of its railway cut. For Vancouver lives only as the distributing point, counting house, port, and bazaar of half the nation.

Logging camps, mills, paper towns, the new aluminum town of Kitimat, the copper mines of Britannia, the salmon canneries, the milkshed of the Fraser Valley, every wharf along 5,560 miles of shoreline, every acre of cultivated land in the interior far back across the Rockies and the central plains pour their products into Vancouver. It processes, sells, and ships them, and takes its profit on every last pound.

The retired sailorman, evidently thinking me a stranger, flung out his arm at the city's serrated profile. "I knew her," he said, "when she was built of wood and hardly went past Georgia and Granville. Outside of that, stumps, just stumps. Now look at her!"

I looked at her, as I had often looked for nearly fifty years, in amazement and alarm.

To the west the black hound's nose of Stanley Park was thrust eagerly into the harbor gate. A green steel web hung lightly over the First Narrows and crawled with automotive spiders. Those friendly marine pups, the double-ended municipal ferries, panted across the inlet, and a sleek white Prin-

cess swept in through the front door, a train of foam behind
her, like a dowager making an impressive entrance into a ball-
room.

The business skyline on the south shore was rising steadily
higher every day, the unfleshed skeleton of a new skyscraper in
every second block. Beyond them on the whale's back of
alluvial soil southward to the Fraser, and eastward to the margin of the wilderness, every vacant lot was sprouting a new
house to serve a population that has never ceased to grow.

No other city in Canada, I thought, and few in the world,
had been planted in such a setting, between mountain, sea,
and forest. To be sure, the setting had been heavily overlaid by
man's toil and folly, but around the wharves the seagulls still
screamed, the smell of wood and sap and salt spiced the autumn
air, and a high tide brought whispers of the Pacific and the
gorgeous East, as when the first white men saw this shore. Captain George Vancouver had found it good. He had not fore-
seen the improbable monument to be built here in his honor.

Yet there was something strange and alarming about Vancouver's city and its people. What? I tried, though a prejudiced
coastal man, to consider the question impartially as a stranger,
but only a coastal man would ask it or understand the answer.

"Look at her! By God, will you just look at her?" the sailorman said, and I looked at her, I remembered the small town I
had known in boyhood, and I asked myself again what had
happened to Vancouver. What had made the human creature
of this coast so different from all other Canadians and even
from all British Columbians east of the Coast Range? Why
had his spirit totally changed in my own lifetime?

The sailorman seemed to guess my question. The beer barrel rolled slowly around a wooden pile so that its owner could
look me in the eye and see if I was to be trusted with a deeper
communication. He fastened on me a leer of insinuation and
disclosed his mind.

"This town," he said, "is the damndest, wickedest, bloodi-
est-awful town in America! More crime, more trouble, more
scandal. Oh, she's wicked! Why, I could tell you . . ."

His voice trailed off as if he dared not reveal the final horror. I knew anyway. I had read the daily headlines in the Vancouver papers. After living long near the stews of British Columbia politics, I could have told this disillusioned Vancouverite a thing or two.

He brightened up to assure me that Vancouver would soon have a million people and more. Nothing could stop her. "By the livin' God," he said for the third time, "will you just look at her?"

He did not have to urge me. I could not keep my eyes off her—this distillate of jungle and ocean, this mixture of beauty and ugliness, this ever spreading fungus of wealth and slums, this woodland clearing where man has heaped up overnight the brassiest, loveliest, craziest of all Canadian towns, and now worships his inferior masterpiece in childlike wonder, fierce greed, and a sure conviction of superiority.

Well, I looked at her, I imagined for a moment what men could have made here to match nature's masterpiece, and I was tempted to weep.

Another hoarse gurgle came from the teetering keg. "She's big, all right," the sailorman concluded, "but she's not what she used to be, not by a damnsight. She's seen her best days."

Perhaps he was right. Anyway, I thanked him for his verdict —a verdict which all modern residents will deny but all old-timers confirm—and strolled up Granville Street to meet by appointment one of Canada's great men.

Lawren Harris, publicly a genius of the painter's art and privately a philosopher, took me and my questions in hand and led the way to the Vancouver Art Gallery without a word of explanation. None was needed.

The walls of the gallery were covered by the paintings of the late Emily Carr, whom I remembered in Victoria, fifty years ago, as a dumpy old maid of quick temper and sharp tongue.

She had captured, as no one else has ever captured, the primal fact of the Pacific coast. She had invented almost a new art form to illuminate the dark tide of vegetation pouring from the mountains to the shore.

There, on canvas, was the force of geography, climate, and steaming growth which had conditioned men's outdoor life from the beginning and, by its terrible presence, had shaped his spirit.

I saw at once what Harris meant, and it answered my question. Coastal men, or most of them, had severed the human roots growing in this forest soil for more than a century. They still live on the forest, but are no longer of it. They have retired into imagined urban security, forgotten their beginnings, and, as Miss Carr seemed to be saying, have lost their way.

But the works of the dead Victorian spinster (so poor that she painted some of her best pictures on cheap, perishable wrapping paper) remind the urban creature that the primal fact of the coast remains. The forest stands at every Vancouver street end. Butchered, it always rises again. Indestructible, it awaits the day of man's departure, when it will repossess its own.

Everywhere in Vancouver, beyond the business district, the forest asserts its title deeds and imposes its green caveat on men's work. The trees of the immense park stand virgin and untamed as some of them have stood for a thousand years. Beside the newest skyscraper a solid cedar stump registers, in death, a life far longer and more secure than man's.

The gardener, if he neglects his garden for a single season, will find it surging up in alder, maple, or the first filaments of the conifers. Every new residential area is soon covered by an umbrella of dense foliage. Leave it unpruned for half a century or less, and Vancouver will be lost, like Sleeping Beauty, in impervious tangle.

An acid forest soil of long-accumulated leafmold, a deluge of winter rain, and a gentle summer sun make everything grow, almost unnaturally. They keep most men attached to some fragment of nature even if Vancouver has shut out the presence at its edge. The cultivation of its earth, more than anything else, saves the city's soul. Nearly every man is a gardener. The poorest house has its patch of flowers.

A plutocracy of peculiar brashness and purse-pride controls the metropolis and sets its outward tone. Its so-called Society is ostentatious, naïve, and provincial.

The ordinary citizen, however, is hardly aware of his betters.

He pursues his pleasant little life seldom knowing how the city's economic stomach is fed, who owns the money, what the politicians and the Cadillac set are doing.

He feasts on the crime news, hears that Vancouver is a world center of the narcotic drug trade and a haunt of organized crime, is shocked by repeated civic scandals, but goes through life without seeing a criminal act and is innocent of vice. He carries on the city's unwieldy labors and sometimes glimpses the glory of his surroundings as dawn flushes the mountain snow and as the sun slides into the sea. But collectively he thinks about the nation's problems far less than most urban Canadians because, in this easy climate and Vancouver's opulence, he doesn't have to.

Though it will resent the compliment, Vancouver must be judged an unusually innocent city, despite its contrary reputation. It has wealth, but is too young to have acquired sophistication. It is too successful, too busy in its own business, and too self-adoring to pay much heed to Canada at large, and it customarily goes to the United States for its holidays.

To tell the truth, Vancouver is not a city at all. Like every other Canadian community except Montreal, it is an overgrown town; or, rather, in Vancouver's case, an overgrown camp, repeatedly enlarged by a series of frontier booms until boom is taken as normal, as these people's reward, under a just Providence, for their wisdom in coming here. And what booms they have seen!

Why, less than a century ago no human work stood on Burrard Inlet except a sawmill or two and the saloon of "Gassy Jack" Deighton, whose hamlet was called Gas Town after him. Some sixty years ago Sam Howe, a discerning newcomer, walked through the brush at the town's outskirts, identified the muddy intersection of Granville and Georgia, bought a few yards of brushland there, and became a millionaire. Roy Brown, the great editor of *The Province*, used to tell me of fishing for trout in a clean woodland stream where the city hall now stands like a vertical match box.

Vancouver's expansion, since the first locomotive crawled to the Inlet and changed the political balance of the continent, has left, until recent times, little leisure for cultural pursuits.

The doubtful phenomenon known as progress has been too fast to permit sensible civic planning, with the result that hovels abut on business streets; Hastings and its skyscrapers run suddenly into Skid Row; Granville and Burrard soar on majestic bridges over a manufacturing area whose smoke ascends into the leafy English boulevards and the rich men's mansions of Shaughnessy Heights.

Two generations back, the inhabitants of Vancouver were clearing homesteads in the forest, breaking the earth, and diking the islands of the Fraser's estuary. Even a generation back these were an outdoor people, a pioneer and essentially primitive people. Their town was ruled by men who themselves had felt axes, plowhandles, miners' picks, and ships' rigging in their hands.

Now it is ruled by the softer sons of the pioneers. Hereditary wealth, extracted raw from forest, mine, and sea, enables young men who otherwise would be drapers' assistants or apprentice undertakers to own their fathers' fortunes, command great corporations, manipulate politics, and spend the winter in Honolulu.

All this happened in many parts of Canada, but perhaps nowhere else so rapidly, enthusiastically, and crudely as in Vancouver. The ruling class thus lacks the patina and manners of Montreal's elite, the thinner shine of Toronto, and the sober thrift of Winnipeg. For all purposes of political, economic, and social power, no other major Canadian city is so *nouveau riche* as Vancouver, so self-centered and isolated from the nation. None is so completely conditioned by its easy environment, its genial climate, and that legend of ceaseless sunshine which a winter of almost ceaseless rain and frequent London fog can never destroy.

Such environment, climate, and legend produce able and imaginative businessmen, powerful labor unions, organized crime, and vulgar politics. They have never produced a single statesman of first rank, or second.

Nevertheless, better things are growing in Vancouver. Its real thinking and its hope are to be found on the Peninsula of

Point Grey. There the University of British Columbia's campus looks south across the oily Fraser, north to the white fiord of Howe Sound, and makes any other campus in Canada appear cramped and mean.

The site is not very important. The university's greatness resides in its teachers, in the successive crops of students who have manned British Columbia's industries and leavened the lump of a frontier society, in the scientists, poets, artists, and heretics. These men and women, you might almost say, have started a counterrevolution against the revolution of machinery and wealth.

A few months earlier I had witnessed, in a single evening, the two extremes of Vancouver's life. At the Shaughnessy mansion where I was dining, some youngsters bounded in from the tennis court. Yesterday they had been skiing, half an hour away, on the North Shore. Now they were setting out for a swim in the sea. They planned to spend the week-end cruising in some tycoon's yacht. That was the Cadillac set. Its fathers had once worked with ax and saw.

The older folk repaired after dinner to the Theatre Under the Stars in Stanley Park, where a coterie of impoverished young artists was staging one of its open-air productions in the forest primeval. The giant trees leaned over the stage, etched against the moon. Wild ducks quacked overhead. The smell of salt and kelp blew in from the sea to mix with the clean breath of the jungle. An audience of one thousand people on camp chairs was lost in that grove of cedar, but it had found for itself the primary fact of coastal life.

No other place in Canada, few in the world, could present such a scene—the drama acted for the love of it, the stage taken outdoors as in Greece, Rome, or Shakespearean England and surrounded by vegetation, by mountain and sea on a scale unknown to any Greek, Roman, or Elizabethan. My faith was restored in the young, brash, and innocent civic colossus.

Another day, toward dusk, I crossed the steel spiderweb to the North Shore and climbed the hill past the mushroom growth of new houses. Here faith changed almost to affection.

The sun was making a stage exit through the First Narrows

and hurrying on to an engagement in Asia. A translucent pink sheen flowed across the brown stain of the Fraser's outlet, the multitude of black islands in the Gulf, and the blurred hump of Vancouver Island. Like a contour map, the cargo of silt deposited grain by grain between the inlet and the river since the birth of the planet carried on its surface the final layer of man's habitation. Beyond this narrow neck of land and the river's three gleaming channels, the white ghosts of Mount Baker and the Olympics, far to the south, flitted over the American horizon.

This town, I thought, had everything to make it healthy, wealthy, and wise. A Vancouver man beside me uttered a sigh of skepticism.

"The beautiful," he said, "and damned."

No, not yet damned. As sunset faded, the lights twinkled in parallel lines from inlet to river like sequins on black velvet. The moving lights of many ships cut their curved patterns in the ink pool of the harbor. All that daytime bulk of land, sea, and man's trespass upon them turned suddenly into a jewel-box. Even though man has done his best to destroy it, such beauty can be forgiven anything.

After some twenty thousand miles of travel we were now close to home. We could have reached it in exactly eighteen minutes by airplane, but we preferred the ferryboat.

It pushed through the buttonhole of the Narrows, crossed the sharp line of green and brown where the Fraser dies in the ocean, entered the crooked channel of Plumper's Pass, and wove through those innumerable little islands of the blessed who have put a moat between them and the world. Four hours later the ferry rounded Vancouver Island's southern tip and we caught sight of Victoria. We were home at last.

The molten gold of broom blossom splashed over Beacon Hill, as we had first seen it long ago. The same deranged golfers of that day seemed to follow their uninterrupted lunacy around the Oak Bay links. On the far shore of Juan de Fuca's Strait the Olympic ballerinas, in billowing white skirts, danced their familiar ballet out to the open Pacific. Alas, we didn't see Cadborosaurus, the home-grown sea serpent. He usually welcomes visitors, but was busy at the moment making headlines in the local press.

A Victoria medical man—he could not claim to be a Victorian, of course, since he had lived here a scant twenty years—stood beside us on the deck, and at this sight of home his eyes filled. He blew his nose violently and apologized for an unseemly show of emotion. "I just can't help it," he said.

Being a Victorian, even a mid-Victorian, I understood. We are all affected in the same way. I cannot tell you why, for the setting of Victoria does not compare with the first glimpse of Vancouver or Quebec, and man has not improved it much. The harbor is only an enlarged dishpan, smeared on the north side by the grime of industry but ornamented on east and south by the fat-domed legislative buildings, the Causeway, and the Empress Hotel amid acres of lawn and roses. Only a native could fail to see that Victoria started to make an immaculate portal and abandoned the job, half done.

However, if you keep your eyes fixed on the better half, the introduction to Victoria is startling in its precise, miniature design. It was all contrived by man since Douglas founded his fort beside this harbor in 1843.

The site was strategic but not promising. Douglas faced a sweep of barren rock, a ravine of stinking tidal mud, and the cedar huts of an Indian village.

Even today, though the ravine has been filled and crowned by the Causeway and the splendid hotel, no one but a native would call the business district of Victoria anything but commonplace and rather drab. The main streets are distinguished chiefly by flower baskets hung from every lamp post to titillate the tourists and by a few human relics who totter about, like stage props, in English tweeds.

Yet somehow Victoria has created not only real beauty, outside the business district, but a synthetic, profitable myth of quaintness, eccentricity, and charm well known throughout the world and sold over and over again to unsuspecting visitors. If this is a feat of commercial genius, something more than the profit motive is at work.

A cold-blooded pursuit of tourists' dollars; that bogus invention of the advertising art, "The Little Bit of Old England on the Shores of the Pacific"; that false legend of lotus-eaters in Canada's demi-Paradise; such shopworn exhibits as the rich widow ladies who daily engorge crumpets in the hotel to the delight of magazine writers; the spangled Christmas tree and December roses before the legislative buildings; the imaginary millionaires who do nothing but play golf and make their club a cartoon out of *Punch*—these spurious huckster's labels explain much but not all.

A reality lies behind the commercial façade, and it is too deep for commerce or explanation. No stranger will guess it; no Victorian will reveal it. The tourists drive about in horse-drawn tallyhoes (in deference to the myth) and imagine they have seen a splinter of nineteenth-century England and a colony of human antiques. But the Victorians keep their secret to themselves. No one can put it into words. Even the oft-quoted words of Rudyard Kipling on this scene were only a visitor's ignorant shout after a bibulous night at the Oak Bay Hotel.

The truth will be found in no document, photograph, painting, poem, or song, but you may stumble upon it, some spring evening, in a little garden where an old man is pruning a hedge; in a quiet house a-glisten with family plate and dark English oak; in the Haunted Bookshop and its pungent shelves of treasure or a secondhand store on Fort Street, cluttered with the heirlooms of dead Victorians; in a field of white lilies, blue camassia, and yellow buttercups under the crooked limbs of a native oak; in the park where the children are feeding crusts to the swans and the air is sweet with the perfume of plum blossom, broom, sea salt, and ageless conifers; or again on a winter night when the white rollers are pounding in from the Pacific and the big foghorns are moaning.

The secret is to be found not in the myth but in the reality of the earth and the people. These people know how to live and, more than any other urban Canadians, they live close to the earth; so close, indeed, that they usually vegetate in middle life, mellow in their autumn, and quietly go to seed—not before they have performed their own special prodigy.

I call it special and prodigious because I have never seen in America, or even in England, anything to match the gardens and gardeners of Victoria. Gardening here is not merely a skill, hobby, or cult as in Vancouver. It is outwardly a pictorial art and is spread, without a single break, across a rumpled canvas of some twenty square miles. Inwardly it is a philosophy, almost a religion, and always a passion.

The gardener, whether he tends a city lot or the stupendous ravines of the Butchart Gardens, must be a mechanic, an artist, a botanist, and a believer. Other Canadians may cultivate flowers; the Victorian worships them, nurses them with scientific care, exhibits them in fierce annual competition, debates them at weekly meetings, imports their seeds from the ends of the earth, and, by his labors, usually on his knees in prayer, has acquired a collective vision of beauty, a civic intimation of immortality.

Victoria has given the nation little else in modern times, but this town of apparent lunatics has taught a profound lesson of sanity. The nation can use it. Nevertheless, Victoria's original human growth, mostly out of seeds from England, is steadily retreating before a new growth out of Canada.

The Victoria I knew fifty years ago was indeed a Bit of England, superficially at least. It was managed by an aristocracy of English birth, dress, manners, and accent, yet not truly English, much less Canadian, for that unique species had become purely Victorian, and its mind never reached beyond its island.

Now, despite all the tourist propaganda, this town is purely Canadian. It is ruled by natives who grew up as Canadians and by newcomers from the foreign nation of Canada who are skeptical of quaintness, scornful of the myth, and determined to make a metropolis even though they lack any industrial base or large payroll except the provincial government's civil service. The North American illusion that size is the measurement of worth and happiness has penetrated even this last stronghold of sanity.

Governor Douglas's fort within a two-by-four stockade, the camp of the Cariboo gold rush, the village by the stinking mud flats, have swelled five miles north, east, and west and seem likely to cover most of the verduous Saanich Peninsula before long. However, if Victoria is growing like any other Canadian town, and faster than most, growth here has a subtle ingredient of its own.

Newcomers do not recognize this quality or resent it as mere dullness. Then, before they know what is happening to them, the most progressive young businessmen, the most impatient boosters and Philistines, the retired tycoons from Toronto, or the stolid farmers from the prairies—all that influx of Canadians in search of a final haven—begin to acquire the secret of this place through their pores and soon fall helpless under the spell. They become Victorians. No other town will satisfy them again. Having crossed that Rubicon, the Gulf of Georgia, they have passed the point of no return.

The reincarnation of such a man is a contemporary process of climate and landscape. It has nothing to do with Victoria's stirring history, for no Canadians have neglected their history more than the Victorians. They are too busy writing their private testaments on the earth. Not many of them realize that Douglas's fort was the fragile western anchor of the entire continental boundary and stood alone in the northward path of Manifest Destiny. Not many of them have read the tarnished bronze plaque at a downtown intersection which alone marks the site of that queer stronghold.

Why, hardly one out of ten Victorians has ever paused to inspect perhaps the most significant Canadian monument west of the St. Lawrence. It is not much to see—an absurd little wooden building, in shape rather like a pagoda—and it is stowed away, as if unworthy of the British Columbia capital, behind the stone legislative buildings.

In this ill-shaped cottage, then one of the colonial government's three "Bird Cages," Confederation was completed by a few forgotten men. They joined British Columbia to Canada, and without their decision—taken in grave doubt and under strong pressure to join the United States—there probably would be no Canada at all today; the disjointed colonial atoms would almost certainly have fallen one by one into the awaiting hands of the Americans.

Only the last Bird Cage, a few old houses on the leafy hill of Rockland Avenue, and the English manor house of the lieutenant-governor remind this generation of the odd breed which, for all its stuffiness and pretension, held the border and gave Canada a western coast.

We walked away from Bird Cage to watch, in a little public square near by, an aged Indian artist, Mungo Martin, and his son carve the last genuine totem poles that Canada is ever likely to see. A wise provincial government has thus arranged to reproduce the ancient totems unwisely exposed to the weather and already beginning to decay.

Here was a curious little paradox worth pause and consideration. Down the street a government of radical economic doctrine carved a new province. An Indian carved a lofty cedar, as his fathers carved before him, to incarnate the original gods and demons of this coast. Between the government and the native craftsman there stretched a block of pavement and a gap of centuries. The old gods and demons of the forest, the new gods and demons of the boom, were close together but worlds away. Those two elements, nostalgia and great expectations, continually war for the soul of Victoria.

As my wife and I walked on to Beacon Hill Park, remembering many lost things of childhood, we met a friend from Vancouver, a learned man, a high-court judge. He was trying to feed crusts of bread to the swans, but they arched their snooty necks and ignored this alien charity.

"There," our friend said, "you have the psychic difference between Victoria and Vancouver. This town is so superior that even the swans won't look at good, honest bread. If you were to throw a crust into the streets of Vancouver, all the brokers would leap out of their skyscraper windows with a scream of hunger."

We left that man with his paper bag of crusts, we surveyed the rank weed growth of our own neglected garden in Saanich, and drove up the Island's main road.

Though it is smoothed into a speedway and much of its charm has been destroyed by progress, the Malahat Highway of the tourist advertisements still looked agreeable, and not far off a quiet lake and a cabin built by our hands awaited us at the end of our journey.

White fishing boats flecked the Saanich Arm. Mount Tzou-halem, on which the young Indian braves used to prove their manhood by climbing a sheer precipice, presided regally over Cowichan Bay.

The town of Duncan, in appearance like any other Canadian town, still nourished the last remains of a remarkable society, much publicized but seldom understood—English nobles, generals, admirals, fishermen, hunters, cricket-players, and pukka sahibs. Alas, they are near extinction. On the adjoining Cowichan River a mad priestcraft, also near extinction, still bravely offered the old sacrifices and libations to Rainbow, Cutthroat, and Steelhead.

Nanaimo, farther north, the Island's second sizable community, began when a nameless Indian brought "black stones" to Fort Victoria and assured a coastal coal industry. Later on, Robert Dunsmuir, a penniless miner, lay down for a nap outside Nanaimo and awakened on a broad coal seam to found a dynasty of wealth, build a railway to Victoria, and die in one of his several mansions.

His town is now a commercial suburb of Vancouver, and is served by numerous ferries across the Gulf. Qualicum, with its long beach of warm sea water, is also a Vancouver suburb, the week-end resort of the upper classes. Comox Bay, however, and its town of Courtenay, belong to the Island and enjoy perhaps its most notable view. An arm of the sea is enclosed here almost like an Alpine lake under the glacial stare of Mount Albert Edward. Campbell River used to be only an international haunt of tyee salmon fishermen (their ritual too intricate and sacred for public view), but is now a town that threatens to engulf even Roderick Haig-Brown, one of Canada's few truly distinguished writers and possibly the world's ablest angler.

Men like him are everywhere in retreat before the surge of progress. They have seen their river harnessed for power and its noble falls reduced to a trickle; Butte Lake, the glory of

Strathcona Park, a little way inland, dammed as a reservoir; the old forest cut; the new growth burned in the historic fire of 1938; and a third growth slowly pushed through the ashes.

From Campbell River a man may travel on foot for many days and see nothing but logged-off and burned land over hundreds of square miles. If he travels by air for a few hours he will see, beyond these shaven patches, the dark sea of living timber, wave on wave, to the Pacific. The island and the mainland forest form British Columbia's largest capital asset, but no two experts will agree on its dimensions, value, or future. Is man cutting it too fast or not fast enough? Does British Columbia face a hiatus between old growth and new? Or can he count on an ever increasing crop under his new harvesting methods? Those are the sovereign economic questions of the coast. Foresters, royal commissions, and puzzled provincial governments have never found a sure answer.

At any rate, conservationists, with Haig-Brown as their unpaid press agent, foresee the day when British Columbians, who were long accustomed to regard the whole wilderness as their playground, will be barred from it. The government, for sound economic reasons, is parceling the coastal timber out in vast individual empires, regulating the cut and assuring a perpetual yield. But in Haig-Brown's opinion it is not conserving the natural recreation, the old outdoor character, and probably the people's future health, physical and spiritual.

Today's young trees will never reach the size of their predecessors. Men cannot wait that long. Lumber, as we know it, will soon become almost obsolete in British Columbia's version of the industrial revolution. Its place will be taken by pulp made from small trees in the new mills.

Wherever roads and the logger's machinery can reach, the Island has been physically, as it has been economically and spiritually, transformed during the last two or three decades.

Roads, however, reach only a small part of it yet. The northern half of its nearly three-hundred-mile length is almost uninhabited. Much of its interior has hardly been explored. Most of its dense vegetation cannot be penetrated until a trail is cut.

Every year men are lost and sometimes starve to death a few miles from the main highway. The west coast, of fog, storm, and upright cliffs, has no habitation but a few fishing villages, logging camps, and timber plants.

This island (the largest on North America's west coast) is essentially a range of mountains. They fall steeply into the sea and leave only a narrow shelf on their eastern flank. A country so precipitous and, for the most part, so infertile has little economic use except as the nation's best tree nursery. The trees love this gravel soil. A few acres of bottomland around the mouths of rivers, an occasional alder swamp, laboriously drained, will support a farm, but the island can never be a farming country.

Often the farm is abandoned after hopeless years of drudgery. You will find on every side road the pathetic remains of those lost labors. A fallen barn, a cabin flat on the ground, the almost imperishable "shakes" of its roof alone unrotted, and always in some little field the thickening ranks of new trees pronounce the forest's inevitable victory.

Man's method of harvesting timber, the island's true crop, has changed, like everything else. As a boy I could still follow the broken logs of the skid roads on which oxen hauled the tree trunks to some lake or river. Stationary donkey engines replaced oxen. Then came the "high lead" to lift logs high in the air and deposit them, as neat as kindling wood, upon flatcars.

No logging railways are being built today. The diesel truck has replaced the flatcar. The caterpillar tractor is replacing the high lead. The whisper of the crosscut and the click of the faller's ax are heard no more. Everywhere the chatter of gasoline chain saws breaks the old silence.

The timber industry has learned the value of wood. Half the forest is no longer left in vast windrows of slash, as combustible in summer as gasoline. The little trees and the limbs of the big ones now go to the pulp mills. A hundred acres of first growth, almost worthless a few years ago, is now worth a fortune. Where the big loggers would not take a second glance at some minor stand, the little "gypo" outfits will bulldoze a truck road to cut a dozen trees.

Efficiency and economy have enriched the coast but diluted the color and adventure of the logger's life. A pair of fallers on a flimsy "springboard," as they hacked out an undercut in rhythmic ax strokes, used to be one of Canada's supreme exhibitions of skill and endurance. Now we watched two mechanics and a chain saw nick the six-foot trunk and complete the main cut from the other side in perhaps ten minutes. The tree shuddered, swayed, and fell with a screech of agony like a great wounded bird.

The skill of these loggers, their judgment, athletes' muscles, and ballet dancers' poise when a man's life depends on every step of his calked boots—all this old cunning remains. So does the logger's fabled appetite.

Entering a cookhouse for a cup of afternoon tea, we were greeted by a platter of beefsteak and half a ton of cake and pie. What, asked the indignant cook, had happened to our appetites that we could not consume this light snack?

Yes, and what had happened to the old-time logger of fiction, the Canadian Paul Bunyan, who labored, celibate and sober, for half a year and spent his wages in the orgies of Vancouver's red-light district?

Most of these men live in towns and travel perhaps forty miles to work in a "crummy" (the elegant local name for a loggers' bus). They are tamed, domesticated, and prosperous, but they never escape the woods. Though they cannot utter these things, the shadow of the forest and its slanting streaks of sunlight color their souls. Its sap flows in the veins of their being. The immensity and terror of it lie forever athwart their lives.

The old hand processes of the woods, the camping-places of our childhood, and the faces of many forest men now gone were in our minds as we drove across the Island to the boom town of Alberni, on the west coast, where the smoke of the new pulp mills declares the westernmost leap of the Canadian revolution; then again as we stood among the fir and cedar giants of Cathedral Grove, a little park of first growth on the main road and a sad reminder of other days. In our youth most of the Island roads wound through such a jungle. Man, by his greed and folly, left only one fine but pitiable specimen beside the main Island highway.

At last we were coming to the end of the travels that began on the Atlantic coast. Our road used to wriggle tortuously among some of the largest and best timber in the world. Those trees had been felled long since. Their stumps were covered by a bristling hedge of young conifers. The lonely lake was crammed with log booms, the shore fouled with the litter of a sawmill. The hills had turned brown under the latest devastation. But in the middle of this havoc an old sanctuary remained intact.

The log house of the first settler on this lake still stood in the little field which he had cleared by hand. Two maples planted at his door spread their shade in diameter of fifty feet. He was gone, of course, but his son, with whom I had scythed hay, fished, and hunted in the summer holidays long ago, was waiting for me, immovable on the father's land.

My boyhood friend, now old and deeply lined by toil, led me to the brook. We used to eat our lunch there at harvest time and idly flick trout from the cold, clean water. The green current ran, laughing, through a tunnel of foliage and mossy rock—safe, as I thought, from man's invasion. Today I saw that no inch of Island land was safe if it held a tree worth cutting. The banks of the brook had been shaved off. A debris of slash choked the little stone canyon. No trout swam in our pool.

Beside the ravaged brook, as everywhere, it was bootless to lament the Canadian revolution. But I had my memories, and I wished to confirm them before I left this spot forever.

Certain relics must still survive near by to record the old days. As a boy I could stand between three cedars, the smallest ten feet in diameter, and touch all of them with my hands. Now I found their stumps staring blankly at the sun. They would be here for centuries yet, long after a new forest had risen to conceal their nakedness.

The new forest! I knelt down to examine the earth beneath the slash, the fireweed, the sword ferns, and the first brave shoots of alder. And there I beheld—microscopic but larger by far than all man's works—the first and last fact of the Pacific coast. A seedling of fir, two inches high, held up proudly on its tip a bud, round, purple, and shiny as a jewel.

INDEX

A NOTE ON THE TYPE

This book is set in ELECTRA, *a Linotype face designed by* W. A. DWIGGINS (1880–1956), *who was responsible for so much that is good in contemporary book design. Although much of his early work was in advertising and he was the author of the standard volume* Layout in Advertising, *Mr. Dwiggins later devoted his prolific talents to book typography and type design, and worked with great distinction in both fields. In addition to his designs for Electra, he created the Metro, Caledonia, and Eldorado series of type faces, as well as a number of experimental cuttings that have never been issued commercially.*

Electra cannot be classified as either modern or old-style. It is not based on any historical model, nor does it echo a particular period or style. It avoids the extreme contrast between thick and thin elements which marks most modern faces, and attempts to give a feeling of fluidity, power, and speed.

The Unknown Country

Canada and Her People

Reissue

The late BRUCE HUTCHISON
Introduction by VAUGHN PALMER

"*The Unknown Country* . . . came as close as any text in defining Canada's identity.
Bruce Hutchison was one of a kind." —Peter C. Newman

 Governor General's Literary Award for Non-fiction

For an entire generation of Canadians, *The Unknown Country* defined their
nation. It is a book that speaks to us still. Winner of the Governor General's
Literary Award for Non-fiction, acclaimed by critics at home and abroad, this
book presents an unforgettable portrait of a nation in the making—a portrait
as vivid, lively, and true as when it first appeared during the dark, heroic days
of the Second World War.

Paperback | 400 pages | 5.5 x 8.5" | 9780195438918

The Struggle for the Border

Reissue

The late BRUCE HUTCHISON
Introduction by VAUGHN PALMER

"Vivid and readable . . . Canada–US relations told as an adventure story."—Vaughn Palmer

The boundary between Canada and the United States is famously described as the longest undefended border in the world. But it was not always so. In *The Struggle for the Border*, renowned journalist and award-winning historian Bruce Hutchison tells the little-known story of how that border was established—a story of frontier war, Fenian raids, the burning of Washington, and diplomatic intrigues.

Paperback | 520 pages | 5.5 x 8.25" | 9780195447927

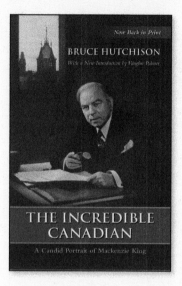

The Incredible Canadian

A Candid Portrait of Mackenzie King

Reissue

The late BRUCE HUTCHISON
Introduction by VAUGHN PALMER

"Bruce Hutchison, abandoning our native caution, has been the first Canadian to bring an historical figure completely to life on the printed page. [A] revolution in Canadian biography." —*Globe and Mail*

 Governor General's Literary Award for Non-fiction

From Canada's greatest political journalist comes *The Incredible Canadian*, the astonishing story of Prime Minister William Lyon Mackenzie King and winner of the Governor General's Literary Award for Non-fiction. Scholar, reformer, spiritualist, Machiavellian mastermind—Mackenzie King seized control of a leaderless party, brought it to power, and then clung to the prime minister's office longer than anyone else in the history of the British Commonwealth. Bruce Hutchison saw it all firsthand.

Paperback | 464 pages | 5.5 x 8.5" | 9780195438901

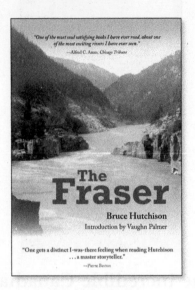

The Fraser

Reissue

The late BRUCE HUTCHISON
Introduction by VAUGHN PALMER

"One of the most soul satisfying books I have ever read, about one of the most exciting rivers I have ever seen." —Alfred C. Ames, *Chicago Tribune*

In *The Fraser*, Bruce Hutchison—one of Canada's great storytellers—relates the epic saga of the river whose history is one with that of British Columbia and her people. Hutchison's masterful narrative draws in the reader with its tale of gold rush and fur trade, heroism and despair. Vivid and exciting, *The Fraser* is a dramatic portrait of Canada's colourful past.

Paperback | 378 pages | 5.5 x 8.5" | 9780195438925